Jeffrey Richardson Brackett

The Negro in Maryland

A Study of the Institution of Slavery

Jeffrey Richardson Brackett

The Negro in Maryland
A Study of the Institution of Slavery

ISBN/EAN: 9783744731713

Printed in Europe, USA, Canada, Australia, Japan

Cover: Foto ©ninafisch / pixelio.de

More available books at **www.hansebooks.com**

THE

NEGRO IN MARYLAND

A Study of the Institution of Slavery

By JEFFREY R. BRACKETT, Ph. D.

BALTIMORE
N. MURRAY, PUBLICATION AGENT, JOHNS HOPKINS UNIVERSITY
1889

JOHN MURPHY & CO., PRINTERS.
BALTIMORE.

CONTENTS.

CHAP.		PAGE.
I.—Introduction,		1
II.—Indians and White Servants,		11
III.—Slaves,		26
IV.—Manumission,		148
V.—The Free Negro,		175

THE NEGRO IN MARYLAND.

CHAPTER I.

INTRODUCTION.

We are not called on, happily, to bring up from our past politics those questions of slavery over which so many lances were broken—until arguments were ended by the sword. The object of this study is simply to trace, as clearly as possible, the growth of African slavery, as an institution, in Maryland.[1]

Nor will it be necessary to study the institution of slavery

---

[1] A residence of several years in Maryland has not alone fixed this limited field of inquiry. It is true, no doubt, that the lot of the slaves in Maryland was, as a rule, much better than that of those on the large plantations in the thinly settled portions of the Southern States. Thus, for instance, the system of special magistrates' courts, for trial of slaves for serious offences, was not known in Maryland. But Maryland was settled early; its slave code was rigorous; becoming a Border State, its slave property became less secure; the number of slaves remained large, while the free blacks became more numerous than in any other slave State; and earnest efforts were made for colonization. A study of the growth of slavery in detail, with reference to these conditions, may be of more value to the student, to-day, than a more general, and necessarily less accurate, study in a wider field, or one directed more to the severities to which slavery made the blacks liable—which are already well known.

Any work of such a nature must be very imperfect. The writer can give only what he has gathered, and asks any person who may be interested in the subject, to communicate to him any further facts.

Baltimore, Md., 1889.

among the ancients, for the presumption is that the planters on the Chesapeake acted by their own impulses and for their own interests, with little knowledge of, or regard to, what other men had done, two thousand years before. But to begin with the settlement of Maryland, without noticing the ideas of the age concerning slavery—ideas which the settlers brought with them—would be as unfair as to begin a history of the United States without notice of the Thirteen Colonies.

The slavery of antiquity, the right to hold a person for debt, or as a captive taken in war, was based on no strict race or religious grounds. Romans enslaved captive Germans, as Germans, afterwards, in their turn, enslaved Romans. But this slavery died out in Western Europe early in the Middle Ages; and Christians ceased to enslave Christian captives. The semi-servile condition of villeinage which grew up at that time, declined quickly with the decline of the feudal system, long before the settlement of America.[1] It is significant, that just at the time when Columbus turned to the court of Spain, to become the discoverer of America, Ferdinand of Arragon had succeeded with some difficulty in bringing cer-

---

[1] Villeinage varied somewhat in different parts of Europe, and has survived in some countries almost to our own day. In general, to all others but his lord, the serf was as a freeman. In England, villeinage died out early, the Peasants' Wars of the fourteenth century giving the death blow. The last case, we are told, in which it was pleaded in the courts was in 1618. That class distinctions may have accustomed men easily to the existence of any form of servitude is worthy of consideration, but villeinage cannot be said to have had any vital influence on the rise of African slavery. The only case in which we find mention, in the early records of Maryland, of the laws or customs of England on villeinage, as affecting slavery, is the answer of Lord Baltimore to the Lords of Trade, in 1678 (Md. Arch., V., 267), on the subject of conversion of the blacks. A law was made, he says, to encourage baptism of slaves, "by which it was and is declared That as in former times The Baptizeing of Villaynes in England was not taken by the Lawe of England To be a Manumission or Infranchiseing of the Villaynes soe neither shall it be in this Provynce as to Negroes or Mulattoes," &c. See chapter on Slaves. The Court of Appeals declared, afterwards, that slavery and villeinage were entirely different.

tain nobles to grant freedom to their serfs, of European race and Christian faith, and was also pushing vigorously the conquest of Grenada, by which thousands of Saracens were scattered as slaves in Southern Europe.

Christians had ceased the enslavement of Christian captives, as a rule; but the custom of ransom, of which we read in the chronicles, was a survival of slavery. The beaten warrior became subject to the terms of the victor. At the battle of Poitiers, in 1356, the English—so the old chronicler Froissart tells us—had French prisoners twice as many in number as themselves, and deemed it advisable to ransom them on the spot. Many were set at liberty and others kept; "for whosoever made any prisoners, they were solely at his disposal, to ransom or not, as he pleased." Several of the English archers had four or six prisoners, and a number of those who could give no ransom were put to death. One Sir Edward de Roucy felled to the ground an English knight who was following him from the field. Dismounting and placing his lance on the Englishman's breast, he called on him to surrender under penalty of death, as his prisoner, rescued or not. The defeated knight surrendered, accompanied Sir Edward, and afterwards ransomed himself. At the battle of Chevy Chace, in 1388, one Sir Matthew Redman surrendered to a Scotch knight. "Rescued or not?" cried the Scot. "I consent," answered Sir Matthew, "you will take good care of me?" "That I will," said the Scot. Then Sir Matthew, putting up his sword, said; "now, what do you require of me, for I am your prisoner by fair conquest?" "And what is it you would wish me to do," replied the Scot. "I should like," said Sir Matthew, "to return to Newcastle; and, within fifteen days, I will come to you in any part of Scotland you shall appoint." "I agree," said his captor, "on your pledging yourself, that within three weeks you be in Edinburgh; and wherever you may go, you acknowledge yourself as my prisoner." So they parted, and in a few moments, the Scot himself was captured by the Bishop of Durham. He philosophically exclaimed: "I have made a prisoner, and am now one myself: such is the chance of war."[1] In 1441, Charles VII. of France brought a number of English prisoners to Paris. After suffering shocking treatment, those who could not pay their ransom, by far the largest number, were bound hand and foot, and thrown into the Seine. Not till the seventeenth century were agreements entered into by the nations of Europe for the regulation and exchange of prisoners.[2]

But it was in Christ only that all men were brethren. The captive heathen or infidel became usually the slave of his Christian conqueror. It was due chiefly to the conquest of the Spaniards over the Moors and to the rising trade of the Spaniards and Portuguese with Africa, that there grew up for Europe a new form of chattel slavery. And if the zeal of the earlier church had helped the fall of the old slavery, the zeal and bigotry of good churchmen of this age certainly had a part, conscious or unconscious, in the rise of the new. "Whole droves of slaves," wrote Bodin, in 1576, "are sold and that openly in all parts of Portugal, as if they were beasts."[3] By the trade with Africa, negro slaves were brought, to a limited extent, to Portugal and Spain. Prince Henry of Portugal, in 1442, insisted that negroes should be brought there; "for whatever number he should get, he would gain souls, because they might be converted to the faith, which could not be managed with the Moors."[4] "And certainly," adds the old chronicler, "his thought was not vain, for as soon as they had knowledge of our language, they readily became Christians." It is not necessary to dwell on the extreme zeal of the Church in that age—so well seen in the Inquisition. "It was the received opinion," says Prescott,

---

[1] Froissart, Johnes' Trans., Vol. I, 219, &c.; II, 373.
[2] For much of interest on this subject see Ward's Inquiry into the Law of Nations (R. Ward, London, 1795).
[3] Commonweale, Knolles' Translation, p. 43.
[4] The Conquerors of The New World: Sir A. Helps, pp. 28, 36.

"among good Catholics of that period, that heathen and barbarous nations were placed by the circumstance of their infidelity without the pale both of spiritual and civil rights."[1]

By the discovery of America, Europeans met a people, the Indians, not akin to them in race or religion. Columbus, in his diary, speaks thus of Ferdinand and Isabella: "Your highnesses as Catholic Christians and princes, lovers and furtherers of the Christian faith, and enemies of the sect of Mahomet, and of all idolatries and heresies, thought to send me, Christopher Columbus, to the aforesaid provinces of India to see the aforesaid princes, the cities and lands, and the disposition of them and of everything about them, and the way that should be taken to convert them to the sacred faith."[2] It is true, indeed, that the conversion of the natives was steadfastly enjoined by the sovereigns, and carried out by certain of their subjects. But in the treatment of the Indians by the Spaniards we see plainly the spirit of the times. A number of Indian slaves were soon sent to Spain, some of them by Columbus. Isabella ordered back those who had not been taken in just war. The Spaniards were little suited to work the mines in the Indies. They had gone out expecting largely to pick up precious metals; they found by experience that riches were to be won only by toil. The natives were soon impressed into their service. The matter was carried to Spain, and the right to enslave the unoffending heathen was debated there by learned men. It was finally determined that a qualified servitude would be beneficial to both Spaniard and Indian; the former might the better work his plantation or his mine, the latter might gain from the religious and social influences of his employer. The rights

---

[1] Ferdinand and Isabella, Part II, ch. 8. The Mahometans enslaved captives of another faith; Capt. John Smith was a slave among the Turks. Europe felt the converse working of her old rule, later, when the Barbary States exacted tribute, as ransoms.

[2] The Conquerors of The New World, p. 102.

thus granted were terribly abused; in a few years, from overwork and ill-treatment, the numerous populations, of men unaccustomed to toil, had dwindled away. At first, the capture of cannibal Indians had been forbidden, but as they persisted in idolatry, they too were enslaved.[1]

At the very beginning of the sixteenth century, permission had been given to carry to the Indies such negro slaves as had been "born in the power of Christians"—that is, negroes from Southern Europe. The rapid decrease of the Indians, and the cruelties practised on them, had roused a number of zealous friends to them, among the Spaniards. About 1511, says the chronicler Herrera, "the King of Spain issued fresh Orders for promoting the Conversion of the Indians, and their being well instructed in the Christian Religion. Nor did he take less care of the civil Government, directing among other things, that those People should not be oppressed, and that for easing of them, numbers of blacks should be carry'd

---

[1] A proclamation was addressed to the Indians not under the Spanish rule. They were called on to acknowledge the grant of the new world by the Pope to the Crown—a grant made in certain writings which they might see if they wished. They were to acknowledge the Church, the Crown, and to receive the ministration of the priests. Due time was given them to consider this. If they came under the Spanish rule, His Majesty would greet them with all love and affection and leave them their wives and children free, and give them many privileges and exemptions. But if they did not, "by the help of God I will enter with power into your land," reads the threat, "and will subdue you, and will take your wives and children and make slaves of them, and sell them as such, and take all your goods and do all the mischief I can, as to vassals that do not obey and will not receive their Lord, and I protest that all the death and destruction which may come from this is your fault, and not his Majesty's or mine or that of my men." And we are told in the old chronicle, how the Spaniards would sometimes halt in the dark before an Indian village, and the commander would read this to his men and the trees of the forest, as a prelude to pillage and slaughter. An officer was afterward employed by the King to report which of the Indians were cannibals, "barbarous People, Enemies to Christians, and Man Eaters." Certain ones could not be determined, but it was declared that those named as cannibals might be attacked, taken, and sold as slaves. (Herrera, Stevens' Trans., I, 1, 14; II, 8, 6).

over to work in the Mines, because one of them (i. e. one negro slave) did more than four of the Natives."[1] The production of sugar increased the desire for negroes. Soon, with the entire sympathy of the court and by the advice of those friendly to the Indians, negroes were extensively introduced. The service of Indians was thus supplanted by African slaves.

With the demand for negro labor in the New World, the slave trade increased, and soon extended from the Portuguese and Spaniards to the Dutch and English. "Although servitude in these latter times was left off," wrote Bodin in 1576, " for about three or four hundred years, yet is it now again approved, by the great agreement and consent of almost all nations."

The early treatises on war reflect plainly, no doubt, the spirit of the times. The Spaniard Victoria, professor at Salamanca, writes, a few years before Bodin, that in wars between Christians—although, by the law of nature, warriors who surrender or are captured might be slain—the usage and custom of war, which had become a part of the law of nations, had ordered that prisoners might be redeemed by ransom. But this mitigation of the extreme rights of war was not applicable to infidels. It was not lawful to kill or carry into captivity innocent persons, and women and children were presumed to be innocent, even in wars with the Turks; but in a war against pagans, which might be said to be perpetual and without hope of obtaining satisfaction, doubtless the women and children captured from the Saracens could be detained as slaves.[2] So Ayala, the Judge Advocate of the Spanish army in the Netherlands, says in his Treatise on War, in 1581, that an ancient and laudable custom had substituted for enslavement the practice of ransoming prisoners of war; but that the older usage still existed between Christians and such infidel nations as Turks and Saracens.[2]

---

[1] Herrera, Stevens' Trans., I, 9, 3.
[2] Wheaton's Law of Nations, Introduction.

Albericus Gentilis, called from the continent in 1587 to be professor of civil law at Oxford, wrote that there was no slavery in wars of Christians, for such were civil wars, as all men were brothers in Christ. I do not hesitate, he adds, to say that the law of slavery is just, for it is the agreement of the law of nations.[1] Grotius, the historiographer of Holland, states in his famous work on the Rights of War and Peace, published in 1625, that even among Christians the custom still continued of keeping captives till their ransom was paid —it being generally agreed that Christian prisoners taken in war were not to be "made Slaves, so as to sell them or force them to hard Labours, or to such Miseries as are common to Slaves." And what Christians, he adds, in this case observe among themselves, the Mahometans likewise do among themselves.[2] Bynkershoek, an advocate and judge at the Hague, stated in his Public Law, in 1737, that prisoners were often released even without ransom. As slavery had fallen entirely into disuse among Christians, he says, "we do not inflict it upon our prisoners. We may however, if we please, and indeed we do sometimes still exercise that right upon those who enforce it against us. Therefore the Dutch are in the habit of selling to the Spanish as slaves, the Algerians, Tunisians and Tripolitans, whom they take prisoners in the Atlantic or in the Mediterranean; for the Dutch themselves have no slaves, except in Asia, Africa and America."[3]

---

[1] Thomas Aquinas pleases me, says Gentilis, in saying that slavery is natural; not, indeed, according to first intentions by which we have all been created free, but from second intention, since nature allowed delinquents to be punished. (Albericus Gentilis: De Jure Belli, Holland's Ed., ch. IX, p. 314, &c.)

[2] The right to enslave captives, says Grotius, taken in solemn war, was granted by the Law of nations for no other reason, than that the captors might be tempted to forbear the rigor allowed them, of killing their prisoners either in, or after, the fight. Among Christians it was generally agreed that prisoners were not to be enslaved, and that with reason, "for they are, or should be, better instructed by the great Recommender of every act of charity." (Grotius: De Jure Belli, Barbeyrac's Trans.)

[3] Bynkershoek: Quaes. Juris. Pub., Du Ponceau's Trans., Book I, ch. 3.

While scholars were writing thus in their studies, the African trade was increasing. From time immemorial, indeed, the Africans, in their inter-tribal warfare, had been accustomed to enslave their prisoners; but the native traders must have caught from the Europeans something of the greed for riches that so strongly marked that age. It was an age of great activity and discovery. Marvellous reports came to Europe of the riches of the New World. In Florida, the Spaniards sought for the fountain of youth. Theatre-goers in London, at the beginning of the seventeenth century, heard that gold was to be had for the picking up, in America. "Why man," says one fellow, "all their dripping-pans are pure golde ... all the prisoners they take are fettered in golde; and for rubies and diamonds, they goes forth in holy-days, and gather 'hem by the sea-shore."[1] An old Spanish historian— who softens, says Prescott, the excesses of his countrymen— tells us of an Indian chief of Cuba, who, having carefully watched the Spaniards in the neighboring islands, and hearing that they were coming to Cuba to settle, called together his people. And putting them in mind of their many sufferings at the hands of the Spaniards, he told them that the Spaniards acted for a great and beloved lord, whom he would show them. Then he took from a little palm-tree basket a lump

---

In 1661 and 1664, the States-General ordered their admiral to sell as slaves all the pirates he might take.

Pufendorf says, in 1672, that the ownership of acquisitions by capture in war was then a subject of dispute. "The idea that captives in war are slaves," wrote John Adams to Granville Sharp, the English philanthropist, in 1786, "is the foundation of the misfortunes of the negroes. This principle is honored and admitted by all the powers of Europe, who pay tributes to the States of Barbary." Memoirs of Sharp, I, 374.

[1] Marston's Eastward Ho; 1605. The excesses of the Spaniards were, doubtless, far greater than those of the English, who cannot, however, in their part in the slave-trade, be exonerated from avarice.

Sir Henry Maine says, in his Ancient Law, ch. V, "The simple wish to use the bodily powers of another person as a means of ministering to one's own ease or pleasure is doubtless the foundation of Slavery, and as old as human nature."

of gold, saying, this is the lord of the Spaniards. Then they danced around the basket, and "when they were spent with Singing and Dancing before the little Basket of God," he bade them not keep "the Lord of the Christians in any Place whatsoever, for tho' he were in their Bowels, they would fetch him out, and therefore they should cast him into the River, under Water where they would not find him; and so they did."[1]

---

[1] Herrera, I, 9, 3.

CHAPTER II.

INDIANS AND WHITE SERVANTS.

The Colony of Maryland was settled in 1634, under the proprietary government of Lord Baltimore. The royal charter, we may mention as passing, spoke not only of the spread of English territory, but, as charters usually did, of the zeal of the founder for spreading religion among a savage people who knew not God. The right to initiate all laws was soon secured to the Assembly by the Proprietor, and, although legislation remained subject to veto, the authorities in England interfered little in those internal affairs of the Colony which interest us most. Several cases of this interference we shall have to note, later. We begin with the little settlement, of some few hundred persons, about St. Mary's, on a peninsula by the lower Potomac. There met the Governor, the appointee and representative of the Proprietor, the half dozen councilmen, and the freemen or their representatives, in assembly.

The colonists at once, on landing, met with the Indians, a heathen race unknown to them in England. These pagans, as the white men called them, seemed friendly, and intercourse between the races began auspiciously. But the Indian saw with aversion the spread of the settlement, and the whites lost property and finally even a few lives at their hands. In 1639, it was declared a penal offence for anyone, without the consent of the government, to leave the English plantations to live among any Indians who were not christened.[1] Some of the Indians were soon open enemies. The commission issued by the Governor, in 1640, to the commander of an expedition planned against a certain tribe, which had refused to make satisfaction for sundry insolences and rapines, authorized him to attack these Indians, with any company of Englishmen that would be willing to go, "and against them and their Lands and goods to execute and Inflict what may be inflicted by the Law of warr and the pillage and booty therein gotton to part and divide among the Company, that Shall perform the Service."[2] We find another proclamation, dated a few days later, forbidding all Englishmen, under penalty, from doing any injury to a neighboring tribe which, in peace and amity, the Colony had taken under its protection. The commission to the leader of an expedition against the unfriendly Sesquihanowes, in 1643, expresses the confidence of the authorities in his forwardness to vindicate the honor of God and of the Christian and English name upon those barbarous and inhuman pagans, and bids him do all things needed for training his men, vanquishing the enemy, and "disposing of the spoils," and all things that any general might do by the law of war.[3] In 1652, an expedition was planned against the Indians of the Eastern Shore, who had committed serious depredations and murder. It was ordered that one man out of every seven men in the Colony should be armed and equipped by the six remaining at home, and that all the Indian prisoners brought back, unless otherwise disposed of by the Provincial Court, should be divided, according to their value, in a general division among those who had armed and sent forth the fighting men—who, in turn, were to share the other plunder. The captain was ordered to "make Warr upon and through God's Assistance by all possible meanes to

---

[1] Bozman's Md., II, 134.
[2] Md. Arch., III, 87.
[3] Md. Arch., III, 133.

Vanquish, destroy, plunder, kill or take prisoners at yor discretion all or any the s^d Indians either by Sea or land, and being Soe taken to put them to Death by the Law of warr or to Save them at your pleasure."[1]

An act of 1715, when the Southern Colonies were involved in an Indian war, provided—among permanent regulations for the militia—that any booty, plunder or Indian prisoners should be given by the commander to the soldier who took the same—to encourage men to enlist in such service.[2]

Indian slaves are occasionally mentioned in the old records. About 1660, one Indian was sold, as a punishment for petty larceny, and brought one thousand pounds of tobacco.[3] But, while Indians taken in war might be enslaved, kidnapping of friendly Indians was early and always forbidden. It was declared felony, in 1649, to take or sell any friend Indian, without license from the Governor—and felony might then be punished with death. At the end of the century, the same offence was made punishable by fine and imprisonment, at

---

[1] This expedition was given up, on account of bad weather. Md. Arch., Vol. III, 285.

[2] Acts of 1715, ch. 43 (Bacon's Laws of Maryland), continued indefinitely in 1722. The captain of an expedition in 1647 had been ordered to make no distribution until he should arrive at the fort, and give a just account to the authorities of all plunder taken.

The practice of the Indians in requiring ransom, often, is well known. The Assembly of Maryland was petitioned, in 1650, to ransom two children held by hostile Indians. Nine hundred pounds of tobacco was asked for the elder and six hundred for the younger; and the estate of their father, deceased, was not sufficient for this. The Assembly, stating that the public charges were then very heavy, directed that any of the colonists who chose to redeem them should be entitled to their service, in return, until they were twenty-one years of age. Bozman's Maryland, II, 396.

We find an English soldier who had escaped from the Indians, in the French and Indian War of 1756, telling the Governor that, had he not escaped, he must have served his Indian captor all his days, for saving his life.

[3] Mention of Indian slaves, in the Provincial Court Records, 1658–1662, pp. 143, 148, 187, 484, &c.

discretion of the Governor and Council; and this act was continued later. The reason, as stated in all the laws, was that no breach of peace might occur between the colonists and the neighboring Indians.[1] In 1722, a resident of- the Province was brought before the Governor and Council, committed for examination by the justices of Somerset county, for having sold or otherwise disposed of an Indian boy, of a tribe friendly to the English. On examination, the man confessed that the boy, in consideration of five pounds in money, a horse bridle and saddle, and two suits of clothes, indented to live with him as a servant for a term of thirty years, and that he afterwards sold the boy to a gentleman in Philadelphia, for fifteen pounds. In Virginia, he stated also, it was customary for Indians to be bound out, and this same boy had been previously a servant there. Thereupon the Council decided that as the man had already satisfied the Indians, and had suffered more than three months' imprisonment, he should be mildly dealt with; and he was fined five hundred pounds of tobacco and imprisoned one day.[2] In articles of peace made in 1666 between the government and a number of Indian settlements, it was stipulated that in case of danger from any hostile Indians, the Governor should appoint a place to which these friendly Indians might bring their wives and children for safety, and that these, if the men chanced to be killed, should remain free and not be servants to the English.[3] All disputes between Englishman and Indian were for many years heard before the Governor and Council. After 1700, cases involving not over twenty shillings were decided at first by special commissioners, and afterwards by any justice of the courts. After 1756, the county courts heard cases of greater value, and decided the rents of Indian lands, &c.[4] We find several

---

[1] Md. Arch., I, 250. Acts of 1692, 1705, and 1715. See Prov. Court Records in Md. Arch., IV, pp. 392, 399.
[2] Council Records, 1721–1728, p. 47.
[3] Md. Arch., II, 26.
[4] 1700, 6; 1717, 14; 1756, 9.

interesting cases concerning Indians. In 1642, a grand jury indicted for murder a certain planter, one Elkin, in that, when moved by malice and the instigation of the devil, he had shot an Indian, known as a king among a neighboring tribe. When brought before the court of the colony, the Governor and secretary on the bench, Elkin pleaded not guilty. The Proprietor's attorney gave as evidence the examination of Elkin, duly attested and with Elkin's signature, in which was a confession that he killed the Indian, and an account of the affair. But the jury gave a verdict of not guilty, saying that they so decided because they understood the deed had not been committed against the peace of the Proprietor or the King, because the party was a pagan, and because they had no precedent in the neighboring colony of Virginia to make the offence murder. The Governor thereupon directed them that those Indians who had been injured were in peace with the authorities, and that they should not take notice of what other colonies did, but of the law of England. After reconsideration, they found the prisoner guilty of murder in his own defence. Being told that this verdict was a contradiction, they reconsidered again, and found that the prisoner killed the Indian in self-defence. But the Governor refused to have this verdict entered, and called for another jury, to hear the same evidence. This jury found Elkin guilty of manslaughter. It is not uninteresting to note that proceedings were taken to have all the members of the first jury grievously fined—for having given an unsatisfactory verdict, contrary to the verdict of the second jury, from the same evidence. The foreman was then fined, by the court, the sum of two thousand pounds of tobacco. And he was soon fined one thousand pounds more, for contempt of court, for having said at the first trial of Elkins, when the court was "importunately pressing & charging the Jury . . . & arguing & pleading the crime ags^t the prisoner," that if an Englishman had been killed by the Indians, there would not have been so many words over it.[1] The penalty given Elkins is not stated, but we find him afterwards a resident of the Colony. In the next year 1643, a coroner's jury returned that an Indian lad had been shot and killed by one John Dandy. Dandy at once entered security, in the sum of three thousand pounds of tobacco, to answer the charge of homicide. It is interesting to note that the Indian had been christened, before his death. The grand jury returned that the bill was true, and the petit jury gave a verdict of guilty of felony and murder. Two years before, Dandy had been sentenced to death for some serious offence, but on petition of a great part of the Colony, the Governor had commuted the sentence to service to the government for three years. He was by trade a blacksmith and gunsmith, and, no doubt, a valuable man to the young colony. And now, again, he saved his own neck, being sentenced to fill the unpleasant office of public executioner. He was released from this four years later, having proved himself of service to the public.[2]

Lord Baltimore directed in 1651 that certain lands should be set aside as homes for some friendly Indians.[3] When a queen of one of the Indian settlements in Maryland complained to the Governor that, though her people had retired to the bounds of their territory, as allotted them, the English plantations had advanced so near that their crops were injured

---

[1] Md. Arch., IV, 177, 180-183.

[2] Md. Arch., IV, 255, 260; III, 98, 187. Also, Md. Arch., V, 480-482, 517.
Treaties were frequently made between the Colony and Indian tribes. In one, for instance, with certain Eastern Shore Indians, in 1659, it was agreed that the Indians were to restore stolen goods, that any Indian who should kill a white man, should be given over, with any abettors, to the government, for justice according to law; and that the Indians, if injured by whites, should appeal to the neighboring county commissioners, while the English, vice versa, were to appeal to a certain Indian chief. By another treaty, a few years after, with a tribe recently hostile, the right was reserved to the English of slaying any Indian who might be found killing cattle or hogs. (Md. Arch., III, 363, 433.)

[3] Md. Arch., I, 330.

by the colonists' cattle, the Governor issued orders that no Englishmen should settle within three miles of the Indians.[1] To a number of neighboring tribes of friendly Indians grants of land were secured by acts of assembly: it being most just, the acts read, that the ancient inhabitants of the Colony should have dwelling places in their native lands, free from the encroachments and oppression of the English.[2]

Soon after the planting of the Colony certain restrictions were laid on the Indians, and on the intercourse between Indians and English. To give or sell arms or ammunition to an Indian was felony, unless leave was gotten from the Governor. Nor could a colonist keep an Indian over night at his house, without leave. A few years later, permission was given to take arms and ammunition from any Indian who had not a license to carry them.[3] Nor could an Indian be entertained by a white at any time. A few Indians had been allowed to carry arms for the use of certain colonists, doubtless for hunting; but these licenses were withdrawn.[4] It is evident that these restrictions depended on hostilities between the Indians and the whites. In the game law of 1730, to preserve the breed of wild deer, there is special exemption for friendly Indians, who could kill all the deer required for their own use. The sale to the Indians of liquor in large quantities was forbidden, to prevent disorders by drunken Indians. By an act of 1756 a census was to be made, by the local authorities, of all the Indians settled in Maryland, and those who wished to leave their towns were ordered to procure passes. This was during the French and Indian war.[5]

An act of assembly, in 1650, in recognition of the Proprietor, states as the greatest blessing enjoyed by the Colony, the

---

[1] Md. Arch., III, 489, in 1663.
[2] Md. Arch., II, 200; 1723, 18, &c.
[3] Bozman's Maryland, II, 45, 286.
[4] Md. Arch., III, 143, 260; IV, 235, 359.
[5] 1715, 16; 1756, 13.

privilege of planting Christianity among a "people that know not God, nor had heard of Christ."[1] But we hear of no pains taken to convert the natives. In the plans for the settlement of all the Colonies, in fact, there is set forth this righteous end, but history shows that earnest efforts were no more made to reach it—than the black and Indian slaves, enslaved as captive heathen, were freed after they were converted. Another act, for the confirmation of peace with certain Indians, declares that the articles shall be kept, for the preservation of the people of the Colony, and for the honor of the Proprietor and the English nation, "which will undoubtedly suffer by breach of faith even to a heathen."[2] The treatment of the Indian by the government of Maryland seems indeed to have been most fair. But it should not be overlooked that this policy would have been dictated, if from no other reason, by prudence and even by necessity. The Colonies were not founded without the aid of the gun; and the words of John Archdale, the Quaker governor of Carolina, are of significance wider than the experiences of that Colony alone. "And, Courteous Readers," writes this staunch friend to the Indians, "I shall give you some farther Eminent Remark hereupon, and especially in the first Settlement of Carolina, where the Hand of God was eminently seen in thinning the Indians to make room for the English." For not only had the Indians there been cut off largely from previous inter-tribal war, "but, again, it at other times pleased Almighty God to send unusual Sicknesses amongst them, as the Smallpox, etc., to lessen their numbers; so that the English, in Comparison to the Spaniard, have but little Indian Blood to answer for."[3]

---

[1] Md. Arch., 1, 300.
[2] Md. Arch., 11, 131.
[3] Gov. Archdale, of Carolina, tells of his interview, in 1707, with four Indian prisoners about to be sold as slaves to the West Indies, as was usual. They were Roman Catholics, having been taught probably by the Spaniards or French. The Governor adds, that on finding they were Christians, he thought in a most peculiar manner that they should be free. See Carroll's Hist. Coll'ns of S. Carolina, II.

Should we digress to glance at other Colonies, we should find only better examples of the custom of enslaving Indian captives, and of the distance usually "observed betwixt Christians and Barbarians, as well in warres as in other negotiations"—to use the words of the Commissioners of the New England Colonies to the commander of the expedition against the Narragansetts, in 1645. The famous Body of Liberties of Massachusetts allowed such slavery, and captives in King Philip's war, at the close of the century, were sold.[1] In Virginia, while Indians captured in war became slaves for life, by act of assembly as well as by the custom, there was doubt for a time as to the proper lot of those who might be sold to the colonists by other Indians. This is a most interesting point to notice, as such Indians were practically in the same position to the colonists as were the negroes from Africa—sold by the traders to British merchants. When the king of one of the Virginia tribes sold a boy of another tribe—whether a captive in war we do not know—to one of the colonists as a

---

When one of the tribes in Maryland asked the pleasure of the Governor, in 1665, as to its removal from its old home, to which the whites were constantly approaching, the Council decided it would be safer for the Colony to keep these friendly Indians within its command. In 1694 the Governor asked the Assembly what answer should be made to a certain tribe of Indians, which had recently tarried in Maryland, if it should return and ask leave to settle. It was at the time of the French and Indian wars at the North; and the Assembly said it did not seem fit at that time to receive any strange nations of Indians. Whereupon the Council composed the following beguiling message for them, should they return: That Maryland is a country dealing in tobacco and not in furs; and as they have had an invitation from the government of New York to settle in that province, they are advised that such parts as New York and Pennsylvania, which trade mostly in furs, will be the most proper for their abode. In answer to queries by the government in England, about 1760, the Governor stated that there were in the populous parts of Maryland only one hundred and twenty Indians. These lived on lands allotted them by the Assembly, and were very orderly. (Md. Arch., III, 534. Council Proceedings, 1694-1698; 1753-1767.)

[1] For slavery in Massachusetts, see the admirable work of Dr. George H. Moore (Appleton & Co., New York, 1866).

slave, an act of assembly declared that the king had no power to sell an Indian of another tribe, and that "the said Indian be free, he speaking perfectly the English tongue and desiring baptism." This was about 1660. Some ten years later, the term of service of Indian prisoners, sold by their Indian captors, and not Christians, was fixed at twelve years and no longer, except children, who were to serve until thirty years of age. But, about ten years later still, all such Indian prisoners were declared slaves for life.[1]

We do not know how many Indian slaves there were in Maryland, for they were classed with the negro slaves. The Indian certainly was little suited to be a slave, by disposition and habit.[2]

If we find mention of slaves but here and there, in the early records of Maryland, we are constantly meeting with white servants.[3] These—Christian servants, as they were frequently called, in contrast to Indians and Africans—were

---

[1] Hening's Statutes of Va., II, 155, 283, 491. A law of North Carolina, as late as the war of 1760, provided that hostile Indians should be the slaves of their captors. In South Carolina, especially, kidnapping seems to have been carried on; but steps were taken to prevent it, afterwards. The captives taken in the wars, early in the eighteenth century, had to be delivered to the receiver of the Colony, to be sold in the West Indies. (Hewatt's So. Carolina, I, 91; Statutes of So. Car., II, 311, 321.)

[2] Numbers of the Indian captives in the various Colonies seem to have been sold to the West Indies.

Any number of Indian slaves would have been a very dangerous element in the Colonies. Cotton Mather tells us that the colonists in Massachusetts found certain Pequot Indian prisoners not able to "endure the Yoke," for few of them continued any considerable time with their masters. Various acts of the New England Colonies, about 1712, forbade the further importation of any Indian servants or slaves, as they were of a malicious, surly and revengeful spirit, and hard to govern withal.

[3] Where we use the word servants, we mean white, indentured or hired, servants; not negroes.

mostly natives of Great Britain who wished to try their fortunes in the New World, but had not means for their passage and necessary expenses. So they entered into written agreements with persons of means, to serve these faithfully for a certain number of years, in return for transportation, clothes and living. The number of servants in Maryland seems to have been quite large, some colonists bringing as many as twenty or thirty or more.[1] We hear of one who brought in over sixty. They were a desirable class in all the Colonies, important in settling the country, and counterbalancing any danger from Indians and negroes. Persons already in America often entered into service, too; and the punishment for some offences was servitude. To prevent fraud and injustice, one of the earliest laws enacted in Maryland limited the time of service, where no time was specified in the agreement, and fixed the freedom dues to be given by the master.[2] It was provided, later, that all agreements of service should be entered at the courts; and no indenture made during service was to be binding for an extension of time.[3] We have a copy of articles of indenture made in 1647.[4] In return for six thousand pounds of tobacco, the man binds himself for three years, to obey, to serve, according to his master's commands; not to absent himself without permission; and not to steal. On the other hand, the master agrees to provide sufficient lodging, food, clothing and washing. It was found at once that servants would run away, so the courts were empowered to add to the time of service, to compensate the masters. The entertainment of others' servants was also strictly forbidden.[5] And when white servants ran away with slaves, they were obliged to recompense the owners of the slaves. After 1715, a reward of two hundred pounds of tobacco was offered every

---

[1] Neill's Founders of Md., 77. Md. Arch., III, 256, 259.
[2] Md. Arch., I, 80.
[3] Md. Arch., I, 352, 409; II, 351.
[4] Md. Arch., IV, 327.
[5] Md. Arch., I, 249, 489. 1715, 44.

colonist who should capture a runaway servant, and an Indian captor was given a match coat. No servant could go beyond ten miles from home without a pass from the master or overseer, under penalty of being caught as a runaway. One who entertained a servant over night became liable to a fine of five hundred pounds of tobacco. Later, the fine was raised to one hundred pounds an hour, or a whipping, if the fine could not be paid. Nor was a servant secure, if he escaped the Colony. On complaint from his owner, the courts would send him back[1]—as slaves were returned. Treaties with Indians stipulated that runaway servants were to be returned. In 1637, the question as to the privilege of servants to rest on Saturday afternoons, was raised in the lower House of Assembly, and it was declared that no such custom was to be allowed.[2] Working on Sunday, however, was not customary. By act of 1715, masters who did not provide sufficient food, clothing and lodging for their servants, or who unreasonably burdened them beyond their strength, or kept them from necessary rest, or beat or abused them excessively—the whipping must not be over ten lashes for any one offence—were liable, if found guilty by the county court, to be fined not over one thousand pounds of tobacco for the first or second offence. On a third offence, the servants would be set free. Any magistrate, on proper complaint of the master, might order a servant to receive more than ten, but not over thirty-nine, lashes. Complaints between masters and servants were heard before the Provincial and county courts, on the petition of either party. As many goods were stolen and sold, trading was forbidden with servants who had no license therefor.[3]

It is evident that this service was radically different from slavery, in that it resulted either from crime or voluntary contract. On the expiration of his term the servant became a

---

[1] Md. Arch., IV, 224, 319.
[2] Md. Arch., I, 21. Bozman's Maryland, II, 136.
[3] Md. Arch., I, 500; 1715, 44.

freeman and a citizen. For some years[1] it was the law that fifty acres of land should be included in the freedom dues, lands being given masters for the servants they imported. Some of these servants were well educated men. We find an advertisement of sale, in 1774, of a schoolmaster, an indented servant, who had two years to serve, with the postscript that he was to be "sold for no fault, any more than we have done with him. He can learn (i. e., teach) bookkeeping, and is an excellent good scholar." Of the servants imported by one of the most prominent colonists, one became a sheriff and five went into the Assembly.[2] This very same gentleman, the military commander of Maryland for many years, presented to the Governor and Assembly, in 1663, a petition which began with the statement that he had, for nearly thirty years, at great cost, benefited the Colony by yearly importations of servants, many of whom had been of "very good Ranck and Quallity;" nor had he ever before been charged with a breach of his promises or duty to them, though it was well known that the care of so large a family was never met by their labor. It appears that this worthy captain had consented, several years before, to take as a servant for seven years the ten-year-old daughter of a poor neighbor, at the neighbor's request. This fellow now falsely alleged that the captain had agreed that the girl should do nothing else than wait upon his wife, and be cared for as his own child—a most ridiculous charge, says the petition, for the lady was about to return to England, and who would be at the trouble of taking such a raw and ill-bred child there, where servants of all sorts might be had on easier terms! The petition then desires

---

[1] Md. Arch., I, 97, 496.
[2] Gambrall's Colonial Church Life in Md., 165; Neill's Founders, 77. A resident of Baltimore, appointed woodcorder in 1781, was found to have been a servant at the time when the oaths of allegiance to the States had been taken, after separation from Great Britain. So the commissioner administered the oath before confirming him in his office.

the serious consideration of the court to the statement of the girl's father in begging that his daughter may not be made a slave—a term, says the captain, so scandalous that if it be admitted to be the title or condition of the apprentices in Maryland, no free-born Christians will ever be induced to come over as servants. Therefor, he prayed that his reputation might be vindicated, and the abused servants and apprentices of Maryland be righted.[1] And yet the lot of the servant was not unlike that of the slave. He was a piece of property, practically. In the inventories of estates, his services are charged as worth so many hundred pounds of tobacco; one man might own his services to-day, and another to-morrow. By a deed of bargain and sale, of 1641, a man-servant was sold from one colonist to another, in different hundreds, for four milch cows. The Provincial Court held that the agreement of a servant to dispose of himself for the satisfaction of his master's debts was valid, and ordered execution on him, as on any goods.[2] About 1700, the Governor and Council received a complaint from a certain inhabitant, that a servant of his, a schoolmaster, whom he had corrected for being impudent and refractory, had applied to a magistrate for a peace-warrant against him. He declared that the servant had been insubordinate and had threatened to send his wife sprawling; while the servant, in turn, accused his master of trying to break his head. The Council considered the matter, and decided to order the magistrate not to countenance the servant, for it was not customary to allow servants to swear the peace against their masters—and it might be very inconvenient. Cases of cruelty to servants were sometimes before the courts.

---

[1] Md. Arch., I, 463. The House, according to the captain's request, ordered the case to be tried again. Do., 481.

[2] Md. Arch., IV, 156, 327.

Council Proceedings, 1704-1708, 8. A letter from Gen. Oglethorpe to the trustees of Georgia, in 1739, tells how 69 "heads of German servants" had been delivered to different persons on credit; one Christie got "5⅔ heads;" the widow Harris got 2, &c.

When the English courts took up the policy of transporting felons, a number of the worst convicts were sold as servants into the Colonies. Before the Revolution the custom of service had practically died out; but it was a common custom at the time when slavery was planted in the Colonies. It must have tended, like the sharply marked class distinctions of that age, to make smoother the pathway for the growth of slavery.

CHAPTER III.

SLAVES.

When, and by whom, the first negroes were brought to Maryland, we do not know; but it was soon after the settlement. We find Governor Calvert bargaining with a certain shipmaster, in 1642, for the delivery of thirteen slaves at St. Mary's.[1] The increase of the blacks—so much is certain—was very slow at first.

One of the first acts of Assembly, declaring "the liberties of the people," assured to all Christian inhabitants all the rights enjoyed in England by natural born subjects, except, of course, in so far as those rights might be changed by provincial law—and excepting slaves. And the early acts for the regulation and protection of servants expressly stated that nothing contained in them should affect any slaves whatever. The rule in the courts was that justice should be administered, where provincial law or custom was silent, according to English precedent. The royal charter to Lord Baltimore had ordered that the laws to be enacted in the Colony should be consonant to reason and, as far as conveniently might be, agreeable to the rights and customs of England.[2] But the first colonists brought with them from England no precedent for giving any especial rights or privileges to Indian or negro—nothing but the distance felt in that age between Christian and

---

[1] Md. Arch., IV, 189.
[2] Charter of Md., Md. Arch., I, 41, 80, 409, 487; III, 53, &c.

heathen. There were no Indians in England, and few if any negroes. Even later, when a number of negro slaves were held in England, mostly as body servants, and sales of them at auction not infrequently took place, there was no legislation touching them. We have seen how the Colonies dealt with the Indians according to their own ideas of justice or prudence. British merchants, indeed, under the patronage of the British government, supplied the slaves; but the colonists otherwise built up their slave legislation as they saw fit. Just as a nobility, an incident of the growth of English society, existed in England at the time of the settlement of the Colonies and yet took no root in them, so slavery became an incident of the condition of the Colonies, and the slave codes grew up as a matter of local law. Thus, we can trace in the legislation and in the court reports, and in the life of the plantation and the town, of such an unit as Maryland, the entire growth of a slave code.[1]

---

[1] We use the word negro, or black, to include mulattoes. When the distinction is to be drawn, the word mulatto is used.

The legal view of the introduction and growth of slavery in the Colonies has been elaborately treated by Mr. John Codman Hurd in The Law of Freedom and Bondage (Little & Brown, Boston, 1858).

The writer of a recent Constitutional History of England says that slavery was legalized in the colonies by British statutes encouraging the slave-trade. A number of negroes were brought to England as servants, some of them from the colonies. An article in the *Gentleman's Magazine* of London, in 1764, speaks of the encouragement given to the practice of importing negro servants, and states that the number of such in London alone was supposed to be nearly twenty thousand. In the famous Somerset case, eight years after, Mr. Dunning asserted that there were in England fourteen thousand slaves brought from the colonies. Even as late as that time, negroes were occasionally sold in England. One negro boy in London brought thirty-two pounds, at auction, and another, at Richmond, brought the same. A boy was advertised to be sold at auction at Liverpool, in 1779. The visitor to Hampton Court or Warwick Castle, to-day, will see busts of black servants, with metal collars about the neck. In 1677, there was tried in England a case of trover for one hundred negroes, and the court held that as negroes were usually bought and sold among merchants, and were also infidels, there might be property in them sufficient to maintain trover. As late

Slaves had not increased much in numbers in the Colonies before a most interesting question arose concerning them— What was the effect on the status of a slave of his conversion to Christianity? And the extent to which doubts on this matter spread, and the length of time which those doubts lasted, show that the knowledge that a religious distinction was the basis of this chattel slavery was not confined to students of law alone. It was not unnatural that in popular belief freedom was associated with baptism. In the first case concerning slaves, in English courts, in 1677—in which the court held that trover would lie for the negro, as they were heathen—the argument was advanced that in England negroes could be no more a property than villeins could. But the court said they were held as goods by usage, and should therefore be given to the plaintiff, "until they become christians, and thereby they are Infranchised." During the session of the Maryland Assembly of 1664, a message was sent the Council by the House, requesting the former to draw up an act which should oblige negroes to serve for life, the assembly thinking this very necessary to prevent the damage that masters of slaves might sustain by such slaves pretending to be christened, and so pleading the law of England.[1] And so a law was made that all negroes

---

as 1694 judgment was given that trover would lie for a negro, for he was a heathen. After that, judicial opinions differed; and in about a century, public opinion changed so far as to support Lord Mansfield in his decision in the Somerset case, by which slavery in England ended. The abolition of slavery in the British colonies was brought about only after further and arduous efforts by the abolitionists and philanthropists. See Taswell-Langmead's Const. History of England, p. 300, note. British Statutes; 10 Will., III, c. 26; 5 Geo., II, c. 7; 23 Geo., II, c. 31. Bandinel's Slave Trade, p. 71, note. *Gentleman's Mag.*, XXXIII, 45, XLI, 521. Memoirs of Granville Sharp, I, 140. Cases of Butts *vs.* Penny and Gelly & Cleve, quoted in Hurd. In the colonies, as we see, ideas of English law were often very uncertain.

[1] Butts *vs.* Penny, in 3 Keble, 785. Md. Arch., I, 526–533. In Chamberlayne *vs.* Harvey, twenty years later, the question as to whether baptism was a manumission was raised, but the court gave no answer, holding that trover would not lie for a negro. In Carthew's R., 396.

or other slaves already in the Province, or to be imported thereafter, should serve for life. This was made more explicit seven years later, by an act entitled "an Act for the Encouragcing the Importacon of Negros and Slaves," which declared that conversion or the holy sacrament of baptism should not be taken to give manumission in any way to slaves or their issue, who had become or should become Christians, or had been or should be baptized, either before or after their importation to Maryland, any opinion to the contrary notwithstanding. Because, as the act says, several of the good people of this Province have been discouraged from importing or purchasing therein any negroes or other slaves; and such as have imported or purchased any there have neglected—to the great displeasure of Almighty God and the prejudice of the souls of those poor people—to instruct them in the Christian faith, and to permit them to receive the holy sacrament of baptism for the remission of their sin, under the mistaken and ungrounded apprehension that their slaves, by becoming Christians, would thereby be freed.[1] So the law remained. To a question of the Lords of Trade as to the number of negroes converted to Christianity, Lord Baltimore answered, in 1678, that all he could say was that in many other parts of America masters were refusing, "out of covetousness," to allow their negroes and mulattoes to be baptized—of an idea that baptism would work as much loss to them as the death of their slaves; but when this opinion became current in Maryland, a law was made declaring that as in former times the baptism of villeins in England was not taken to be manumission or enfranchisement, so it should not then be taken to free negroes and mulattoes. And there have been found good effects since, adds the proprietor, masters generally being willing to instruct these in the faith of Christ.[2] We find little else in Maryland to

---

[1] Md. Arch., II, 272. Reënacted in 1692, and, in other words, in the permanent act of 1715 (44).
[2] Md. Arch., V, 267.

throw light on this most interesting subject. One colored man, a native of Madagascar, who had been a servant in England, and had then been shipped to America as a servant, was detained as a slave in Maryland. On petitioning for freedom in 1692—which was given him, the court finding that he had been shipped as a servant only—his plea was that he had been baptized and educated and had served two apprenticeships, and was therefore free by the laws of England. We find the zealous Thomas Story publicly reproaching a clergyman of the English church, at a yearly meeting of Friends at West River, in 1699, for taking negroes into the brotherhood of Christ in baptism, and yet keeping them slaves.[1] The idea that baptism implied freedom seems to have lingered long in all the Colonies, even where there was direct legislation to the contrary. In 1729, in response to an appeal from some of the American colonists—evidently, according to Bishop Berkeley, in order to increase the conversion of the blacks—the Crown-Attorney and the Solicitor-General of England sent over their opinion that baptism in no way changed the slave's status.[2]

---

[1] Prov. Court, Liber C, 162. Janney's History of the Friends, III, 66. According to that zealous missionary of the time, Rev. Dr. Bray, the whites of Maryland abstained largely from baptism themselves.

[2] This opinion seems to have been especially called for in Rhode Island. Works of Berkeley, Vol. III. See, also, Pearne *vs.* Lisle, Ambler's R., 75.

In Virginia there was enacted, in 1667, that baptism did not give freedom, so that divers masters, freed from doubt, might endeavor to spread christianity among the blacks. By the Act of 1670, all servants *not christians and imported by sea*, were to serve for life. But this was changed twelve years later, having been found inconvenient in preventing the introduction of slaves from neighboring colonies: inasmuch, we read, as many Negroes, Moors and others, born in heathenish, idolatrous and Mahometan countries, have been gotten as slaves therefrom by some well disposed christians, who have then brought them to the christian religion, out of a pious zeal, and have since had occasion, or may have occasion, to bring them into Virginia to be sold—where they can sell them only for the limited time of service of a white christian servant, and must then either carry them elsewhere, where they can be sold as slaves for life, or else depart from their just right to

Until a few years only before slavery was abolished, the old religious distinction that underlay that institution was still to be read in one law of Maryland. The testimony of no negro or Indian would be received as evidence at law in any case in which "any Christian white person" was concerned. The word Christian was struck out in 1846.

The clever political student Bodin, writing in 1576 of slavery in Southern Europe, noted with some reproach that—like the Mahometans, who converted but still kept in bonds their Christian prisoners—the Portuguese and Spaniards were keeping in perpetual slavery the Moors and negroes whom they had taken as heathen but had converted.[1] In Maryland and the other Colonies there was probably no widespread and serious opposition to the continuance of this bondage of the children of enslaved Indians or Africans, whether heathen or Christian. Thus slavery was based on a race distinction; though we

---

them, to their great damage, and to the great discouragement of the importation of slaves. (Hening's Statutes, 1667, 3; 1670, 12; 1682, 1.) About 1700, there appeared in print in New England an earnest plea for the religious instruction of the negroes and Indians. The writer, who says he does not know why freedom should follow conversion, asks what hindrance there is to the baptism of those people. It is a notorious matter of fact, he answers, that masters discourage those poor creatures and hinder them from coming to baptism, though many desire it. Talk to a planter of the soul of a negro, and his actions, if not his words, will tell you that the body of the black may be worth twenty pounds, but the souls of a hundred will not yield him a farthing. The true reason is, that custom of giving them their freedom after they become christians. (Moore's Slavery in Mass., 93.) An English clergyman in Carolina, in 1709, wrote to the secretary of the Society for the Propagation of the Gospel, that a few of the two hundred and more negroes in his neighborhood were taught of the christian religion, but their masters would by no means permit them to be baptized, from a false notion that a slave is thereby freed, by law. Another missionary wrote, soon after, that he had with much importunity prevailed on a certain person to allow him to baptize three of the negroes. (Hawk's North Carolina, II, 310, 332.) So fixed had these ideas become in Rhode Island, as stated by Bishop Berkeley in a sermon at London, in 1732, that but few negroes there had been baptized.

[1] Commonweale, Knolles' Trans., 43.

must be careful in supposing that such changes were plainly seen, or that most men acted from theories. As a rule, men were thinking of material prosperity. Most of those who theorized on the subject, echoed, without doubt, the voice of that New England writer, who appealed for the religious instruction of the negroes: Some persons, nay, some nations, he says, seem to be born for slaves; particularly many of the barbarians of Africa, who have been such almost from the beginning of the world, and who are much better off when slaves among us than when free at home, to cut throats and eat one another, especially if by slavery of the body they are made capable of freeing their souls.[1]

However the matter of religion or race may have entered into slavery, the "color line" was not drawn as sharply in Maryland at first as it was afterwards—although "negroes and other slaves," as we read in the old acts, were certainly deemed a most abject class. As an illustration of this, as well as of the newness of many questions which the few legislators at St. Mary's had to answer, we place here several laws, which might properly be considered also under the head of crimes and punishments. In drawing up the act of 1664, to prevent slaves from pleading freedom by baptism, the Council asked the lower House what it intended should become of such free women of the English or other Christian nations as married negroes or other slaves; should they serve as long as their husbands lived, and should their issue be bond or free? Suits had evidently arisen over such issue, and some damage been caused to the masters of the slaves. In a few hours, the House sent back their answers—that women so married should not serve during their husbands' lives, and that their children should serve to thirty years of age. But the act, which was soon passed—reciting that divers freeborn English women, forgetful of their condition and to the disgrace of their nation,

---

[1] Moore's Slavery in Mass., 94; quoting from the Athenian Oracle of about 1700.

intermarried with negro slaves—declared, that such women as might so marry thereafter should serve the slaves' masters so long as the slaves lived, and that children of such marriages already made should serve until they were thirty years old, but that the children of such marriages made thereafter should be slaves "as their fathers were."[1] By the act of 1681, children born of white servant women and negroes were free.[2] After 1692, the issue of a union between any white woman and any slave or *free negro* became servants for a long term.[3] By the act of 1715, ministers and magistrates were forbidden, by fine, to marry any white to "any Negro whatsoever, or Mulatto Slave." By this, a white and a free mulatto could marry. And an act, two years later, to provide penalties against the parties marrying unlawfully, under this act of 1715, made a free negro or mulatto liable to service for life—except mulattoes born of white women, who had to serve, like the whites, for only seven years.[4] Again, by act of 1728, free mulatto

---

[1] This act declared that "Negroes or other slaves" should serve for life, and that "all children born of any Negro or other slave shall be Slaves as their FFATHERS were for the terme of their lives." There must have been then no free blacks in the colony—or we are left to reason that children followed the condition of the father instead of the mother, entirely contrary to custom, as we find it later. (Md. Arch., 1, 526, 533.) The act of 1681 declared simply that all children of slaves were to serve for life.

[2] The mother also became free; and her master, if he knew of the marriage, was liable also to a fine of 10,000 pounds of tobacco, and so was the minister or magistrate who performed the service. (Acts of 1681, W. H., 174.)

[3] By this act of 1692, also, the white woman who married, or became with child by, a slave or free negro, became a servant for seven years, to the use of the parish clergy or the poor. If a servant and if her master had not known of her offence, she first recompensed his loss by service. The black served for life, except that a free black, for having a bastard child by a white woman, served seven years. There was the same heavy fine against the master who allowed such a marriage and against the person who performed it. And there was, also, the provision that any white man who married with, or had child by, a negro woman, should be put to service for seven years. (1692, L. L. 220.)

[4] Service for seven years at the disposition of the county court, for the benefit of the public schools. By act of 1715, the fine against minister or

women who might have children by "negroes and other slaves" were to be punished by the same penalty as white women for the same offence—which was declared to be as heinous for a free mulatto as for a white.[1] So, the act of 1717, which remained the law of evidence for a long period, excluded the testimony of any Indian or slave or free negro or mulatto servant, in cases at law in which any Christian white person was concerned, but left the free mulatto, apparently— the free mulatto born of a white woman, surely—as free to testify as was a white.[2]

Africans might be more or less colored, but they were not all slaves, of course. And kidnapping came to be recognized

---

magistrate was made 5,000 pounds of tobacco. Any white woman who became a mother by a slave or free negro had to serve seven years, as before, and the free black served the same time. The children of such unions served until thirty-one years old. There was, also, the same service of seven years for white men, the fathers of illegitimate colored children. All service was disposed of by the courts. (1715, 44; 1717, 13.)

[1] All free negro women, also, having illegitimate children by white men, were liable to the same punishment as white women for having children by negroes. Forasmuch, says the preamble, as such relations, as between a free mulatto woman and a slave, or a free negro woman and a white, "are as unnatural and inordinate as between white women and Negro Men, or other Slaves." (1728, 4.)

[2] 1717, 13. See Evidence, in chapter on The Free Negro.

In 1788, a committee of the House of Delegates reported in favor of abolishing those parts of these laws which inflicted penalties on the children. Two years later, they were abolished; it being contrary to the dictates of humanity, and to the principles of the Christian religion, says the preamble of the act of repeal, to impose penalties on children for the offences of their parents. (1790, 9. Code of 1860, Art. 30, 128.)

Several cases, under these laws, came to the Court of Appeals.

In 1681, the Lord Proprietor brought with him to Maryland a white servant called Irish Nell. She married a slave, evidently before the passage of the act of 1681. Perhaps indeed the act was called for by this marriage. The descendants of those children of Nell, born after the act— which exempted from servitude the children of such marriages made thereafter—petitioned in vain for freedom. See 1 H. & McH., 210; 2 H. & McH., 137. Also 3 H. & McH., 380. The cases cited from the Maryland Reports down to 2 Gill, are from Brantly's edition.

by all authorities as a crime, by custom if not by positive legislation.[1] But it is evident that the status of a black, or of his ancestry, could not often be easily shown.

The chief justice of Calvert county was asked by the Governor and Council of Maryland, in 1760, to examine carefully one Cousins, captain of a brigantine, who had recently imported a number of negroes into the Province,—as word had just come to the Governor that several of these negroes had declared that they were not slaves but freemen; that one of them in particular, called Capt. Gray, was the son of an African of some consequence; and that Captain Cousins had treacherously stolen them away. See, therefore, ends the letter, if Cousins be guilty of the crime whereof he is accused; and if the evidence be sufficient, have him brought before the Council at once. The depositions of the mates, a boatswain and a sailor of the brigantine, were soon sent to the Council. The seaman testified that he had sailed from Liverpool with Cousins on a slaving voyage to Guinea, and that there the negroes were purchased; all of whom he believes were slaves, except, perhaps, the one called Captain Gray. This Gray, he

---

[1] The Massachusetts Body of Liberties, of 1641, restricted slavery—except, of course, for crime—to lawful captives taken in just war, and to such strangers as might be sold to, or might willingly sell themselves to, the colonists. A few years after, a kidnapped negro from Africa was sent home, by order of the General Court—which felt bound, so reads the resolution, to bear witness against the "heinous and crying sin of man-stealing." (Moore's Slavery in Mass.)

The British statute, for extending and improving the trade to Africa, at the middle of the last century—which declared that trade to be very advantageous to Great Britain, and necessary for supplying the Colonies with sufficient negroes at reasonable rates—provided that no master of a ship trading in Africa should by force or fraud, or any indirect practice, carry away from that country any native thereof, or allow any violence to be committed on the natives in prejudice of the British trade. (23 Geo. II, 31.) In 1779 a captain of a Liverpool slaver was prosecuted by the African company for having sold a free negro, whom he had hired as a sailor. He was fined five hundred pounds, as a warning to the other commanders engaged in the trade. (Macpherson's Annals of Commerce, III, 638.)

understood, had been a servant to a freeman on the coast of Guinea, and was employed by his master in carrying slaves out to the ships. While thus at work, he stole a scarlet jacket from Captain Cousins, who never allowed him to go on shore afterwards, but offered to return him if another slave were given for him. But those to whom this offer was made refused to exchange him, saying that he was a scandal to his country, and they would not give for him a slave four feet high. The seaman further stated that he had heard that servitude was the common punishment for crime in that country. The mates and boatswain swore that Gray was not only taken in theft, but had been concerned afterwards in cutting the ship's cable, and so endangering her loss; and that the other negroes in question had been left on the ship as pledges by the traders, for some seven weeks or more before she sailed, without any offers to redeem them, and that as many goods had been given for them as for other slaves. The Council deemed the complaints groundless, and Captain Cousins was discharged. A petition for freedom, of a certain woman—held, it so happened, by a parish—came before the General Court of Maryland in 1796. The fact was admitted, without question on either side, that the petitioner was descended from a negro woman who had been imported many years before from Madagascar. The counsel for the petitioner claimed that the act which stated that all slaves imported, and their issue, should be slaves, related to those brought from countries whence slaves were customarily exported. A person brought from any country where the slave trade was not carried on, and sold in Maryland, would not lawfully be a slave. Madagascar was not a place whence slaves were usually brought; and Vol. 6 of the "World Displayed" was cited. On the other hand, the counsel for the parish quoted three works of geography and travel, in which there was stated that in Madagascar the petty kings make war on each other for plunder and slaves, and are accustomed to sell slaves to Europeans. The court dismissed the petition, holding that, as Madagascar was a country where the slave trade was practised, and Maryland was one where slavery was tolerated, the petitioner, in order to receive her freedom, would have to show that her ancestor was free in her native country.[1]

The act of 1664 and its successors, declaring the children of slaves to be slaves, did not operate, to quote the General Court of Maryland in a decision in 1799, to make all negroes slaves, but merely created a presumption that they were such, which presumption could be rebutted.[2] There was growing up slowly, during the eighteenth century, from manumission or free ancestry, a small free black population. If one parent of a child was free and the other was a slave, the status of the child—as under Roman law—was that of the mother.

The existence of slavery in Maryland was stated plainly in many acts of assembly and in a constitutional amendment of 1837. But, as the courts in some of the free States began to require owners of fugitive slaves to prove the existence of slavery in the State where the slaves belonged, an act of 1839 declared that in Maryland from the earliest settlement, negroes and mulattoes had been held as slaves, and were then held and might be thereafter held as such, as the property of their owners; and that the owner of any slave was entitled to his service during his life, unless the slave could show that by the grant or devise of his owner, or of some former owner of his or of his maternal ancestor, a shorter period of service had been prescribed. A negro was presumed to be a slave. If he petitioned for freedom, the question to be tried was his right thereto, not the right of his master to hold him in slavery. The slave must bear the burden of proof. Nor was the fact that a negro went at large and acted as a freeman, deemed a proof that he was free.[3]

---

[1] Council Records, 1753–1767; Sept. 22d, 1760. 3 H. & McH., 278.
[2] 4 H. & McH., 193.
[3] 1839, 42. 6 G. & J., 86; 9 G. & J., 112, 127. See chapter on Manumission.

The acts of the Assembly of Maryland of 1671 and 1692—which, as we have seen, declared that the children of slaves were slaves, and that conversion did not affect slavery—were entitled, acts to encourage the importation of negroes, and were passed because several of the good people of the Province had been discouraged, so we read, from importing them.[1] But the number of those brought in was small, until about the beginning of the eighteenth century. Governor Nicholson wrote the Board of Trade, in 1698, that some six hundred servants had recently been imported and four or five hundred negroes were expected during the summer.[2] There is mention of some three hundred slaves brought into Patuxent Bay in August, 1700. The Board of Trade in London was constantly asking after the state of the slave importations. The Governor of Maryland wrote, in 1708, that the trade had been rising and was then a "high" one; that some six or seven hundred blacks had been imported in the ten months past.[3] Two years later, came word that the negroes were increasing. The Public Record Office in London has a list of the "Christian" men, women and children and also of negro slaves, in Maryland, in 1712.[4] The whites numbered

---

[1] In the same way we find early laws of South Carolina declaring that negroes are necessary for the development of that Province.

A prominent member of the Massachusetts Bay Company wrote his brother-in-law, the elder Winthrop, in speaking of the Narrragansett Indians, about 1645, that "if upon a Just Warre the Lord should deliver them into our hands, we might easily have men woemen and children enough to exchange for Moores, (i. e. negroes) which wilbe more gayneful pilladge for us than wee conceive, for I doe not see how wee can thrive untill wee get into a stock of slaves sufficient to doe all our buisines, for our children's children will hardly see this great Continent filled with people, soe that our servants will still desire freedom to plant for themselves, and not stay but for verie great wages. And I suppose you know verie well how wee shall maynteyne 20 Moores cheaper than one Englishe servant." (Moore's Slavery in Mass., 10.)

[2] Steven's Hist. Index, vols. 4 and 5.

[3] Records from the London Office, quoted in Scharf's Maryland, I, 376.

[4] Steven's Index, vol. 8. Scharf, I, 377.

nearly thirty-eight thousand, the negroes over eight thousand. In three of the southern counties, the blacks far outnumbered the whites. In the years following, both races increased fast, but the blacks faster than the whites. By 1750, the whites may have been nearly a hundred thousand, the blacks nearly forty thousand.[1] In 1790, there were over two hundred and eight thousand whites, and nearly half as many slaves; the eight thousand and odd free blacks making the proportion of white to black as less than two to one.

The great staple of colonial Maryland, as of Virginia, was tobacco. The Governor of Virginia wrote of the tobacco trade, in 1726, as the one by which the governments of the Colonies subsisted. Tobacco was the common currency. Cotton seems to have been planted somewhat before 1700, but it was spoken of by one high official to another as prejudicial to the planting of tobacco and the King's interest. So great was the production of tobacco that efforts were made by the colonial authorities both to improve the staple by more limited crops, and to turn the interests of men to other things—but it was hard to make men agree to the first, and to both aims the policy of the mother country was bitterly opposed. Hardly had a generation passed, after the foundation of the Colony, before laws were enacted, to encourage the production of hemp and flax, and manufacturing and tanning. But it was little use to urge men to work the iron ore, when an act of Parliament, encouraging the exportation of pig iron from the Colonies to England, forbade in them the erection of any furnace or forge. By 1750, the trade of Maryland, chiefly in tobacco, was carried on by British vessels of some twelve thousand tons, total burden—the shipping of the Province being forty or fifty small craft, only. Among the queries sent, some ten years later, by the authorities in England to the Council of Maryland was the question: are there any trades or

---

[1] The early estimates of population in the Colonies seem as a rule to be very untrustworthy. We must take them as approximations.

manufactures in Maryland which are hurtful or may prove hurtful to Great Britain; and, if so, how may they be suppressed, divided or restrained? And in reply we read, that the chief branch of trade was the importation of goods and manufactures from Great Britain, supposed to be worth annually more than one hundred and sixty thousand pounds, and, in return, an annual export of about twenty-eight thousand hogsheads of tobacco, bringing to the producers and the merchants together, before it reached the English markets, nearly three hundred thousand pounds. Perhaps eighty thousand pounds worth of other produces were shipped—corn, wheat, pig iron, skins, lumber, &c. This trade was carried on in some hundred and twenty British vessels of eighteen thousand tons, total burden. The boats belonging in the Province numbered about thirty only, of thirteen hundred tons in all, and had been mostly engaged in the West India trade; but that trade had not been very profitable, and there was little probability of its increase. As to manufactures or trades in the Province which might be hurtful to Great Britain, there were none.[1]

Even as late as this time, we must remember, the bulk of the population of these Southern Colonies had not gone far from the coast. Maryland, like Virginia, had been well suited for agriculture in its physical characteristics. For years the settlements had been mostly dotted along tidewater, plantation after plantation, with few towns. Endeavors made to build large towns and ports by act of assembly were far from successful.[2] The flat fields were cut up by a network of rivers and creeks. A short row in a boat would often save near neighbors miles of travel over wretched roads. Up these inlets came the British vessels, to give to the planters the manufactures that he seldom saw otherwise, and to take away the

---

[1] See Md. Arch., V, 16, 266. Council Records, 1749, 390; 1761, 316 (416?); 1756, 117.

[2] As 1683, 5; 1684, 2; 1688, 6, &c.

tobacco and breadstuffs from the very fields where they were raised.

The British ships brought not only the manufactures, but the slaves. The colonists themselves were anxious, at first, as we have seen, for supplies of blacks. In how far they were influenced by ideas that black labor was cheap and advantageous labor, peculiarly suited to those flat coast lands, hot and malarial in summer; or in how far competition between these tobacco regions may have really ruled out any other labor, we do not venture to answer.[1] But to the British, the slave trade only supplemented the policy of discouragement of manufactures and encouragement of tobacco. Acts of Parliament, at the beginning and middle of the eighteenth century, encouraged it as highly beneficial to both mother country and colonies; and it was pursued to the benefit of the British Crown, as well as of the merchants. Of the twenty-two hundred and ninety negroes imported into Maryland from 1699 to 1707, all but a hundred and twenty-six came in London vessels.[2]

Towards the close of the seventeenth century the public charges of the Province had been growing burdensome. Efforts were being made to increase the facilities for education. The seat of government was moved to Annapolis. In 1689 war broke out between Great Britain and France, to bring new burdens on the Colonies threatened by French and Indians. The same Assembly which reënacted the law to encourage the introduction of slaves in 1692, laid a new duty of fourpence a gallon on

---

[1] The introduction of slavery into Georgia suggests most interesting questions of this kind. The only labor allowed in Georgia, by the rules of the Trustees of the Colony, for some twenty years after the settlement, was white labor. Many considerations, as the nearness of hostile Spaniards and Indians, and the unfavorable character of part of the settlers, prevent any hasty answers; but climate, especially in the production of rice in the lowlands, and the fact that the same produces could be bought much cheaper on the Carolina side than on the Georgia side of the Savannah, were certainly strong influences on those Georgians, by far the great majority of authorities and citizens, who finally secured the introduction of black labor.

[2] Doc. from Public Record office, quoted in Scharf's Md., 1, 377.

imported liquors, to discharge the arrears of government, to pay soldiers, to repair courthouses and prisons, and for other charges. Two years later this was continued, and a duty was laid further on several commodities exported, as furs, beef and bacon, for the maintenance of the free schools. The next year, in addition, a duty of threepence a hogshead was put on tobacco, for a year; and ten per cent. on all "European commodities" exported, for three years; as well as a tax on certain local offices.[1] Over three hundred pounds had then to be sent towards the support of the colonial forces in New York. It was then—when the Province was so destitute of ready money, to pay the soldiers in arms for its defence, that a member of the House of Delegates offered to loan certain sums until he could be reimbursed from the treasury—that the first duty was laid on slaves imported, and on white servants, too. The majority of the Assembly declared for ten shillings a head on negroes; all agreed on two shillings sixpence for servants. The receipts were thereupon to be applied to the building of a statehouse and other expenses. We should note that at the same session, there was passed an act to restrain large assemblages of negroes. There were rumors of movements by papists and negroes—it is interesting to note how European politics were reflected in the Colonies, often amounting only to a little talk, and some legislation. At the next session the duty on both negroes and Irish servants was made twenty shillings a head—with a penalty of five pounds on any smuggling merchant or shipmaster—to raise supplies and to limit the importation of Irish papists. The full title of the act of 1704, which continued this, was an Act for imposing threepence a gallon on liquors, "and twenty Shillings per poll for Negroes, for raising a Supply to defray the public charge of this Province; and twenty shillings per poll on Irish Servants, to prevent the importing too great a Number of Irish papists into this Province." But by act of the same session, liquors and negroes could be

---

[1] 1692, 22; 1694, 19, 23.

imported without duty in vessels owned wholly by residents of Maryland, to encourage the inhabitants to adventure their ships abroad more freely. In 1715 the same exemption was offered, in addition, for Irish servants imported in home vessels. The next year an additional duty of four pounds a head was laid on Irish servants and on negroes, for the old reasons; but this act met with the dissent of the Lord Proprietor. So the next Assembly laid twenty shillings more a head on them, making the total duty forty shillings, except for those imported in home vessels. So the duty remained for years, except that after 1728, home vessels had to pay half duty; and after 1732, Protestant servants from Ireland could be imported free, as from elsewhere.[1] These duties were to be laid on all importations, by land or water; but after 1721, residents of Maryland, who owned slaves in other colonies, and persons coming to Maryland to settle—as complaint was made of the hardship such persons had to suffer through the duties—were allowed to import their servants free, if not for sale.[2]

We have no grounds for presuming that the early duties on negroes were laid for any other reason than that given in the acts—the payment of public charges. But by the middle of the century there was evidently some opposition rising to the further large importation of them. Maryland was not such a frontier, nor was its black population so large in proportion to the whites, as to cause its citizens the anxieties which were felt in South Carolina, where the laws, which had not long since

---

[1] Proceedings of House, May, 1695; 1695, ch. 9; 1696, 7; 1699, 23; 1704, 9, 67; 1715, 36; 1716, 6; 1717, 10; 1728, 8; 1732, 23. After 1735, no duty had to be paid for any servant or slave who might die, or be exported by the importer, within three months after importation. (1735, 6.) When the House of Commons asked, in 1736, for the laws in force by which duties were laid on various articles of trade, the Governor of Maryland answered, for negroes, forty shillings. This evidently referred to the duty for those imported on English vessels; and the home commerce, as we have seen, amounted to little.

[2] 1721, 9.

spoken of the need of black labor, now called for whites, and ascribed the faster increase in the blacks to the "afflicting providence of God." But when, during the French and Indian war, the Maryland Assembly argued with many words the expediency of requiring indentured white servants to do military duty, as called for by the Governor, one objection thereto was that the importation of servants would decrease, for planters would import more blacks, who were never subject to military duty. When a country, answered the Governor, is in danger of being lost to the enemy, it is no time for its government to enter into critical dissertations as to whether the enlistment of servants may not tend to lessen the importation of them, for planting, and to increase that of slaves.[1]

In 1754 new duties were laid, to meet the demands for His Majesty's service in the French and Indian war. A pedler had to pay four pounds for his license; each wheel of a carriage cost the owner five shillings a year; twenty shillings a head was put on all servants imported, to serve for seven years or more, and five shillings on most others. On negroes, ten shillings a head was added to the existing forty. When larger expenses had to be met, later, some new duties were laid. The duty on servants for long terms was abolished, and twenty additional shillings per head was put on negroes.[2] When these new duties ceased, a year after the war ended, there was laid a duty of two pounds a head on negroes, over and above the still existing duty of forty shillings.[3] But, as before, any

---

[1] Council Records, 1756, 90.

[2] Among the provisions of this act were a tax of 5 shillings a year on all unmarried men worth from £100 to £300, and 20 shillings on those of greater means; for every billiard table, £3; for every horse imported from any colony for sale, a duty of 40 shillings; a tax of 1 shilling on every 100 acres of freehold property, except lands owned by papists, who paid 2 shillings, &c. 1754, 9; 1756, 5.

[3] 1763, 28. The acts 1715, 36; 1717, 10, seemed to have continued in force. So the total duty, to 1771, was eighty shillings a head. The money was applied to the schools.

person coming to Maryland to live, from any part of the King's dominions, could bring in his servants free. And the duty would be remitted also on slaves exported within two months. Eight years later, in 1771, there was placed a further additional duty of five pounds a head—excepting, as before, those brought in by persons coming to settle, and excepting those exported within four months—on importations by land or water. This ceased in 1778, but within two years, under pressure of war, taxes and duties were rated anew. As before, nothing had to be paid on slaves brought in, not for sale, by persons coming to reside. Otherwise, there was a duty of fifteen pounds on every slave who had lived in the States for full three years, and of five hundred pounds on every other.[1] After two years, in 1782, as enough of the required funds had been raised by taxes and sales of State property, some of these new duties—as those on iron and tobacco exported—were taken off; and it was declared that all those on imports should cease as soon as Congress should lay the expected duty of five per cent., except the duty on slaves. And at the same session the tax rate on all property was reduced by a third.[2] The next year—when the favorable condition of the State finances allowed the removal of the extra duties and taxes laid for redeeming the bills of credit—was passed the act which forbade the introduction by land or water of any slave for sale. A citizen of the United States who might come to Maryland to live, and should actually live there a year, could bring in any slaves who had belonged to him elsewhere—if they had been in the country for three years. The previous whereabouts of the slave was to be fully proven to the collector. Servants of travelers were specially

---

[1] This act (1780, 8,) is entitled an Act for sinking the quota of Maryland of the bills of credit issued by Congress. It put a duty, also, on iron and tobacco exported, a tax on marriage licenses, &c., &c. The title of 1771 (7) is simply to place an extra duty on negroes imported. Payment under 1780, 8, was in pounds currency.

[2] 1782, 50, 54.

exempted, but they could not remain indefinitely, or be sold in the State. And any slave imported contrary to law was to be set free.[1] The number of blacks had grown to be about eighty thousand, nearly a half of the number of whites. They had increased faster than the whites during the preceding decade, if we may trust the estimates of population.

The wishes of the Colonies, now the States, had changed during the century. The result of the change is well known: how negroes were forced on the southern Colonies—despite frequent remonstrance from some of them—by the mother country.[2] Virginia had been foremost in remonstrance, and now forbade all slave trade from without her borders, in 1778. The Maryland Act of 1783 was much the same as this Virginia Act of 1778; but the high duty of 1780 on negroes fresh from abroad was practically a prohibition of the foreign trade. Aside from the duties, we find no remonstrance against the slave trade on the part of the colonial Assemblies of Maryland. Later, when the question of the prohibition of the foreign trade was before Congress, the Assembly of Maryland resolved, in 1805, that their senators and representatives should be instructed and requested to use their utmost exertions to obtain an amendment to the Constitution, by which Congress, when it was deemed expedient, could put an end to all further importation. And the same resolution was sent to the Governors of all the States, with the request that it be laid before the different Legislatures, for their concurrence and adoption. Again, the next year, similar messages were sent the Maryland congressmen, declaring the prohibition of the slave trade to be a most desirable measure.[3]

---

[1] 1783, 23; 1782, 29. Scharf's History of Maryland, III, 291, says that a bill against importation was presented in the House in 1767, but was not passed. The manuscript Journals of Assembly do not give any session that year.

[2] See Bancroft, Part III, ch. 16.

[3] Res., 1805, 11, 12; 1806, 6, 14.

The old duty of forty shillings was not collected, as we have seen, on slaves brought into Maryland by citizens who had estates in other colonies or by persons about to become residents. But all importations had to be entered at the customs, and no slave could be sold for three years. The act of 1783 allowed importation to residents only, and limited it then, to slaves who had been in the country for some time, and who were not for sale. But some fault was soon found with such sweeping restrictions. Several citizens of Virginia who owned lands in Maryland asked leave of the Assembly to bring in some of their slaves from Virginia, to cultivate those lands. A bill in their favor passed the House but was defeated in the Senate. For several years following, similar bills were similarly defeated. One citizen of Maryland, who had married a Virginian who held slaves in trust, and had also carried certain slaves into Virginia, received permission in 1791, by a special act, to import all these slaves. The Senate then urged upon the House a bill amending the law of 1783. Should we reciprocate, reads their message, the privileges given by Virginia, and allow Virginians to bring their slaves over the Potomac, under careful restrictions, surely "no political disadvantage will accrue" to Maryland. Whereupon the House passed the bills—by a vote of thirty-eight to seventeen—so that citizens of Maryland holding land, in their own or in their wives' rights, in Virginia, Delaware or Pennsylvania, and owning slaves employed on those lands, might bring these slaves into Maryland, to be worked for their benefit, and not to be sold; and provided, further, that the slaves were residents, or children of residents, of the States mentioned, before 1783. Citizens might bring in, also, any such slaves acquired by inheritance or marriage in other States. And Virginians holding lands in Maryland might bring in their slaves, to cultivate these. To prevent fraud, the slaves—as well as the title to them, if acquired by inheritance or marriage—had to be recorded in all cases at the county office; and they could then be carried to and fro, at the pleasure of the owner.[1] The next year, a former citizen of Maryland who had been living in Delaware for two years, obtained an act to allow him to bring back the negroes he had taken away with him, and their issue. The proprietors of several iron works which lay near together on both sides of the Potomac, were allowed to carry back and forth male slaves used on the works, provided that no Virginia slaves should be sold in Maryland unless under *fieri facias*. Slaves could also[2] be carried to and fro, by certain parties, between Maryland, Virginia and Washington, for work on certain public buildings; but they were to be removed from Maryland within a year from the completion of the work, or they would become free.[3] Further doubts as to the act of 1783 were settled by a provision, of 1794, that residence of a year in Maryland, by persons coming there to settle, was not necessary before slaves could be imported; but no slaves or their increase, so brought in, could be sold until the importer had lived in Maryland for three years, barring the case of disposition by will or at law.[4] Since 1783, slaves could be brought to Maryland by citizens of the United States only. In 1792, some of the French inhabitants of the West India Islands fled from the revolutions there to Maryland. So a new law[5] declared that such French subjects who should settle in Maryland during the disturbances at home might retain their slaves, but the number that they could keep, after the expiration of a year from their coming, was limited to five domestic servants to the master of a family, and three to a single man; while

---

[1] House Journals, 1787, p. 111; 1788, 52; 1789, 31; 1791, ch. 19, 57.
[2] 1792, 45, 48.
[3] 1792, 75. This was not to become a law unless a similar act was passed by Va.
[4] 1794, 43. See also 4 H. & McH., 143.
[5] 1792, 56. When the act was repealed, five years later, the authorities of Baltimore were authorized to rid the city of any of these slaves who might be deemed dangerous to the peace; for it was said that many of them had been disorderly and were under suspicion. (1797, 75.)

any surplus slaves, not exported, became free. Such Frenchmen as merely sojourned in Maryland could keep the same number for their own use, but could not dispose of them.

When the House of Delegates received petitions in 1795 from certain residents of Charles and Prince George's counties, for changes in the law so as to allow the introduction of slaves—by land, we presume—the committee reported that they were opposed, "upon principles of policy," to an entire repeal of the law, but advised that it be made more clear and explicit. In the next year a petition was received from a citizen of Talbot county, that he might bring back to Maryland a negro whom his mother had carried away, and in whom he had certain rights. It was found that the slave had been removed during the infancy of the petitioner, at a time when he could give no consent. The committee, again, and this time with success, urged a general law. The act of 1796, which, in many ways, long remained the law, reiterated the prohibition of the importation of any slave by land or water, for sale—declaring, as before, that such slaves should be thereby free—but provided that citizens of the United States, coming to Maryland to settle, could bring in within a year any slaves which they owned at the time of their removal, if the slave or the mother of the slave had resided in the United States for three whole years previous; but neither the slaves nor their increase could be sold—except in settlement of an estate or by process at law—until the importer had lived in Maryland for three years. Travelers had to carry their servants away with them. If a slave were carried away by any person during the infancy of, or without the consent of, the real owner, that owner might bring the slave back at any time.[1] A resident of Maryland, possessed by inheritance, in

---

[1] House Journal, Nov., 1795, pp. 6–29; 1796, 57, &c. Acts of 1796, ch. 67. As to freedom from importation, the Court of Appeals held, in 1820, that this applied to voluntary importation on the master's part only. 5 H. & J., 69.

his own or his wife's right, of lands in an adjoining State, and of slaves used on those lands, might bring the slaves into Maryland to his own land, for his own benefit and not for sale. Conversely, a resident of an adjoining State possessed by inheritance of lands in Maryland and the owner of slaves at home, might import the slaves, to work them on those lands only.[1] In both cases, the slaves must have been residents, or descendents of residents, of the States in question, before 1783. And careful record had to be made, within three months, in the county office.[2] After the slaves had been properly recorded, they might be removed as often as the owner should choose without repeated record. Any citizen of Maryland who acquired property, by marriage, bequest, in course of distribution or as guardians, in any slave who was a resident, or the descendant of a resident, of the United States before 1783, might remove such slave into Maryland for the purpose only of employment for his own benefit, and not for sale. Such slaves had also to be properly recorded; and they could not be sold for three years. Over twenty years later,[3] there was added the condition, that slaves so imported should be used by the importer only in his own immediate service and not for any other purpose whatever. By a supplementary act of 1797,[4] executors and administrators of citizens who should remove into Maryland and die within a year, might import within a year any slaves, with their issue, that had belonged to the deceased and had themselves, or their mothers, been residents of the United States

---

[1] By 1798, 76, citzens of Maryland or of an adjoining State, inheriting lands in Md. or the adjoining State, and owning slaves used on them, might import the slaves for use on their own lands.

[2] If the slaves were acquired by inheritance, the testator's name, the date and place of record of the will, must all be recorded; when by marriage, the name of the person from whom the title was derived, was necessary.

[3] 1818, 201. It was further declared that such slaves did not have to be brought in within any limited time.

[4] 1797, 15.

for three years previous. So, guardians of the children of such citizens might import such slaves within a year from the beginning of their trust; and the children on becoming of age, might also bring in such slaves and their issue, within a year.

We have noted that occasionally, under authority of special acts, slaves were brought from Virginia to Maryland for specified occupations and for limited times. Thus, in 1794, leave was given the Potomac Company to import slaves, with the condition that they would be freed, if not removed within a year from the completion of the work in hand. Several years after, as several citizens of Maryland were in the habit of hiring out their slaves to this same Company in Virginia, and as doubts had arisen whether the slaves could be brought back after a year's residence away, without being entitled to freedom, a further act declared that slaves might be hired out to the Company, but that they should be deemed free unless returned within a year from the end of the work. It appeared proper, so reads the act, that citizens of Maryland might have the privilege of hiring their slaves to the best advantage, "when no injury to the State can result therefrom." When, in 1803, a citizen of Virginia petitioned the Maryland House of Delegates for leave to bring in certain negroes, the committee of the House reported that it was inexpedient to extend the privilege of importation.[1] The proprietors of a stage line between Philadelphia and Norfolk, got leave in 1799 to use their slaves as drivers, to and from Maryland, on condition that every driver be duly recorded. In that portion of Maryland ceded to the District of Columbia, a number of slaves, belonging to citizens of Maryland, had been hired out or otherwise employed. An Act of 1802 allowed the importation of such slaves, and their issue; and it was further made lawful for citizens of Maryland and of that part of the District which had been ceded by Maryland, to remove to and

---

[1] House Journal, 1803, 79.

from the District at pleasure such slaves, and their descendants, as had been brought into the District from Maryland.¹ Other border counties found the law oppressive; and it was finally enacted, in 1812, that slaves might be hired out in any adjoining county of another State—where the laws of that State did not forbid—as often as the owner wished; and, conversely, slaves owned in the adjoining counties could be brought into Maryland, to be hired out. In either case, no record had to be made, but the slaves must be returned within a year.²

Hardly had the Revolution ceased when a number of citizens of Maryland began active efforts to abolish slavery. Some were political leaders. Many of them were of the Society of Friends. In December, 1785, the House of Delegates received the petitions of several citizens of Queen Anne's, Kent, Caroline, Dorchester, Worcester, Talbot and other counties, relative to an abolition of slavery. These petitions were read a second time on the day following, and were rejected by a vote of thirty-two to twenty-two. It is interesting to note that the votes of the members from the counties named—and many delegates were not present—were about equally divided, pro and con.³ Two years later there was presented to the House an address and petition for the emancipation of slaves, from the yearly meeting of the Friends in Baltimore; but these were refused also, by thirty votes to seventeen.⁴ The Maryland society for promoting the Abolition of Slavery and the Relief of poor Negroes and others unlawfully held in Bond-

---

[1] 1802, 68. See 3 H. & J., 379, 382; 1813, 56.
[2] 1812, 76.
[3] House Journal, 1785, pp. 36-39. Of four of the largest slave-holding counties, Calvert, Charles, Prince George's and St. Mary's, only one of the delegates present voted to receive the petitions.
[4] House Journal, 1787, pp. 34-36.

age, was organized in 1789. Its membership was soon between two and three hundred, and a building in Baltimore was devoted to its use. Its work began at once by a petition presented to the House of Delegates, on November 12th. On the next day the House received, also, an address of the Friends, of the same purport. These were referred to a committee of seven members, who reported the next day, through Mr. William Pinkney. It should be the wish of every free community, they said, to bring about the abolition of slavery. As both a sudden and compulsory abolition are exceptionable —the former being dangerous, the latter in violation of acquired rights—no opportunity should be neglected of attaining abolition "by silent and gradual steps, with the consent of the owner." So, all restriction should be removed from the voluntary emancipation of slaves.[1] Within a week, a bill was introduced in the Senate, to promote the gradual abolition of slavery, and to prevent the rigorous exportation of blacks from Maryland. It was read the first time and laid on the table. Consideration of it was postponed, some days later, to the first week in December. It was then committed to Mr. Nicholas Hammond, who had introduced it, together with Mr. Charles Carroll and Mr. John Hall, with the resolution to request the House of Delegates to appoint a committee for conference. Accordingly, the following message, brought in by Mr. Charles Carroll, was sent to the House the following day:

"A Bill for the gradual abolition of slavery, and for preventing the rigorous exportation of negroes and mulattoes from this State, has been originated in this House, and lain some time for consideration. The great importance of this subject, whether considered with a view to the persons whom it concerns, or to the advantage and happiness of the community at large, appears to be such as to require peculiar investigation, and the most serious attention of the legislature.

---

[1] In 1752, manumission in any way during the last illness of the master had been forbidden.

Hence it is conceived that a discussion of this subject by a joint committee of both Houses will be proper, that by a candid exchange of sentiments such a system may be reported as will be thought most agreeable, as well to the sense of both branches of the legislature as to the sense of our fellow citizens." But this proposition of the Senate the House refused by a vote of thirty-nine to fifteen.[1] The members from the large slave-holding counties voted against it, and those from the others were divided. The Senate ordered that the bill be referred to the next Assembly. At the next session the Senate received a petition from the Abolition Society, and referred it to the House. When this petition was read the House voted, by twenty-six to twenty-two, to refer it to a committee. There was then put the question, that the committee be instructed to express their disapprobation of that part of the petition which referred to the gradual abolition of slavery; but this was defeated by a plurality of two votes. And nothing further seems to have been done at that session.[2] But the work of the abolition societies had not been in petitions alone. In 1791 the House of Delegates received complaints against the society in Baltimore for its interference between certain slaves and their masters. The committee on Grievances and Courts of Justice, to whom the matter was referred, reported that the owners had been unjustly brought to much unnecessary trouble and expense. So large and influential was this Abolition Society that an individual who should be brought to law with it had better give up his slave than defend his rights. In this case the Society had acted in an indecent and

---

[1] House Journal, 1789, pp. 10-14, 64-5. Senate Journal, 1789, 5-34. A letter in Hazard's Register (Vol. X, 411) from a gentleman of Baltimore, written in 1832, states that Charles Carroll of Carrollton, introduced in the Senate of Maryland, in 1797, a bill by which all female slave children were to be bought by the State, educated and bound out to the age of 28, when they were to be free; and other slaves under 45 were to be free at a certain time. This, we presume, was the plan of Mr. Carroll in 1789, as the Senate Journal for 1797 does not make any mention of abolition.

[2] Senate Journal, 1790, Nov. 15th.

unjustifiable manner—so said the committee. The House, after considering the representations of the Society in defence, voted by a large plurality that its action could in no way be justified upon any principle by which good citizens ought to be moved. Although a resolve that the Society had become unnecessary, oppressive and repugnant in principles to the laws of the State, was lost by three votes, the work of the Society as a body had to be discontinued. Other societies were formed of not large membership. A number of slaves were assisted to get freedom, and a few petitions and memorials sent to the legislators from time to time, but only to meet with disapproval.[1]

During this period, however, there was a noticeable increase in the number of slaves manumitted. Manumission by will or otherwise during the last illness of the master, which had been forbidden in 1752, was allowed once more by the general act of 1796, on Slaves—by amendment of the Senate.

When, in 1823, a communication was received in the House of Delegates from the Governor of Ohio, on gradual emancipation in the United States, the committee of the House reported that they deemed it inexpedient then to express their views thereon.[2] In the Assembly of 1827, there was presented to the House a petition of sundry inhabitants of Harford county, for the abolition of slavery in the State. It was referred to a committee of nine—one member from Harford, Baltimore, Prince George's, Talbot and Worcester counties, each, and two from Cecil and Montgomery. On the day following, this committee reported, that they were compelled to acknowledge the inexpediency of submitting, at that time,

---

[1] House Journal, 1791, pp. 82–106. Griffith's Annals of Baltimore, 127. Poole's Abolition Societies, 72. House Journal, 1791, 19, 31, 38; do. 1792, 24; do. 1801, 66. Mr. Jefferson stated that there was not as much disposition for abolition in Maryland as in Virginia. We may add that there was very little in Virginia, however much many leaders like Mr. Jefferson may have desired it.

[2] House Journal, 1823, 139.

any system of legislation for abolishing slavery. But they expressed their entire confidence that the time was fast coming when Maryland would be relieved, through the plan of colonization, from "this grievous national calamity." "We cannot now, for obvious reasons," they continued, "follow the examples which have been set us by our sister States to the north and east of us. With them the evil to be subdued was a pigmy, with us it is a monster; with them a superfluous and decaying limb was to be removed; with us the destroying worm is to be sought for in the root. There, the system, full of health and vigor, submitted cheerfully to the simple cure; here the disease, exhibiting itself in its greatest strength and worst form, must receive a different treatment, and be gradually subdued by persevering, but not abrupt remedies."[1] This report was read and left, apparently, on the table. A memorial was presented in the House, in 1829, from sundry citizens of Frederick county, asking for a law which should declare that all children born of slaves should be free after a certain time. In 1832, a committee was ordered to enquire into the expediency of such legislation, but there seems to have been no result.[2] An amendment was added to the State constitution in 1837, to the effect that the relation of master and slave should not be abolished unless a bill for the purpose should be passed by an unanimous vote in each branch of the Assembly, and should then be published at least three months before a new election of delegates, and should be then confirmed by unanimous votes of the Houses in the next session thereafter; nor then, without full compensation to the master for the property of which he would be deprived.

Exactly how far the feelings of the people of Maryland were voiced in these actions of their legislators, is as hard to judge to-day—as it is hard to learn whether the "sundry

---

[1] House Journal, 1827, 320, 342.
[2] House Journal, 1829, 427; 1832, 89.

citizens" who signed these abolition petitions were six or a score or a whole community. There were citizens, and some of them prominent citizens, always ready and anxious to further any steps towards gradual abolition, but the people of Maryland, as a whole, did not care evidently to do away with slavery, or felt unable to solve the problems that a larger free black population would bring, or looked too long and too trustingly to colonization as the remedy for the evil.[1]

Several efforts were made, also—especially at the same time with those early efforts for abolition—to restrict or prevent exportation of slaves from Maryland. In 1789, in the House of Delegates, Mr. Pinkney had spoken of this as a species of traffic inhuman in itself, and disgraceful to the government.[2] Two years later, several petitions were presented in the House, from the Friends, from the Abolition Society in Baltimore, and from certain citizens of Caroline and Kent counties, for legislation to prevent the exportation of slaves and free negroes. These were referred to a committee of seven—one member, each, from Baltimore town, Baltimore county, Annapolis, Queen Anne's and Harford counties, and

---

[1] In 1830, there were several anti-slavery organizations in Baltimore—a "National Anti-Slavery Tract Society," a Branch of the Society of Md., &c.—but these seem to have been small and of little vitality. A small number of prominent citizens of Baltimore and the counties associated together, in 1846, to initiate a movement towards gradual emancipation; but public opinion, in the growing hostility between North and South, would not support any such plan, and it was abandoned as wholly impracticable. (Baltimore and the 19th of April: Hon. Geo. W. Brown, p. 113.)
Note resolutions of the Assemblies—1841, 16; 1843, 57; 1849, 37.
We may add that the Bill of Rights of Maryland, of 1776, did not state that all men were free and equal—as did the Bill of Rights of Virginia and the Declaration of Independence. It gave to "every freeman" remedy at law for injury to person or property, &c.

[2] House Journal, 1789, 9-14.

two from Dorchester, headed by Mr. Pinkney. In a few days, they reported that they could not conceive how, while the citizens of Maryland continued to hold slaves—a property recognized by law and secured by the Constitution—the exportation of slaves could with any warrant be prohibited. They did not see that justice or policy required such an interference with the rights of the community. Nor could they forbear from suggesting that such petitions would only make worse rather than better the condition of the slaves, by tending to destroy the spirit of acquiescence among them, by which alone their happiness could be secured, and to fill them with regret for evils that did not admit a remedy.[1] With this report the House concurred. At the next session, another memorial of the Friends was received, read and referred, but with no result. In 1800, there was received a petition from sundry inhabitants of Kent and Queen Anne's counties, for an act to prohibit the sale of slaves—without the State only, presumably. This was referred to a committee of seven, two from Anne Arundel, two from Kent, and one each from Charles, Dorchester and Queen Anne's counties. Over a week later, this committee reported that they had given the subject the serious consideration which its importance merited. They considered that the property in slaves acquired by citizens of Maryland, under the faith of laws existing before the Revolution, and sanctioned by express compact on the adoption of the new government, was secured by society to individuals on the general basis of property. And where the rights of such individuals are to be resumed by the public for the general advantage, a reasonable compensation must be made. They would not deny the power of the legislature to meet any great regulations of civil policy which the uncertain events attending every social institution might render necessary, particularly such an institution as slavery with them; but, as they were not aware of the necessity then of any such changes, they could not consent to pro-

---

[1] House Journal, 1798, 19, 31, 38.

hibit generally that use of their property which the needs of slave-owners might make indispensable. Nor did they believe that the transportation of the blacks to a warmer climate more suited to their physical natures, was either inhuman to the blacks or impolitic to the State. They deemed the gradual diminution of the black population of Maryland—a people so different by nature from the whites—and a substitution in their place of a white yeomanry, to be objects highly desirable. Yet, with all this, they could not for a moment doubt that the right of property in slaves is, and ought to be, a right limited by the laws of humanity and Christianity. The legislature is bound to repress vices of cruelty, and to encourage charity and philanthropy. While they would refuse to prohibit generally the sale and transportation of slaves to the South, they would so far restrain the same as to prevent the violation of those ties of nature which even savage man respects, and which society should protect with a religious reverence. And to this end they offered the resolution, that a law should prohibit the sale—except in consequence of the commission of some crime or offense—of any slave to be carried out of Maryland, by which an acknowledged husband or wife, according to the relations customary among slaves, would be separated from each other, or by which a mother would be separated from a child under a certain age. This report was read, but nothing seems to have resulted from it.[1] The next year the House received further memorials of the same purport from the Friends and sundry citizens. After some weeks a similar resolution was reported, fixing the limit of age under which a child could not be taken from its mother at ten years. But this resolution was rejected by a vote of thirty-eight to twenty-one.[2] In 1818 a petition from citizens of Washington county, that the existing traffic in slaves might be restricted, was likewise referred to a committee; but without result. In

---

[1] House Journal, 1800, 58, 77.
[2] House Journal, 1801, 44, 66, 80-84.

1832 there was presented a petition from the justices of the orphans' court of Somerset county and certain citizens of Somerset and Worcester, for an act to restrain registers of wills from engaging in the purchase of negroes for transportation and sale. The committee on Grievances and Courts reported against the petition.[1] By this time the policy of the State was to free itself as much as possible of the black population. Any slaves for life could be carried out or sold away from the State, except such as were brought in for the purpose of transportation and sale.

As manumissions increased there was an increase in the number of those slaves who were to be free at a certain time. During their terms of service they were as other slaves. The law provided for the careful record of the deeds under which they were to be free, and that those who were brought into Maryland, being slaves for a term of years only by the law of the State whence they came, should serve for the prescribed length of time only. It is easy to see how injustice might arise from the transportation and sale elsewhere of these blacks, as slaves for life. As early as 1789, the attention of the House of Delegates was called by the Society of Friends and by others, to the exportation by fraud or violence of slaves for terms of years; and a committee stated that the honor of the State was deeply concerned in giving exemplary punishment to such a practice. For a generation thereafter, efforts for stringent and effective legislation were frequently made, especially by the Society of Friends.[2] The general act of 1796 gave a penalty of eight hundred dollars—or work on the road for not over five years, in default—for anyone who might transport, knowingly, from the State, and sell as a slave for life, any black entitled to freedom at any age. And there was the same penalty for bringing in and selling such in the State.

---

[1] House Journal, 1818, 96; 1832, 204.
[2] House Journal, 1789, 9-14; 1790; 1791, 31; 1795, 53, 65; 1803, 15, 18, &c.

But a committee of the House of Delegates reported, in 1801, that the removal of these servants and other acts of inhumanity to the unhappy blacks called loudly for the interposition of the legislature; on which the House went to the extent of resolving, by vote of fifty-four to five, that the severest penalties should prevent the sale, South, of slaves for terms of years. Finally, in 1810, there was enacted that no such slaves should be sold to anyone who had not been a *bona fide* resident of Maryland for a year. The penalty, as for any sale for a longer term than that which the black had to serve, was five hundred dollars. That for actual kidnapping had been fixed the year before at between two and ten years imprisonment.[1] During the session of 1816, the House passed, by a vote of thirty-four to twenty-three, a bill which required the formality of a bill of sale, acknowledged before witnesses and containing a description of the slaves transferred, in the case of sale and removal of slaves where the person about to remove them had not been for two years an actual resident of the county where they had been held. This was defeated in the Senate by a tie vote. But an act of the next session provided that purchasers of any slaves for removal from the State should take copies of duly acknowledged and recorded bills of sale, in which the slaves should be identified. A slave for a term of years could not be sold to any other than a resident of the State of over a year's standing; nor could a resident purchase as agent for a non-resident, under penalty, in either case, to seller or buyer, of not over two years' imprisonment. And all sales of slaves for terms of years were clothed with the formalities of bills in writing, under hand and seal of the purchaser, and of the seller or his agent; which should give the term of service, the interest of the seller, and the residence of the purchaser; and should be duly acknowledged before a justice of the county, and be recorded within twenty days. If

---

[1] See 1783, ch. 23; 1790, 9; 1796, 67; 1804, 90; 1810, 15. Act on Crimes. 1809, 38.

these formalities were fraudulently omitted, the servant became free; and magistrates were authorized to examine any persons on whom reasonable suspicions were fastened. The penalties of this act were extended in 1834 to all cases where a resident of Maryland should purchase or receive, knowingly, with the intention of sending away, a slave for a term of years; and where residents should remove and then sell such slaves, taken with them.[1] These formalities for the sale of slaves entitled to freedom, and the penalty of not over two years' imprisonment for any illegal sale of them, remained the law. But notoriously vicious servants were often sold, for transportation, under the authority of the courts, by act of 1833—the court being satisfied that the master had warned the slave of that penalty, and the slave being provided with an authorized copy both of the order of the court and of his title to freedom.

We find the Assembly of 1818 giving permission to a resident of Cecil county to remove a negro girl, a slave for a term of years, to Pennsylvania, on condition that he give bond with security, not to sell or remove her out of that State. So, in 1829, certain trustees were allowed to sell several negroes for their unexpired time of service, in Delaware—but to no other than an actual resident of that State; and the conditions of the permission of sale were to be mentioned in the bill of sale; and they must secure a bond for one thou-

---

[1] House Journal 1816, 98. 1817, ch. 112; 1834, 266. The minimum imprisonment became eighteen months. A society called the Protection Society was organized at Baltimore about 1817. Many valuable blacks were aided, and incorrigible servants were quietly transported. (Griffith's Baltimore.) A bill for a "Protection Society of Kent county" was rejected by the Senate in 1827. A few years later, a number of slaves were bought in Maryland, to be taken to Louisiana; but difficulties arising at the custom house in Baltimore, owing to the informalities in the bill of sale, the matter was carried before a justice of the city court. As the negroes, on being examined, acknowledged themselves to be slaves, a special act of the Assembly allowed the transportation as if the bill had been drawn according to the forms prescribed by law. (1821, 15.)

sand dollars, with good security living in Maryland, that the slaves should not be removed from Delaware during the time of service. And the act declared, further, that the trustees or their heirs might maintain an action on the bond, should the slaves be removed, and any damages would be used in bringing back their slaves and for their further benefit. In another case, a citizen of Delaware was allowed to take from Maryland a negro woman, in whom he owned an unexpired term, on condition that he first gave bond with security, to be kept in the clerk's office of the county from which the slave was removed, that he would not keep her in servitude after the expiration of her term of service. Again, a citizen of Prince George's county was authorized to sell a negro woman out of Maryland, if he specified in the bill of sale that she was to be free at a certain time, and if he took security from the buyer that she should not be disposed of for longer servitude. Another citizen of the same county was given leave, two years later, to take with him to Virginia his servant for a term of years, provided the negro should appear in person before the orphans' court and signify his willingness to go, and also that the master should furnish him with a certified copy, under seal, of the instrument under which he was entitled to freedom. Again, in 1840, a special act allowed the removal of a girl to Virginia, provided that she should give her consent, and that the master should first file with the county clerk a satisfactory bond to the State of Maryland for one thousand dollars, with security from a citizen of Maryland, for the faithful and safe return of the girl to the State by the master or his executors as soon as she finished her term of service, should she then desire to return. She must return, if at all, within twelve months after becoming free. And in case she desired to return but was detained, the district attorney must bring suit on the bond, and any money recovered should be used for the Colonization Society. Before she left, the county clerk was to give her, at the expense of her master, a certified record of her right to freedom. Thus several exceptions to the laws were made. But all petitions for special acts were not granted. A bill passed the House, in 1835, to allow a certain clergyman to carry out of Maryland a colored apprentice, the son of free parents; but the Senate would not pass it. Two years later, a bill was introduced in the House to allow a certain resident of Prince George's county to carry with him to Mississippi a servant for a term of years. By the recommendation of the committee on Colored Population, these bills were amended so as to require the master both to give bond in the sum of two thousand dollars, that he or his heirs or executors would liberate the slave at the proper time, and in all respects comply with the conditions of the permission given him, and, also, to have a copy of the permission recorded in the office of the county in Mississippi to which he should remove. This bill the Senate rejected; and refused to reconsider, when asked by the House.[1]

In 1820, a bill was introduced in the Senate, to repeal all laws that forbade the importation of slaves into Maryland, provided that no slave imported should be manumitted within ten years. This bill passed the Senate by a vote of seven to five, but was defeated in the House. Two years later, leave was asked in the House for a bill of similar purport, but the committee reported that the laws were satisfactory in giving sufficient latitude for importation. The House refused to agree to this by a vote of thirty-seven to thirty-four; and then the bill was referred to the next Assembly. There, a bill was again passed in the Senate and defeated in the House.[2] From time to time, special acts allowed the importation of

---

[1] See 1818, ch. 205; 1829, 2, 55; 1831, 233; 1834, 1; 1836, 201; 1840, 111. House Journal, 1837, 56, 165, 208.

[2] Senate Journal, 1820, 19. House Journal, 1820, 82; 1822, 162. Senate Journal, 1823, 18.

slaves, in answer to the petitions of the owners. And not a few such petitions were rejected.¹ In 1823, as—so the preamble of the act reads—the numerous special acts of legislation had been of great expense to the State, and no inconvenience could occur from a general law embracing most cases —there was enacted that any citizen of Maryland who acquired " by marriage, bequest, course of distribution, or as guardian, or by gift, or in any other lawful manner," any slave, a resident of the United States, might at any time bring such slave into the State for the purpose only of employment there " for his own immediate service." Slaves so brought in had to be recorded. They could be neither sold nor manumitted until they had been residents for three years. There seems to have been some doubt, thereafter, as to whether slaves imported under this act could be hired out within three years. One special act allowed certain negroes who had been brought back to Maryland with their owners, then minors, to be hired out, without danger of their freedom being thereby acquired. Another allowed a citizen of Harford county to hire out several negroes, "in the same manner in which he might or could have done had the said negroes been born slaves" within the State. Again, the executors of a citizen of Maryland who had died in Florida, were given permission to import certain slaves belonging to the estate, and to hire out or sell them, as directed in the will, as if they had never been out of Maryland.² But—the Legislature having been roused by the Southampton insurrection—the proviso was added, that, if the

---

¹ For instance, leave was asked to introduce in the House, in 1829, a bill to authorize one of the members, from Caroline county, to bring into the State, as a hireling, a negro to work at a forge. Leave was then refused. Later, a bill was reported, by leave; was then amended, to limit the privilege of keeping the black to five years; and was finally rejected. (House Journal, 1829, 176, 359.) The acts varied considerably in particulars, such as the times within which the slaves must be registered at the county clerk's.

² 1823, 87; 1827, 176; 1831, 10, 273.

negroes should refuse to go to Liberia, they should be sold out of the State.

The slaughter of a number of white persons of Southampton county, Virginia, in the summer of 1831, by the negro Nat. Turner and a few followers, roused the attention of the whole country. This so-called insurrection was wholly local, was put down at once, and showed no tendency in the slaves as a people to rebel against their masters. But many empty rumors of uprisings went abroad, far beyond Southampton county.

The year 1831 is a landmark in all legislation in Maryland affecting the negro, slave and free. It was then that the State actively took up the policy of the colonization in Africa of its free blacks. There was further enacted—it was the autumn of 1831—that it should not be lawful after the first of June following to import into Maryland any slave for sale or to reside there. This did not apply, however, to the rights of non-residents, under laws then in force, to remove their slaves to or from islands belonging to them in the Potomac. Nor should the act prevent persons who lived in Maryland, or an adjoining State, and held land in the two States, not over ten miles apart, from removing their slaves to and from those lands, solely for the cultivation of the same. Such slaves so brought in must be recorded within thirty days with the county clerk. Any person importing a slave contrary to the act should forfeit the slave, who, in turn, would be entitled to freedom on condition that he consent to be sent to Liberia or to leave Maryland at once.[1] Otherwise he was to be sold by the sheriff to the Col-

---

[1] 1831, 323. The Court of Appeals held, in 1837, that the importation of a slave contrary to this act, so as to entitle the slave to freedom, must be by the owner or with his approbation or authority. (8 G. & J., 269.)

If a slave returned from another State where he had resided, even with his owner's permission, the owner could not hold him—though the return was against the master's consent. (9 G. & J., 14. 1837.)

But the Act of 1831 did not prevent owners from sending away, or taking away their slaves, to travel, or sojourn temporarily. The plan of permanent residence elsewhere must actually be consummated. (9 G. & J., 127.)

onization Society, for the sum of five dollars and prison fees, to be carried to Liberia. If the Society would not take him he was to be sold, on condition that the purchaser would take him beyond Maryland to reside. All justices of the peace were bidden to hold for court, and, if necessary, to commit to jail, any persons importing slaves contrary to the law. At the next session of Assembly, 1832, the House received some thirty-eight petitions for leave to introduce slaves. No special act seems to have been passed, but a supplement was added to the act of 1831, because—so reads the preamble—the introduction of slaves ought to be prohibited except in a few special cases, and all cases of hardship should be embraced under one law, according to some general principles. The supplement[1] declared that slaves for life who should be hired out or loaned to service for limited times in a State adjoining Maryland, or in the District of Columbia, might be returned to Maryland; but the importer must be a resident of Maryland as well as the owner of the slaves—at the time both of exportation and importation. Persons who had already acquired land in Maryland by inheritance or otherwise, or by purchase with intent to become residents, and who were about to become such, could bring in any slaves owned by them before the act of 1831 was passed; but the proper record must be made and the affidavit of the owner given that the conditions of law had been properly complied with, and that the slaves were slaves for life, and were not imported for sale. Persons living in the District of Columbia, east of the Potomac, and holding lands in Maryland, might move to those lands from their residence any slaves for life, and the increase of such slaves, who had belonged to them and lived either in Maryland or the District before the act of '31. Also, residents of Maryland removing for a limited time to the District, might bring back at pleasure any slaves carried with them. Those, too, who owned land in an adjoining State,

---

[1] 1832, 317. The importation of such hired slaves had been allowed by an act passed a month before. (Ch. 40.)

and worked on those lands any slaves who belonged to them and had gone from Maryland, might bring back such slaves at any time. Citizens of Maryland who should leave home for a time, in the service of their State or of the United States might bring back with them any slaves for life that they had carried away; and in case of their death, their representatives might return them; but there must be entered on record, before removal, the usual list of the slaves, together with a declaration of the reasons for the departure from the State, and also of the purpose of returning, and another record must be made within a month after the return. It was enacted, lastly, that where any slave owned in Maryland by a citizen of the State should have been married before the law of 1831—in regular marriage ceremony by a minister of some recognized religious body in the State—to any slave owned in any adjoining State, it should be lawful for the owner of the slave in Maryland to bring in the husband or wife. But the fact of the marriage must be proven by the purchaser, or some credible white person, and put on record within a month. This act was strongly opposed, passing the House by a vote of thirty-six to twenty-nine.[1] At the next session, the Senate passed a bill relaxing somewhat the strict prohibition of the previous year, but imposing a tax on such slaves as might be imported, for the benefit of colonization. The House amended by cutting down the proposed taxes by a half, and then passed the bill by a vote of forty-one to twenty-eight. It enacted that any citizen of Maryland might import slaves for life acquired in another State by marriage or bequest, or in course of distribution; also, that any persons residing out of Maryland, and removing there with a *bona fide* intention of becoming citizens of the State, might also import their slaves, the intention of residence being shown

---

[1] One member moved to repeal the policy of colonization, and State taxes for it, as the passage of this bill of 1832 would admit more blacks than were removed by 1831, 281. The motion was lost by 45 to 21. The bill was introduced by the chairman of the Committee on Colored Population.

by affidavit duly filed in the county office within a month. In all cases, a list of the slaves had to be filed in the county office, with a statement that the list was true, and that the slaves were not to be sold and were slaves for life; and at the same time there had to be paid for the use of the Colonization Society, the sum of fifteen dollars for each slave between the years of twelve and forty-five, and five dollars for a slave either younger or older.[1] There was further enacted the next year, that any officer of the army or navy called by the service into Maryland, might bring with him his slaves, on condition that they be not sold, and be taken away when he left. A further supplementary act to the stringent provisions of '31, now allowed citizens of Maryland, or of the District of Columbia east of the Potomac, who had, or might acquire, lands in the District or the State, respectively, to move back and forth at pleasure any slaves for life who were natives of the State or of that part of the District. Also any resident of Maryland thereafter appointed executor, trustee or guardian in the State or an adjoining State or District, could carry to and fro from the adjoining State or District, and hire out in Maryland, if deemed advisable, any slaves for life held in trust, on condition of due record in the office of the county to which these might be at any time removed. Such slaves, of course, could not be sold.[2] Certain residents of Charles county had received by bequest in Virginia a number of slaves, but had exchanged them for others. A special act ended their fears by allowing the other slaves to be brought in. Several other acts allowed the removal of certain slaves between Maryland and Virginia. In one case there was a proviso that they should be used solely for cultivation.[3] By the act of 1831, those persons owning lands in both Maryland and an adjoining State, not over ten

---

[1] House Journal, 1833, 205, &c. 1833, ch. 87. A special act also admitted nine slaves, on payment of the taxes. The case was not included under the provisions of the general act.

[2] 1834, 75, 124, 284.

[3] 1835, 50, 74, 172, 194, 274.

miles apart, might carry their slaves to and fro. The ten mile restriction was now done away, and citizens of either Maryland or Virginia who owned lands in both States anywhere could move their slaves at pleasure, paying the taxes for colonization when the slaves were recorded.[1] As no provision existed for the introduction of slaves gotten by gift, there was enacted further that any citizen of Maryland might import any slave for life, acquired by gift in the United States, but on condition not only that the slaves be duly recorded and the colonization fees paid, with an oath that the gift was a *bona fide* one, but that none of the slaves or their descendants could be manumitted in Maryland unless the owner should provide for their removal.[2] In 1836 the question of changing the laws so as to admit slaves without restriction was reported adversely by a House committee. It seemed best, they said, to continue the policy then being tried, which promised well; and cases that were especially deserving, in the judgment of the Legislature, would always find relief.[3] But three years later, there was enacted that any citizen of Maryland, and any person coming to Maryland to reside, might bring in from any part of the United States any slave for life. A person moving into the

---

[1] 1835, 329. Apparently, the tax had to be paid on the first introduction, only. A special act, in 1843, allowed a certain citizen of Virginia, owning land in Maryland, to move his slaves at pleasure, but limited their use to work on those farms, and said the colonization fees need be paid only once. (1843, 38.)

[2] 1835, 61, I. e. Removal under the act of '31, for decreasing the free black population.

[3] See House Journal, 1836, 384. 1837, ch. 351; 1844, 42; 1846, 244. In one case, a citizen of Anne Arundel was allowed to bring back from Louisiana fifty slaves, who had been taken there for temporary work. Again, a gentleman of Virginia asked and got leave to bring with him, whenever he wished, a black boy who had been his servant in Maryland, before his removal to Virginia. Again, a certain owner of lands in both Maryland and Delaware could carry to and fro his slaves including children born to them in Delaware. At least two slaves owned in Virginia were hired out in Maryland, the owners being required to put them on record and pay the fees.

State must file within a month an affidavit of intention of residence; and, in all cases, the slaves must be recorded, with sworn affidavit, that they were not imported for sale and were slaves for life, and the fees for the Colonization Society must be paid. Three years later, again, the privilege of carrying to and fro slaves for life, from the United States, and not for sale, was given to any person entering the State, to remain temporarily or permanently, on condition of proper record and payment of fees. Thus, step by step, were lessened the stringent provisions of '31.[1] In 1847 the House committee reported unfavorably the suggestion of a repeal of all restrictions; but two years later, all laws were repealed which prohibited or in any way taxed the importation from any part of the United States of any slaves for life. But no slave whatever could be imported for the purpose of sale and transportation, under penalty—when the slave was actually sold, to be taken away—of not less than two nor more than five hundred dollars. Nor could any slave sentenced to transportation as a punishment for crime, in any other part of the United States, be imported into or held in Maryland.[2]

The total amount received by the Colonization Society from these duties on the introduction of slaves, during seventeen years, had been nearly twelve thousand five hundred dollars—the number of slaves brought in must have been a thousand or more.[3] In 1850, there were over ninety thousand slaves in the State—some ten thousand less than there had been a half century before. In 1860, there were eighty-seven thousand. But the free blacks—having increased dur-

---

[1] 1839, 15; 1842, 213; 1845, 113.
[2] 1849, 165. The penalty for importing a convict slave was from $100 to $300; for holding one in the State, the loss of the slave, who was sold for the benefit of the State.
The Baltimore *Sun* of May 2nd, 1851, mentions the arrest of a man for importing a slave contrary to law.
[3] Report of Committee on Colored Population to Constitutional Convention of 1850-51.

ing that decade by three times the decrease in slaves—numbered nearly eighty-four thousand.

The Code of 1860 read, simply, that anyone could import any slave for life from any part of the United States, except those who were guilty of any crime, or had been banished from Maryland.

From the very settlement of the Colonies the indentured white servants frequently caused their masters vexation and loss, by running away. Laws to prevent this were soon made in Maryland. Any persons suspected to be runaway servants or criminals were to be taken up and kept until either they could prove their freedom and pay four hundred pounds of tobacco, or their masters claimed them and paid the same sum. It is interesting to note that a law of this kind, of 1669, was to be communicated to the sister Colonies to the North, that fugitives might be held there for their masters.[1] For a hundred years, law after law was made, but despite stringent regulations—of passes required, and penalties threatened—some of the servants would not stay in service. Finally, white indentured servants ceased to form a class in the population, and when men spoke of a runaway they meant a negro.[2]

Some of the negro slaves soon followed the example of the white servants. In a quarrel between the Dutch of New Amsterdam and the government of Maryland, in 1659, the Dutch declared that unless their runaway servants were sent back to them, they would keep all the servants and negroes

---

[1] Md. Arch., II, 224, 523.
[2] We read in an act of 1786 (43) that many apprentices had been running away. The Baltimore *Sun*, for Jan. 6, 1858, gives the case of a white apprentice, who had absconded and was sent back by the magistrate. In the latter years of slave-holding, as to-day, a white apprentice had sometimes to be given back to his master.

that had fled to them from Maryland.¹ The courts allowed masters of runaway servants to recompense themselves for their losses by holding the servants for a longer term. Slaves for life were evidently incapable of paying any such penalty. An act of 1663 required English servants who should run away in company with negro or other slaves, to repay the master or owners of the slaves, by direction of the courts.² The act of 1669 makes no mention of slaves. That of 1676 was intended chiefly for servants, though slaves are included, and declared that former acts had proved ineffectual, in not giving sufficient encouragement for the seizure of runaways. So, servants were forbidden to depart ten miles from home without a note of leave, under penalty of being arrested as runaways, and having to serve, at the end of their terms, ten extra days for each day of absence. Any person who should detain a servant, knowing that he or she was unlawfully absent from home, would be liable to a fine of five hundred pounds of tobacco for every night the servant was on his place. Those who carried away any servant or slave should pay the employer or owner treble damages and costs. As the act applied to servants, "whither by Indenture or according to the Custome of the Countrey or hired for wages," it is evident that any passer by was liable to be examined, and perhaps delayed, by any zealous citizen. So, the better to insure against detention or arrest, persons traveling beyond their own county were directed to get a pass, under the county seal, for which they had to pay one shilling or ten pounds of tobacco. Any person who should take up a runaway or one without a pass who could not give a good account of himself, was entitled to two hundred pounds of tobacco or other satisfaction. If he lived in the Northern Colonies or in Virginia or Delaware, except in certain parts adjacent to Maryland, he was entitled to twice that sum for a runaway returned to

---

¹ Md. Arch., III, 372.
² Md. Arch., I, 489.

Maryland.[1] In order that runaways might more easily be returned, the plan was adopted of making Annapolis a clearing-house, as it were. Not only were runaways brought there, but notices were to be speedily sent there, from all parts, of servants or negroes in custody, whose masters were not known; and a list of these was to be kept posted by the sheriff. The commissioners in each county were also to post notices, at the offices of the courts, of such runaways as might be taken thereabouts.[2]

In 1709, an Indian who had been kept for some time in one of the county jails, was discharged by special act of assembly, and the distinction was then drawn that persons, *other* than negroes and mulattoes, who should be found traveling without passes and committed as runaways, should not be detained over six months, if they could not before prove their freedom. On being released, such persons had to pay or work out the costs. After 1719, servants and slaves who had not been taken away by their owners, might be sold at auction, and the balance, after all costs were deducted, was secured to the owner, should he appear within reasonable time.[3]

In treaties made by the Governor of Maryland with various Indians, in 1661 and 1663, there is the stipulation that the Indians are to return any runaway "Englishmen." Later, the neighboring Indians were encouraged to seize runaways by the reward of a blanket or its value. Treaties with them forebade their harboring servants and slaves, who were to be given over to the nearest English plantation. The backwoods offered a near retreat for runaways. As a certain tribe of Indians had evidently been regardless of the rights of the good people of Maryland in their servants and slaves, the Governor and Council decided, in 1722, to send to these a messenger with a treaty of peace and friendship, and the promise of a reward of

---

[1] Md. Arch., II, 523. Re-enacted in 1692 and 1699. See also LL. 3, 40.
[2] Council Proceedings, 1695/6, H. D. 2, p. 297.
[3] LL. 3, 385. Re-enacted in 1715, 44, 35. 1719, 2; Repealed, 1802.

two blankets and a gun to every Indian who should return a slave. These allurements were evidently unavailing, for three years later it was decided to send again, to invite some of the chiefs to Annapolis. The messenger was to endeavor to persuade them to come, by all reasonable means, including a present of a calico shirt and pair of scarlet worsted stockings to each chief, and the distribution of four other shirts among such as the chiefs should name. Feeling sure of the success of this mission, the Council decided that whatever negroes should be brought down by the Indians should be held in custody until the Assembly should decide what to do with them. But neither chiefs nor slaves came, and another messenger still seems to have been sent without result. At that time a sum of money was appropriated from the treasury for the encouragement of the seizure of runaways.[1]

Honest people of Maryland were somewhat troubled by the escape of debtors to foreign parts, and after 1715, masters of vessels could not lawfully carry away any persons whatsoever without the proper passes from the authorities. But servants and slaves were still evidently able to get away, for there was enacted in 1753 that captains of boats over eighteen feet long, keel, should not enter or take permit to sail, at any custom house, without taking an oath against concealing any such on shipboard, or taking them away. They might be properly hired for work on a vessel, but otherwise the captain became liable to a fine of twenty shillings and costs, for every hour he allowed a servant or slave on board. Ten years later this act was made perpetual, the preamble stating that it had appeared very beneficial.[2]

When word came to Annapolis, in 1697, that two negroes, a man and a woman, were outlying in the neighboring woods, the man being armed with a gun and threatening the life of

---

[1] Md. Arch., III, 433, 486. Council Records, 1700, X, 238; 1722, 51, 131, 140, 1725/6, March 23.
[2] 1715, 19; 1753, 9.

anyone who tried to take them, the Governor ordered an officer of the county to raise the neighborhood, to apprehend the negroes by force and to give them to the sheriff at Annapolis, to be imprisoned against the appearance of their master. If the posse was not successful in arresting them, the rangers would be put on their track. In 1723 there was enacted that any runaway negro, or other slave, who should outlie in the woods and resist those persons who were legally empowered to capture him, might be killed, without offence or penalty on the part of the pursuers. An act of 1751 secured from prosecution any person who might kill a slave, deemed to be guilty of any serious offence, and resisting arrest. The value of the slave so killed, was paid to the owner by the public. But this was so qualified, two years after, that the person should not be secured against trial, but should not be punished in any way, if the killing was found by the court to have been done justifiably.[1]

As sheriffs sometimes neglected to advertise runaways, a law of 1792 provided that advertisements, with minute particulars, should be continued until the prisoners were released in course of law. After 1802, sheriffs were to advertise runaway servants or slaves in some public newspaper printed in Baltimore, in Washington and in Easton, besides any other notices they should see fit to post, within fifteen days after the capture. The runaway was to be fully described. If the owner did not apply for him within sixty days, and give security for all costs, the sheriff should advertise him for sale, wait at least twenty days, and then sell him to the highest bidder. All the proceeds after

---

[1] Council Records, H. D. 2, 442. 1723, 15; 1751, 14; 1753, 26. In 1738 several negroes who had broken jail, and others who had run away, were outlying in Prince George's county, and had done some violence. The Council were of the opinion that the magistrates had not exerted themselves sufficiently, so the sheriff was ordered to seize them, and to take, if necessary, the whole power of the county. (Council Records, May 5th.) We read that in 1764 the Governor, having read the letters and depositions relating to the shooting of a slave of Charles Carroll, Esq., by Captain John Ireland, "was pleased to order a *nolle prosequi* and pardon" for the said Ireland. (Council Records, Liber T. R. 169.)

costs were deducted, were to be paid by the county court to the owner, but if he did not apply within two years, they went to the county. No servant or slave so sold could be carried out of Maryland within two years after the sale, under the same penalties as for the transportation of a free black. For every case of neglect to follow the law, a sheriff could be fined a hundred dollars.[1] By the act of 1796, a free black who allowed a slave to use his freedom paper, by means of which the slave escaped, could be fined not over three hundred dollars—half to the master of the slave—or be sold to service in default. But as misuse of these certificates continued, greater care was now prescribed for the issue of them, and a second one was not to be issued to any free black, except on satisfactory proof that the first had been lost. In 1810, the courts before which negroes might be brought as suspected runaways, were ordered to be well satisfied in every case before granting discharges. After 1817, any person who had been duly committed by a magistrate as a suspected runaway, and had then been duly advertised, as before, but had not been claimed within the sixty days, was taken before a judge of the county or orphans' court for full examination. If the judge deemed the prisoner a free man, he would thereupon discharge him. Otherwise he would remand him for a reasonable time, and have the reputed owner notified, but if no rightful owner appeared in that time, the prisoner would then be discharged. In either case, any costs were paid by the county. This radical change of freeing the negro who, while not claimed, could not yet prove his freedom, and of leaving all costs to be paid by the public, was not effected without much strong opposition. The motion to strike it out of the bill was lost by two votes only in the House. At the next session a bill to repeal it passed the House finally, but was rejected by the Senate. It remained the law, save that after 1828, the charges for the care of blacks ultimately discharged, were paid from the State treasury.[2]

---

[1] 1792, 72; 1802, 96.
[2] 1810, 63; 1817, 112; House Journal, 1828, 98.

White servants who ran away and were captured had to recompense their masters by increased term of service. Negro servants for terms of years were dealt with, doubtless, in the same way, but they were few in number before the nineteenth century. By an act of 1804, a master could secure the use of a captured runaway for such extended time as the court should deem just; but the court must be satisfied that the servant had not run away from ill treatment. The servant could be used for the specified time by the master or his heirs, but was in no case to be assigned to anyone living out of Maryland. In 1830, the House committee, in answer to a petition of sundry citizens of Talbot county for further security to slave owners, recommended a bill which allowed the sale for a much increased term, of those slaves, for terms of years, who had run away and been taken. But the bill was amended so that no order for the sale should be granted except in cases where the servants had once before run away; and the matter was then indefinitely postponed. In 1833, it was enacted that the courts could extend the term of runaway blacks so as fairly to indemnify the owners for all loss, or could give orders, on due petition of the owners, for the sale of the owners' rights in them to anyone in or without Maryland, if, as in all cases, the offence had not been caused by the ill treatment of the master. In case of sale, the slave was to be given a certified copy of the papers on which his freedom depended, and of the order of the court for the sale. He could then be taken from the State if the purchaser desired.[1]

Slave owners had always, by the custom of the country, the right to give their slaves reasonable punishment. One of the provisions of the act of 1751, on negroes, was that the owner of a slave who had attempted to run away might, if he chose, turn him over to the county court, to be punished by whipping, cropping, branding or otherwise, as the court should see fit—but not so as to kill him or unfit him for labor. By the

---

[1] 1804, 90; 1833, 224.

same act, any person who should persuade a slave to run away, became liable, if the slave absconded, to pay his full value to the owner, or if unable to do this, to be imprisoned for a year. A white servant, for the same offence, had to pay the same sum, or serve the master for four years. By the act of 1796, on negroes, there was fixed a penalty of not over two hundred dollars—in addition to whatever damages might be gotten at law—for any person who should be convicted of giving a pass unlawfully to any slave or servant, or assisting in any way in their escape. Half of this fine went to the owner of the slave, half to the county. By the act of 1809, on crimes, the stealing of a slave or the act of giving aid or counsel thereto, was punished by indemnification and imprisonment for not over twelve years. In 1818, the penalty for inciting or aiding a runaway to escape, or for harboring a runaway, was fixed at not over six years' imprisonment. This was for a free person, only. In 1827—perhaps the result of a petition from sundry citizens of Montgomery county for greater security for slave property—there was added that slaves found guilty, before any justice, of aiding runaways, should receive thirty-nine lashes.[1] The House of Delegates received, in 1820, a petition from certain inhabitants of Cecil county for a law making a slave who should run away guilty of a felony. This was referred, but evidently without result. In 1838 there was enacted, that any slave who should escape from Maryland with the intention of freeing himself from servitude, against the will of his owner, should be deemed guilty of felony, and, on due conviction by the court, should be sold by the sheriff, at a properly advertised auction, to be transported from the State. The proceeds, after expenses were deducted, went to the owner of the slave. And the purchaser was required to give bonds to the State of Maryland, in a sum equal to the amount paid, that the slave should be removed from the State; and in default of a proper

---

[1] 1818, 157; 1827, 15.

bond, the slave would be sold again. And the Governor of Maryland was directed, when evidence of the escape of a slave was laid before him, to demand the runaway, as a fugitive from justice, from the authorities of the State to which he had fled. Ten years later, the amount of the bond required was doubled, to twice the value of the slave.[1]

The old reward to those taking up a runaway, of two hundred pounds of tobacco or twenty shillings, was changed in 1806 to six dollars. In 1833—as it had been shown, says the preamble, that this was not enough to give the necessary encouragement—the reward was raised to thirty dollars. Constables, too, received special fees for taking up runaways; for instance, those of Anne Arundel county got six dollars for each capture. After 1844, the sum allowed for capturing any runaway slave between the ages of fifteen and forty-five years was fifteen dollars, where the capture took place within thirty miles but more than twenty miles from the slave's home, and fifty dollars, if over thirty miles away. For a slave under or over those ages, the reward was half those sums. But, to entitle one to such reward, the capture must take place beyond the county in which the slave was owned or hired. For a slave taken within a free State, except in the border counties of Pennsylvania, there could be claimed a reward of one hundred dollars, or half the value of the slave, at the option of the owner. Where larger rewards were offered by the owners, these sums were deemed to be included therein.[2]

In 1818, the longest term of imprisonment for aiding or inciting a slave to escape had been fixed at six years. In 1844, this maximum penalty was reduced to five years. Five

---

[1] 1838, 63; 1847, 309.

[2] 1833, 111; 1837, 271; 1844, 273.

In 1829, a petition from sundry citizens of Frederick co. for repeal of the acts on runaways, and that no fees be allowed anyone who might take up a negro who should be found to be free, was laid on the table.

By Act of 1844, a slave once in a free State, one hundred miles from home, was deemed a runaway, so as to entitle the captor to the large reward offered.

years after, however, the minimum term in the penitentiary was fixed at six years, the maximum at fifteen; and so the law remained. A slave convicted of the same offence, received either imprisonment for the same time or not over forty lashes, in the discretion of the court. Later, the penalty of imprisonment was changed to sale out of the State.[1]

Masters frequently sold to the South their slaves who attempted to run away. There remained on the statute books the old law which exempted from punishment anyone who should chance to kill a runaway slave forcibly resisting capture, and which made the State liable to the owner for the value of the slave. In 1807, the House of Delegates received a petition from a citizen of Somerset county, for compensation for his slave who was drowned while pursued as a runaway. The committee reported that the act of 1751 made provision for payment for slaves killed in pursuit; that the slave in question ran into Pocomoke river to avoid being caught, and in consequence was drowned; that no distinction should be made as to the manner of the death, if it was from pursuit, for the result to the owner of a slave was the same. This report, with an appropriation of a hundred pounds, the House accepted by a vote of thirty-three to twenty-nine; but the Senate rejected the bill. In 1856, the State paid a certain citizen one thousand dollars, under the act of 1751, for a slave killed while resisting arrest.[2]

---

[1] 1844, 80; 1849, 296.
[2] House Journal, 1807, 44–59. 1856, ch. 54.
In May, 1852, a runaway slave was killed in Pennsylvania by a resident of Baltimore. The Legislature of Maryland voted several thousand dollars for legal and other assistance to him, declaring that it was believed that the circumstances of the case did not make the killing murder or homicide, to be punished by law. (1852, 330, Res. 12, &c.)
It seems also that masters were accustomed to have committed to the jails by magistrates such slaves as were unruly or desirous of running away, or whom, for one reason or another, they desired to have in safe keeping. To prevent abuse of this custom, sheriffs were forbidden after 1818 to receive slaves from such owners as were engaged in the slave traffic; but others

There was also in force the old law fining a ship-captain—three dollars now, instead of twenty shillings, an hour—for carrying away negroes without passes, and for allowing slaves on board his ship, unless properly hired. In 1824, there was enacted further that no officer of a ship should receive on board or carry away any colored person without a properly authenticated certificate of freedom from a clerk of court of the State, as well as a certificate from the clerk of the county where the vessel sailed, with a description of the black. The clerks as well as the captains were to keep careful lists of all colored persons allowed to sail, and captains had to show these

---

could have their slaves committed to jail and kept there at their expense. Three years after, a bill passed the House to allow sheriffs to receive only such slaves as were committed in due course of law, but this was rejected by the Senate. Some ten years later, a slave escaped from a county jail, to which he had been sent by a magistrate at the master's request. The master sued in the county court to recover damages from the sheriff. He failed there, but the Court of Appeals decided in his favor. "It has been," said the Chief Justice, "the constant practice (with what moral propriety it is not for us to say) for owners of slaves in this State to have them committed to the jails of the respective counties, for real or supposed offences against their owners." (1818, 208. 5 G. & J., 253.)

Within the jails whites and blacks were separated, but they were expected evidently to be given the same food and care, save that any medical care would depend on the master; not being paid for by the public, as in the case of free prisoners.

In 1824, as it was represented that Baltimore was subjected to great expense for the care of negroes committed to jail as runaways—the free black population of the city was fast growing—the sheriff of Baltimore county was ordered to have all supposed runaways brought before one of the judges of the court, within two days, to be examined and either discharged at once or recommitted. The black, if recommitted, was to be advertised in two Baltimore papers, within two days, and twice a week for two months. If not then claimed, he was to be discharged. This act was repealed four years later; the act of 1817, as amended by 1828, 98, being in force for Baltimore as elsewhere. (1824, 171.) The charges to the State for board in Baltimore jail of supposed runaways, ultimately discharged, were in 1830, $237.96; in 1831, $354.13; in 1832, $364.05; in 1833, $270.24; &c. The number of runaways committed were, in 1852, 61 blacks; in 1853, 1 white and 46 blacks; in 1854, 62 blacks; in 1857, 3 whites and 86 blacks; in 1858, 1 white and 82 blacks; in 1859, 2 whites and 99 blacks; &c.

lists to any person who should desire to see them, and had to give every facility for search on their vessels, under a penalty of one hundred dollars. For actually carrying away a colored person contrary to this act, a captain became liable to a fine of one thousand dollars—half to the State, half to the person who should enter suit. In March, 1828, a slave woman left Baltimore on a steamer of the Penn., Del. & Md. Co. The owner warned the captain of the boat that the slave was probably on board, but no efforts were made to find her. The company was then sued for the loss of the slave and judgment given against it in both the lower court and the Court of Appeals. The captain testified that the owner could have searched any part of the boat, and that officers were always stationed on the boats before sailing, to prevent runaways from getting aboard; but the Court held that the captain, if he had been sufficiently informed of the supposed presence of the negro, and had failed to make the necessary search, had acted at his peril, and that his employers were responsible.[1] In 1838, a new law was made, to lessen the facilities of escape for slaves. From that time, no railroad, chartered by the State of Maryland, or vessel navigating the waters of the State, could transport any slave without a permission in writing from the owner, under a penalty of five hundred dollars for every slave, to be recovered from the railroad corporation or the owner or captain of the vessel. One half of this penalty went to the informer, one half to the State. In addition, if any slave escaped by being carried on a railway or vessel, the owner might recover the amount of his loss from the corporation or ship-owners, by an action of debt. But the law did not extend to prevent slaves from travelling in company with their masters or their master's agents.[2] In accordance with this act, officers of boats and railroads were expected by their employers to require proof of freedom or a permit to travel

---

[1] 1824, 85; 6 G. & J., 197, Dec., 1834.
[2] 1838, 375.

from any colored person not known to them to be free. In 1849, a bill to provide, especially, for the inspection of all vessels passing through the Chesapeake and Delaware Canal, for the purpose of stopping fugitives, was ordered in the House of Delegates; but evidently nothing further was done.[1] In 1855, the owner of a slave who was carried on the Philadelphia, Wilmington and Baltimore R. R., and thus helped to escape, recovered over one thousand dollars from the railroad.[2] In August of the same year, a negro boy owned in Somerset county, came to Baltimore on a steamer filled with passengers from a camp-meeting. The officers of the boat had no knowledge that he was on board. The owners of the boat were sued, and judgment given in their favor, in the Court of Common Pleas in Baltimore. But this was reversed by the Court of Appeals, which held that the owners could not escape the penalty by showing that neither they nor their agents knew that the slave was on the boat, although reasonable diligence had been used to prevent runaways from embarking. The law had been made, said the Court, to remedy the great loss suffered by slave-holders; and where one of two innocent parties must suffer, the loss should fall on him who could most easily have prevented it.[3] Another slave owner, at about the same time, got over eight hundred dollars in a suit against the Northern Central R. R. for allowing his runaway slave to use the road.[4] In another case, the runaway slave had been hired out by his master to work on a sailing vessel which ran between Baltimore and Annapolis. His master won five hundred dollars from the owners of the packet, in a suit in the Circuit Court for Anne Arundel county; but this judgment was reversed, the Court of Appeals holding that transporta-

---

[1] House Journal, 1849, p. 132.
[2] In Circ. Court for Harford Co., Baltimore *Sun*, Feb. 3rd, 1855.
[3] 13 Md. Reports, 181. 1859.
[4] Baltimore City Superior Court. Baltimore *Sun*, Feb. 10, 1858.

tion, by the act of 1838, meant the taking away from the owner without his consent.¹

From Georgia or Carolina a runaway slave must make a long journey before reaching free soil—from Maryland the escape would be a short one at the most. For Pennsylvania had abolished slavery in Revolutionary days, and so many of the inhabitants had become opposed to slavery anywhere, that runaways were frequently protected and aided to escape further. As early as 1796, the Maryland House of Delegates received a petition from a citizen of Worcester county, stating that the abolitionists, together with civil officers in Pennsylvania, had taken away his negroes and arrested his person, and praying for aid. The committee reported that the petitioner had been grossly injured in his person and property by some of the citizens in that State, but that it would be improper for the Legislature to interfere and become a party on his behalf, as the federal courts were open to all citizens of the country, and competent to redress all such injuries. With this the House concurred by a vote of sixty to four. A further suggestion that the State should loan money to the petitioner, on sufficient surety, that he might enter and prosecute the necessary suits for redress, was lost by one vote. In 1798 a bill for better security of property in slaves was introduced in the Maryland House of Delegates, only to be postponed; but a resolution was adopted, declaring that slave owners were subjected to great loss and inconvenience from the escape of slaves to Delaware, Pennsylvania and New Jersey, where they remained concealed and protected by the whites, and authorizing the Governor and Council to take measures with the Governors of those States to stop such abuses.² In 1815, sundry inhabitants of Allegany, St. Mary's and Washington counties asked for

---

¹ 21 Md. Reports, 1. 1863. Nor was it necessary, said the Court in this case, that a slave should actually escape, to constitute the offence, under the law.

² House Journal, 1796, 37-40; 1798, 47, 106; Res. 7.

action to prevent the escape of slaves into Pennsylvania. The House thereupon resolved that the Legislature of Pennsylvania be requested to use its authority, as it should deem best, to prevent the citizens from harboring and employing runaway slaves, and to facilitate the return of such to their real owners. This resolution was, however, rejected in the Senate.[1] But at the next session was passed a resolution that such abuses had so increased from citizens of Pennsylvania and Delaware, and the inconvenience to the good people of Maryland had become so great, that further silence was improper. And the Governor was ordered to send a copy of this resolution to the Governors of those States, to be laid before their Legislatures, that some provisions might be made to prevent the evils. Again, the next year, the Governor was ordered to open a correspondence at once for the same object, and it was declared that the abuses were injurious in their consequences even to slaves themselves.[2] In 1820 the Assembly resolved that it was necessary to call the attention of Congress to the constant and ready protection given to runaways by citizens of Pennsylvania. Every possible difficulty, we read, was there put in the way of the recovery of a slave, even in the legal and just efforts of the owner. If legal proceedings favored him, force was not seldom used. Such a state of things was not only vexatious to masters, but tended to destroy the contentment and happiness of the slaves. So the Governor was requested to ask the members of Congress from Maryland to exert their influence to procure measures by Congress to protect the rights of slaveholders.[3] At the very next session of Assembly, the committee on Grievances and Courts reported to the House that they had found true the petition of one of their fellow members, a delegate from Baltimore county, as to the treatment which he received in person from sundry citizens of York

---

[1] House Journal, 1815, 34, 43, 57, 76.
[2] 1816, 68; 1817, 43.
[3] 1820, Res. 281.

county, Pennsylvania, while he was in the peaceable and legal exercise of the provisions of the act of Congress for the capture of fugitive slaves; and the committee urged that measures should be taken by Pennsylvania to stop the practices, not merely of aiding runaways, but of keeping away the owners by threats of personal violence, and of using the civil authorities to force owners to abandon their property rather than undergo imprisonment and trial under a State law against kidnapping. The House thereupon passed a resolution, asking the Governor of Pennsylvania to interpose in behalf of the petitioner, but the matter was dropped in the Senate, as the petitioner had by that time been relieved. Another resolution, however, was sent the Governors of Pennsylvania and Delaware, to remedy the abuses in general. Silence on the part of the Assembly of Maryland was declared to be highly improper, if not criminal.[1] By the next session, again, another member of the House had received opposition and indignity; whereupon a joint committee from House and Senate, at the head of which stood Mr. Reverdy Johnson, entered into communication with the authorities of Pennsylvania. Into the correspondence which followed, and the work done by this committee and those who afterward treated with New Jersey and Delaware, we are not called on to enter.[2] Suffice it to point out the injuries which the people of Maryland felt they were receiving at the hands of their neighbors. These injuries, wrote the joint committee of 1822, had for several years been loudly complained of by the people of Maryland, while due regard was had to the delicate nature of the subject, and of the caution with which it should be treated. Slavery was a calamity, certainly not more deplored by Pennsylvania than by Maryland. All friends of freedom should rejoice at its complete extermination; but that end could not be expected for many years to come. So long

---

[1] House Journal, 1821, 21, 119; Res. 53.
[2] House Journal, 1822, 46, 163, &c.; 1823, 67; 1824, 24, 103, &c.; 1825, Res. 81.

as slavery lasts, citizens of Maryland are as much entitled to their slaves as to any other property; their rights to them are as much secured by the Constitution of the United States as any rights they possess. The existence of our happy Union depends, in a great degree, on preserving harmony among its members. So spoke this committee. All must have agreed that the rights of slaveholders should be protected. In 1837 and 1843, resolutions of the Assembly declared that no State could abridge the rights guaranteed to all citizens by the Constitution of the United States, and called for a law from Congress to make the rescue of a fugitive a criminal offence, to be punished by imprisonment, when remuneration could not be given.[1] A citizen of Maryland met with such experiences in New York, while attempting lawfully to recover a runaway, that the Assembly in 1849 directed the Attorney-General to take all steps for an appeal in the case, if necessary, to the Supreme Court. The negro, so the resolution stated, was discharged by a justice of the Supreme Court of New York, on grounds which amounted to the abnegation of the laws of Congress to secure slave owners their property in runaway slaves. In the same year, several men were brought to trial by the State for helping slaves to escape, and the Assembly, as we saw, tripled the maximum term for that offence. A few years later, the State appropriated over eleven hundred dollars to several persons in Montgomery county for arresting a man from New York who had furthered the escape of slaves.[2] Finally, the Governor, in 1847 and 1852, told the people of Maryland how ineffectual were requisitions on the State of Pennsylvania for the delivery of slaves, as well as for the delivery of a citizen of Maryland who had aided slaves to escape; and how one respected citizen of Maryland had died from violence received in Pennsylvania, and another was shot down there and his son seriously wounded, while engaged in the re-

---

[1] 1837, Res. 79; 1843, Res. 28.
[2] 1849, Res. 21, 32; 1853, 124. House Journal, 1853, Doc. G.

turn of their runaway slaves, according to the act of Congress. There is much significance in the experience of two slaves who ran away from their home in Virginia, in the winter of 1856, and cautiously followed the railroads North. After passing the Gunpowder River, beyond Baltimore, they thought they had crossed the line into Pennsylvania, and applied for work; but they were still in Maryland, and were sent back to Virginia.

In other ways, too, in the newspapers, men were frequently reminded of the insecurity of slave property. In the county papers were the sheriffs' advertisements and the description of runaways, with the rough wood-cut of a black hurrying on, with stick and bundle-handkerchief over his shoulder, and his eyes turned backwards. The Easton *Star*, for instance, told how twelve slaves had just run away from that neighborhood on a certain Saturday night, and that two nights before, and two nights after, several had escaped from the lower counties. The Cecil *Democrat* said that six slaves had gone from that county while their master was away, and that they were doubtless assisted by abolitionists, as one had been seen there-abouts, about that time. Again, the Easton *Gazette* chronicled the loss of five more slaves on a Saturday night. One citizen of Baltimore county lost seventeen slaves together, but found them in Pennsylvania and brought them back. Later still, in 1853, there was a stampede of slaves, as the Cumberland *Telegraph* put it, but eight at least were recaptured across the line. On a certain day in September, 1855, said the Chestertown *News*, ten slaves not only took themselves away, but three horses and two carriages besides; and on October 20th, following, seven more escaped, and on the 26th, eleven more. There were reports, too, of escapes and captures in which weapons were used on both sides.

It is certain that many a slave and free black, especially in the communities where they were known, moved about freely without thought of the need of a pass, or of fear of hindrance. If the laws, as we have seen, were not always regarded, sometimes they were ineffectual. A certain British vessel cleared from Baltimore, in 1852, after the master, as required, had taken the usual oath against shipping runaways. The owners of a slave boy, then missing, had their suspicions, and overtook the vessel down the Chesapeake and had her searched. The boy was found, hidden on board by a colored man, unbeknown to the officers. Two slaves, some years later, got tickets at the Philadelphia, Wilmington & Baltimore Station in Baltimore, on showing a certificate of freedom, but their owner and the police caught them before the train started. But a slave who traveled without a pass was liable to get into trouble. One day in Baltimore, in 1858, several colored men were arrested as runaway slaves, and taken before the Superior Court; where it was found that they were slaves who had come to the city to spend their Christmas holidays, by permission of their master, and that they had left their passes with the captain of the steamer in which they came and were to return home. They were at once released by the court.[1] The slaveholders' convention of Worcester county in 1858, resolved, among other things, that slaveholders should be requested to discontinue the practice of letting slaves leave home without passes.

Scattered here and there in the court reports are convictions of both whites and blacks for aiding runaways to escape. In a few cases, too, both whites and free blacks were found to have encouraged slaves to run away, and then to have betrayed them for the reward.[2] One free black, at least, seems to have earned a livelihood by aiding slaves to escape, for when tried in Baltimore, in 1857, for helping away five slaves, it appeared that he had been for some years in that occupation, was in the employ of three whites, and generally got fifteen dollars for every slave he got away. He had been in the penitentiary before, and was then sold out of the State for thirty years.[3]

---

[1] Baltimore *Sun*, Jan. 1st, 1858.
[2] For instance, Baltimore *Sun*, of Jan. 19th, 1849.
[3] Baltimore City Circuit Court, Jan. 6th, 1857. He brought $350.

In 1846, thirty and more citizens of Kent county were incorporated into a "Mutual Protection Society," for the insurance of slave property. Every person who insured a slave became a member, and the object was to protect the members from loss of slaves who might run away beyond the limits of Maryland. Slaves who were captured were to be sold by the Society beyond the State, and the proceeds went to reimburse members and into the funds of the Society. In 1860, was formed the Southern Slaveholders' Insurance Company of Maryland. Any slaveholder of the United States could have his property insured, and either the runaways were returned or their value paid.[1]

Yet, while slave property in Maryland was thus far from being secure, and many slaves did run away, the great majority of slaves there probably had no thought of leaving home.

In 1854, two slaves who had run away from Worcester county, desired to return home, but feared that they might be convicted as runaways, and sold out of the State. A special act of Assembly, therefore, allowed them to return to their master without fear of such punishment. Some years after, a slave belonging in the same county ran away into Delaware, but soon turned back to go home. On his way he was arrested, lodged in jail in Delaware, and then sent home. By a special act, his mistress was allowed to keep him, inasmuch, we read, as his presence in the slave population was thought by many slaveholders of the county to be calculated to keep his fellows from absconding.[2]

In 1689 rumors went abroad that the Romanists of Maryland were plotting against the government of the Province,

---

[1] See Acts of Incorporation, 1846, 356; 1860, 390. A bill for a "Protection Society" of Kent County had been rejected by the Senate in 1827.
[2] 1854, 291; 1861-2, 134. See also, 1861-2, 245.

and that many and great disturbances were threatened, particularly in Calvert and Charles counties. The Indians, it was said, were in league with the papists. Suspicions must have been cast on the negroes, also, for those Southern counties had a large slave population. But a declaration signed by some fifteen prominent men there, assured the home government that the plot was wholly groundless and imaginary. In 1695, there was passed an act to prevent the frequent meetings of negroes. This soon expired; but it is evident that blacks were regarded by the authorities as a part of the population that could easily be used in political intrigues.[1] Nor were men entirely free of apprehensions from the white servants, some of whom were the refuse of European camps, prisoners of war, and worthless convicts. There were reports of a plot of Irish servants and slaves in Bermuda, and of an insurrection which had been planned and almost carried out in Gloucester county, Virginia, by a number of servants, one of whom betrayed the plans, and four of whom were tried and executed.[2] The Assembly of Maryland in 1705 declared that certain whites were guilty of a conspiracy to seize the Governor and magazine, and, joining with the "Heathen Indians," to cut off the inhabitants of the Province.[3] During all the years of Jacobite disaffection to the Protestant succession in England, the Romanists of Maryland were kept under the eye of government. In 1708, for instance, the sheriffs of the counties were ordered to send to the Governor within a few weeks the number and names of papists—not merely of masters of

---

[1] Pub. Record Office, quoted in Scharf's Maryland, 1, 309. In 1698, the provincial Governors were ordered—at the suggestion of the Board of Trade—to see that the laws for increasing the whites in proportion to the blacks, were duly enforced. There were no such laws in Md., but Gov. Nicholson urged on the Board the evils that might follow from too great increase in the blacks. (Steven's Hist. Index, Vol. IV.)

[2] Virginia Carolorum, 295.

[3] Bacon, 1705, 5. Annals of Annapolis, 108. The ringleader, who was not caught, was attainted, two years later.

families, but of the households, servants and slaves baptized in the Roman faith.[1] In 1739, the Council received the depositions of several negroes of Prince George's county, telling of a most wicked and dangerous conspiracy which had been entered into by the blacks there, to destroy the whites, and to possess themselves of the country. Whereupon, the Governor issued orders for a special commission of Oyer and Terminer for the speedy trial of those who had been taken, and that a guard of twelve men, under the command of the colonel of the county, should be kept at the jail until the execution of any who might be convicted. And, further, the sheriff of Annapolis was ordered not to allow any negroes to enter that city on Sundays without written permits from their masters. On the next day, the Council decided that, in accordance with the laws on slaves, the trials could not be held before the next regular courts should sit, so the sheriff was ordered to take every precaution with his prisoners, and to levy any posse that might be necessary; for there was reason, wrote the Council, to fear that those who were already in jail and the numbers which must be committed, together with their accomplices without, might give trouble. The Governor, further, issued a proclamation to all officials, civil and military, to aid in averting such great dangers as were threatening the lives and property of the people, by the rage and fury of merciless and barbarous slaves. Care was to be taken to enforce strictly the laws against tumultuous meetings of slaves, to secure all slaves who might be found wandering at large and who could not give satisfactory accounts of themselves, to execute all laws for the public safety, and to exhort all the people to be on their guard, for the defence of themselves and their neighbors. In particular, the magistrates were bidden to take notice of the way in which local officers should act, and the major-generals of the Eastern and Western shores were given careful instructions for the practice of the troops,

---

[1] Council Journal, 1701–1708, 125.

to be ready for any possible insurrections or foreign wars. These messages were startling; but this insurrection seems to have been no more than a local excitement caused by a few blacks. The leader was tried and executed. There was a great difference of opinion, indeed, as to the extent of the outbreak and of the dangers from it, the House of Delegates assuring the Council—during some opposition to the appropriations which the Council desired, the following year, on account of the war between England and Spain—that the Romanists of the Province were not inclined to disturb the peace, and that inquiry into the insurrection of the negroes in Prince George's county failed to find anything which could in any way be presumed to have endangered the welfare of the Province.[1] In 1742, the Council feared that there was a conspiracy of certain Indians to destroy all the whites in Maryland; but articles of peace were soon made with them, the action of the Governor was lenient, and within a year their guns were restored to them.[2] In 1745, again, the Romanists were under great suspicion. To one of their leaders Governor Bladen wrote, that their religious duties should be fulfilled, as they surely might be, without such large meetings of people as might give suspicion of designs other than religious exercises. Nothing, said the Governor, could give greater alarm to good subjects of King George than such frequent meetings of whites and negroes under pretence of divine worship.[3] Again, with the breaking out of the French and Indian war, not only were the people of Maryland, particularly those in its distant parts, bidden by a proclamation to be ready for defence, but the colonels of militia in Frederick and Baltimore counties were ordered to hold reviews, and to make returns of

---

[1] Council Records, 1738–1753, 59, &c., 110. The Council seem to have taken the House to be very unpatriotic for being willing to believe no ill-will on the part of the negroes, and so for discouraging the need of military measures.

[2] Council Records, 1738–1753, 162.

[3] Council Records, 1738–1753, 255.

the number of men and arms, and whether there was plenty of ammunition in the counties in case of any rioting or plotting by servants, slaves or others. Should such intrigues be known, the ring-leaders were to be seized by the troops.[1] After Braddock's defeat, according to Governor Sharp's letters, the people were thrown into the greatest consternation, slaves and convicts were well watched, and the militia were ready to quell any insurrections. Soon, indeed, reports came to the Council that the negroes in certain parts had held some tumultuous meetings and intrigues, and the Romanists in several counties had so misbehaved as to give cause for fears of insurrection. So the magistrates throughout the Province were ordered to make examination, and to imprison the offenders; but if the reports were false, to carry the authors before the courts as disturbers of the peace. Inquiries were also to be made into the report that some Roman Catholic priests had recently been absent from their homes. Answers were received from the magistrates in nine counties, and all to the effect that the constables in the various hundreds were wide awake to their duties, that the Romanists were few in number, and that nothing unusual had been done by the negroes.[2] In the troubled state of affairs during the outbreak of the Revolution, several gentlemen requested Governor Eden to give out arms to the people, from fears that the servants and slaves might revolt. The Governor expostulated, stating that such action would tend only to hasten any such evil, but finally gave a quantity of arms to certain regularly appointed persons, in accordance with the militia act.[3] But in both the Revolution and the war of 1812 there was no general uprising of slaves. On the contrary, a number of colored men served

---

[1] Council Records, 1753–1767, 56.
[2] Council Records, 1753–1767, 59, 65–73. Stevens' Hist. Index, Vol. X. Gov. Dinwiddie, of Va., had fears of the negroes at this time. (Dinwiddie Papers, II, 102.)
[3] Letters of Gov. Eden, Scharf's Md., II, 179.

faithfully in the American forces. In the summer of 1793 there arrived in Baltimore some twelve hundred refugees from San Domingo, flying from the horrors of servile insurrection. They brought half as many slaves with them. They were, reported a committee in the Assembly, in a state of distress which exceeded description. The Assembly appropriated five hundred dollars weekly for two months, and thousands of dollars were raised for them besides, throughout the State. The horrors of this insurrection had not been forgotten when, in the autumn of 1831, there came the reports of the revolt of slaves in Southampton county, Virginia. It is certain that fears and suspicions of the negroes were rumored in Maryland. In some of the lower counties, expresses were sent off for arms and men, and some blacks were arrested; but there seem to have been no good reasons for any such apprehensions, and no need for such measures.[1]

Insurrection wholly local and the work of a few negroes only, was not unknown in Maryland. In 1845, several slaves and a free black were arrested for that offence in Charles county. The free black was given forty years imprisonment, and one slave was sentenced to be hung, but most of those who took part in the intrigue were not brought to trial, but were sold out of Maryland by their masters. A memorial, signed by a number of very respectable persons, was presented the Governor, to commute the sentence of the slave from hanging to imprisonment. The Governor signified his willingness so to do, did the law allow the confinement of slaves in the peni-

---

[1] 1831, Res. 27, 65. *Niles' Register*, XLI, 131. In lower Delaware and Maryland, says the current number of *Niles' Register*, awful reports were heaped upon one another by fear, but there does not seem to have been the least foundation for this excitement.

Mr. McSherry, in his History of Maryland, p. 358, says that the intrigues of the party of Nat. Turner extended over a part of Maryland, but that a misunderstanding on the part of those concerned, and timely measures on the part of the whites, prevented the outbreak. Unfortunately, no sources for this are mentioned.

tentiary; whereupon a special act of Assembly directed that the slave might be imprisoned.[1]

Rumors of serious insurrections in Maryland seem to have been as groundless in the latter days of slavery as they had been generations before, when the politics of Europe, reflected in the Colonies, made the royal Governors look on the negroes as ready accomplices of the Romanists, or of the Jacobites, or of the French. In the spring of 1855, a rumor of an uprising of the slaves caused great excitement, in Dorchester county, and the houses of many negroes were searched for firearms, but the papers soon announced that the whole affair was a hoax.[2] Meanwhile the excitement spread to Talbot county. It was feared that the blacks planned some movement during the Easter holidays approaching. A meeting of many and respectable citizens of Easton adopted resolutions asking slaveholders to keep their servants at home—although, says the Easton *Gazette*, there is probably no truth in the rumors.[3] Two years later, a similar report broke out in Prince George's county. The blacks were more carefully watched, but all excitement soon subsided, and people concluded that there had never been any plan or intention of insurrection. In the autumn of 1859 occurred the John Brown raid on the border of Western Maryland and Virginia. Maryland militia were sent for the suppression of the outbreak, and the sheriffs of the Western border counties called out large patroling parties, to prevent the meeting and escape of slaves. For some days the papers were full of nothing else. It was even said that there was to have been, on a certain day, an uprising of all the slaves of Maryland and Virginia. Then began the formation in all parts of Maryland of new military companies. Here, a public meeting was held and a rifle company formed; in other places, cavalry companies were enlisted. The martial spirit is

---

[1] Executive Message, 1845; 1845, ch. 368.
[2] Cambridge *Democrat*, quoted in Baltimore *Sun* for April 13th, 1855.
[3] Easton *Gazette*, April 7th, 1855.

7

up, said one county paper, and our people are their own best defenders.[1] In Frederick, so the local papers stated, strangers had been seen to lurk about the barracks, if not indeed to attempt to enter them; so volunteer companies keep guard at night. There were rumors that accomplices of Brown were abroad, and the patrolers were ordered to arrest all suspicious characters. Again, that some forty slaves had planned to escape from Carroll county on a certain Saturday night, and that horses and wagons were found waiting when the plot was discovered. Afterwards, men learned that one of the first persons shot by John Brown's party was a colored porter at the Harper's Ferry depot, who remained faithful to his trust, and that the aid given Brown by the slaves was trivial. At that time even, there were many proofs that the threatened dangers were exaggerated. On the night of October 19th, the citizens of Frederick were startled by a report that an insurrection was about to break out, and their town was to be attacked. The streets were at once patrolled by bodies of armed men, and various precautions taken; but the report in the newspaper is headed "Another False Alarm."[2] On a certain night, early in November following, an alarm of insurrection and murder was given while services were being held in a church in Somerset county. The congregation, says the local paper, rose from prayers, broke up the benches to provide themselves with weapons, and scoured the neighborhood, but found nothing to alarm them. On the night following, the houses of many free blacks were searched, and a slave who attempted to leave one of the cabins was shot, being mistaken for an insurgent by the excited crowd. This has all, doubtless, adds the paper, grown out of the excitement roused by the affair at Harper's Ferry.[3] The last week in November, the people of another neighbor-

---

[1] See Baltimore and county papers for Oct., Nov., Dec., 1859. 1860, ch. 57, 274; 1861-2, 163.
[2] The *Sun*, Oct. 22nd, 1859.
[3] Somerset County *Union* Nov. 4th.

hood were told that a lady near the Virginia line, a large slaveholder had received a letter stating that the blacks of the Eastern shores of Maryland and Virginia had planned an insurrection which was to be carried out at once. The local paper did not put the slightest faith in the report, but suggested that the citizens should be vigilant and ready for any emergency. A similar report—spoken of by the Baltimore *Sun* as a hoax —had been current on the Eastern shore of Virginia, the week before. At almost the same time, an excitement spread in Talbot county from a threatening letter which was found on a wharf at St. Michael's.[1] Patrols were at once organized and a strong guard made ready to protect Easton. But nothing unusual happened, save these measures, and some unwonted severity, perhaps, shown by the constabulary to the blacks. Once again, Easton was put under arms, from the information of a colored woman; and some person in the county remembered that a suspicious looking man, who might have been Brown himself, had been seen thereabouts before the Harper's Ferry affray.

At these times of reported insurrection, the blacks were without doubt more frightened than the whites. Doubtless, too, many a community in Maryland could have said, at such times, what the paper in Wilmington, North Carolina, added to its account of the excitement that followed the news of the Nat. Turner insurrection: that the subject could not be dismissed without speaking of the good behavior of the slaves thereabouts, who might be entrusted, it was believed, to take part in the defence of the community under any circumstances. In the Civil War that soon followed, the women and children of the South were left largely in the care of slaves, while the masters were fighting for a cause which would have lengthened, to say the least, the existence of slavery.

---

[1] Easton *Star*, Nov. 29th, 1859.

Of the provisions of the act of 1695, to restrain the frequent assemblages of negroes, we know nothing; but the law soon expired. In 1723, the Assembly considered the evils resulting from the large meetings of negroes on "Sabbath and other Holy-days," and enacted that the courts should begin at once the yearly custom of appointing constables, in such hundreds as required them, to suppress tumultuous meetings of slaves. Every constable so appointed was required to visit all suspected places in his hundred, once a month, and could give not over thirty-nine lashes to every negro who might be found away from home without a permit from his master. For the fulfilment of such duties, the constable was to be paid five hundred pounds of tobacco; and he might call on any person to aid him. For a white man who should refuse assistance, there was a penalty of one hundred pounds of tobacco; a negro refused on pain of a whipping. Afterwards, such duties belonged to all constables, under penalty for neglect of not less than one hundred dollars. And any person who refused his aid when summoned, could be fined not more than that sum nor less than twenty dollars. The special pay for the constable was eight dollars; but after 1806, every constable had, before he could receive this, to get a certificate from at least two respectable citizens of his hundred, bearing witness to his industry and fidelity in carrying out the law.[1]

By a law of 1715, persons who entertained or kept away from home any servant or slave for the space of a day or night became liable to a fine of five hundred pounds of tobacco. This seems to have been taken advantage of by persons—many crafty and ill-disposed persons, the act says—who entertained servants and slaves for a few hours at a time and at dead of night, and also enticed these to steal their masters' goods, and to commit other disorders. So the fine was changed in 1748 to one hundred pounds an hour;[2] to be

---

[1] 1695, 6; 1723, 15; 1806, 81; Code of 1860, art. 23, 30 and art. 66, 63.
[2] 1715, 44; 1748, 19.

recovered before a single magistrate, if not over six hundred in all. If the offender could not pay he might be whipped. The penalty afterwards became a fine of two dollars an hour. Servants and slaves who harbored others unlawfully were to be whipped by order of a magistrate. After 1723, also, the owner of a plantation was directed to send home, by whipping if necessary, any negroes who might be found there, without permission or errand from their masters. And any person who encouraged slaves to meet in numbers on his place, except on lawful occasions, became liable to a fine of one thousand pounds of tobacco—afterwards of twenty dollars.

The constables of towns, also, were usually ordered by special acts of Assembly to see, among other duties, that negroes did not gather in noisy groups in the streets, or at meetings, or remain out late at night. For instance, a constable was appointed in 1800 for the town of Cambridge, as the peace of the town was much disturbed by frequent meetings of negroes, and the constable of the hundred had happened to live out of the town. The constable appointed for the village of Newmarket in Dorchester county, in 1804, was to prevent disorderly meetings of blacks there and in the neighborhood, and to give moderate punishment, under the direction of any justice of the peace, to all such as should be found strolling the streets at night, or frequenting the houses of persons other than their masters, without permission.[1] Often, in towns with a considerable black population, a bell was rung at a certain hour in the evening—as nine in winter and ten in summer—and the black who remained out of doors thereafter had to rely on his own good character, or on the carelessness or good nature of the constable, or his heels, to save him from punishment.

These restrictions, both in county and town, were not the result alone of fears of insurrection or of loss by runaways. They were largely for the ordinary preservation of the peace.

---

[1] 1800, 6; 1804, 70, &c.

For instance, the Society of Friends who held yearly meetings in Anne Arundel and Talbot counties, were much annoyed by the numbers of persons who met and drank liquors in the neighborhood of their meeting-houses. Soon after 1700, they petititioned the Governor and Council to have an end put to such abuses. Finally, after several complaints, a law was made in 1725, to forbid the sale of liquors within certain distances of the meeting houses, except at inns. But the orderly Friends were still troubled by the racing of horses and the meetings of negroes—great crowds of idle whites and blacks, they said, drank and behaved riotously there—until, in 1747, horse racing was forbidden, also, and the constables of the neighborhood were specially ordered to disperse all crowds of slaves, at the times of the yearly meetings, if necessary by whipping and by the assistance of a posse.[1] Besides such ordinary measures for good order, there was the need, often, of reasonable discipline in the care of servants and slaves, if the master was not to lose by their picking and stealing, and was to get good work from them. Could they frequent the grogshops, his corn and tobacco might easily be turned into liquor; and were they up for the night, his work would suffer by day. It was as natural for the master of servants or slaves then, to wish them at home by nine or ten at night, as for good housekeepers to make the rule, to-day, that after reasonable hours there shall be no company in the kitchen.[2]

Masters were caused much trouble by the sale of liquor to servants and slaves. The early court records show that care was taken by a license system, to keep inns from becoming nuisances. One landland of St. Mary's, for instance, gave bond in 1660, in the sum of a thousand pounds of tobacco and

---

[1] Colonial Church Life in Maryland, 123. Act 1725, 6; 1747, 17.

[2] The good Friends of Pennsylvania who met in yearly meeting in 1696, not only advised their brethren not to increase slaves among them, but to bring the slaves they had to meetings, to keep them from loose and idle living, and from rambling abroad of First Days and other times. (Janney's History of the Friends, III, 179.)

casks, that he would, for five years, have good order kept at his house, especially at times of divine service, and would not allow servants and apprentices to get liquors or to remain tippling there without their masters' knowledge. Over a hundred years later, an act of Assembly authorized the city of Annapolis to regulate taverns, as, we read, many of the servants and slaves there were injured and their masters deprived of their services, by the sale to them of rum and spirits. After 1780, any tavern keeper in the State who should harbor, or sell any liquors to any servant, apprentice or slave, without written leave from the master, became liable for each offence to forfeit to the master one hundred and sixty pounds of tobacco,— afterwards, ten dollars.[1] To prevent the sale of stolen goods, there was enacted, in 1692, that no one should trade or barter with any servants or slaves without permission from their owners, under penalty of two thousand pounds of tobacco, half to the government and half to the owner of the goods. And if the value of these was over a thousand pounds, the owner, also, could enter suit for damages against the receiver —who, if he could not pay this further fine, received thirty stripes on his bare back. The law afterwards read that no person should buy or get in any way from any slave any goods whatever, or should sell anything to any slave, without written permission from his owner or overseer, under penalty of a fine of five dollars, on conviction before a magistrate.[2] Also, after 1796, any slave who should sell liquor or keep entertainment at any muster-ground, race track or other public place, without his master's permission, became liable to arrest and a whipping by order of a magistrate.[3]

---

[1] See Prov. Court Records, 1658–1662, 397, 411. 1779, 11; 1780, 24; Code of 1860.

[2] W. H. & L., 91; 1715, 44; Code of 1860. These acts, said the Court of Appeals, in 1837, did not imply any right in slaves to deal or make contracts, the penalty on the free person showing the reverse. Servants and slaves had been encouraged to sell stolen goods. (9 G. & J., 14.)

[3] 1796, 67.

In 1666, the House of Delegates called the attention of the Council to a bill deemed very important, to prohibit servants and negroes from keeping pigs for their own benefit; but the Council replied that such a law was not necessary, as every master had the power to forbid swine to his slaves and to his servants—unless the indentures of the servants happened to give them special privileges. In 1723, there was enacted that masters who allowed slaves to keep any horses or cattle or swine, as their own, should forfeit five hundred pounds of tobacco and the animals. There were, afterwards, no such restrictions.[1] A slave could not legally hold property: whether he had possessions or privileges depended, as the Council said in 1666, on the master's will. Generally, the slave had at least a garden and chicken coop, from whose proceeds he got such luxuries as coffee and tobacco. Some masters bought what the slaves raised—even at the risk, occasionally, of paying for a sweet potato or a chicken that was already theirs; others gave their slaves permits to sell and buy; others, still, lay asleep in the big house, while the black quietly did his bartering at some corner store or on some boat in the river. The majority of slaves in the coast States worked by tasks; when the allotted work was done daily, the slave's time was his own. On Saturday afternoons, some slaves had less than the usual work to do, and it was the general custom to give holidays at Christmas and Easter-tide. At such times, the market places of the county towns might be thronged with blacks.

At the session of Assembly of 1787, the House received from the Senate a bill to prevent the inconveniences arising from slaves who were allowed to act as freemen. The first section placed a penalty of five pounds a month on all mas-

---

[1] Md. Arch., II, 23, &c. One of the resolutions of the convention of slaveholders of Worcester county, in 1858, was that slave owners and slave hirers be asked to discontinue the practice of allowing slaves to have corn patches.

ters who should allow slaves to go at large or hire themselves out, except during ten days at harvest time. A motion to strike out this section was lost by a vote of thirty-two to fifteen. The second section provided that no slaves, except such as were generally known to be pilots, should be allowed by their masters, under a like penalty, to run any boat over twenty feet long which was used to carry goods belonging to any other person than the owner of the boat. This section was struck out; but the bill, as amended and passed, excepted regular pilots. And a person who should hire any slave unlawfully, was also made liable to the penalty of five pounds a month. At the session of 1794, there were several attempts made for further legislation—evidently for greater restrictions. One bill, introduced in the House, was to prevent slaves from acting as free in several counties. Baltimore county was added by a vote of thirty-nine to seventeen, and a motion to except Baltimore city was defeated by seven votes—though the delegates from the city were opposed to the bill. Motions to add Anne Arundel, Talbot and Cecil counties were all lost, and the bill as passed was rejected in the Senate. In 1802, the Senate offered a bill for an act by which the penalty on the master who should let out the slave, was raised to forty dollars. This the House would not agree to, although it would tend, the Senate argued, to remedy an evil which had risen to such a degree as to require legislative interference. The House maintained that a fine of twenty-five dollars on both the master and the hirer of a slave was sufficient. The next year, the Senate again brought in a bill, and again the House rejected it.[1] By an act of 1817, there was made an exception of twenty days at harvest time, instead of ten days. The maximum penalty for one who should make any contract with a slave for his services, or who should let his slave go at large or hire himself out, remained twenty dollars a month.

---

[1] House Journal, 1787, 150, &c.; act 1787, 33; House Journal, 1802, 43, 56, &c.

In 1821, a special law required constables in Worcester and Caroline counties to arrest and bring before a justice all slaves, except regular pilots, who might be found going at large or hiring themselves out, or who might not have fixed homes on their owner's estates, or be duly hired out in the employ of some person. If the justice found that the law was being violated, he should let out the slave for the rest of the current year; the proceeds to be given to the county. A constable was entitled to two dollars for thus taking up and letting out a slave. This act was extended, at the next session, to Somerset and Queen Anne's counties.[1]

But competition between white and black was not without some influence, we presume, in bringing about such legislation. A petition was presented the House of Delegates, in 1808, from "the owners of hack-stages, draymen, carters and laborers" of Baltimore, who complained that they were "deprived of employment by the interference of slaves who engross the same." This was referred to the next Assembly.[2] Despite the laws, slaves were often hiring themselves, or being hired out. At the slaveholders' conventions, these liberties were always severely denounced. The papers tell us, for instance, how the grand jury of Anne Arundel, in 1854, gave particular attention to doing away with the custom of slaves hiring themselves out by permission of their masters; and how the citizens of a certain district in Somerset county, at a public meeting early in 1860, expressed their disapproval of the practice of allowing slaves hired out to be masters of their own time, and of that of hiring them out with the provision of their own consent to the agreements.[3] Not a few slaves in

---

[1] 1817, 104; Code of 1860, 66, 29: 1821, 183; 1822, 115. In 1806, sundry citizens of St. Mary's county petitioned, without result, that slaves be prevented from acting as pilots.

[2] House Journals, 1806, 20; 1808, 75.

[3] Baltimore *Sun*, April 28th, 1854; Jan. 20th, 1860. In 1849, a bill to prevent the employment of slaves by merchants, shopkeepers and traders, without the written consent of their owners, was laid on the table.

Maryland, particularly in the cities, were allowed by their masters to live and act as freemen, and also to buy their own freedom by their extra earnings. But this was by the sufferance of others only and by no right of their own. Thus, in one case, the owner of a slave who had been hired out to some third party in Baltimore for a time, finally agreed with him to sell him his freedom for two hundred dollars. This was in 1833, and for two years the negro went at large and acted as a free man, earning in various vocations—now by keeping an oyster house, now a boot-black shop—the money for his freedom. By June, 1835, he had paid, through an attorney or agent, all but twenty-seven dollars, and received receipts on account of his freedom. During the summer following, he went to New York, and was a waiter on a North River boat. On returning in October, he tendered the balance of payment, which was refused by his owner's agent, and he was soon arrested as a runaway slave and sold. The Court of Appeals—on an appeal from the City Court—held that slaves could not enter into valid contracts with their masters, any more than with any one else, nor enforce any alleged contract at law, but agreed with the lower court in setting this negro free—under the old law which declared free any slave who should enter Maryland to remain.[1]

There was enacted in 1752, that slave owners who should neglect to provide for old or disabled slaves, or should allow them to leave their homes, or wander about begging, becoming nuisances to the public, should forfeit four pounds to the

---

[1] 9 G. & J. 14. Bland & Woolfolk vs. Negro Beverly Dowling, 1837. An interesting case came before the Court of Appeals in 1850. Some twenty years before, a certain slave woman was allowed by her master to go to Baltimore, and to live with her reputed husband there—the husband to pay a given sum yearly for her services. When her family became large, this payment was not exacted. She lived as free, renting houses, hiring herself out, &c. She was then seized by a representative of her owner, who stated that there was a report that one of the family was about to run away. There were various questions in the case before the courts. The Circuit Court gave her freedom, but the Court of Appeals denied it. (9 Gill, 120.)

county court for the use of the county. In 1790, because, we read, humanity required that faithful servants should be supported by their masters, another act provided that any master who should allow a slave who was aged, or infirm from any accident, to wander abroad, or to lack proper care and cover, should be examined by the county court, and, if guilty, required to give good bond in the sum of thirty pounds, for future care of the negro. This act, of course, did not apply to a slave who might run away contrary to the will of the owner. After 1796, the bond was one hundred dollars.[1] Aged or infirm slaves who were occasionally left without anyone to support them, were cared for by the levy courts and afterwards by the county commissioners. Some lived and died at the regular almshouses. Old slaves were sometimes left in want by persons who died insolvent, and the county authorities were specially ordered to care suitably for these.

At a council meeting at Annapolis, in 1699, at which some of the King's instructions were read on the conversion of negroes and Indians, Governor Blakiston said he was informed that several masters hindered their negroes, though baptized, from going to church. On being told that there was no law to prevent such abuses, he recommended the passage of one; but nothing seems to have been done.[2] There was enacted in 1723, that no person whatever should work on the Lord's day, nor should command or allow any children, servants or slaves to work in anyway—works of necessity and charity excepted. Nor should children or menials be allowed to profane that day by unlawful pastimes and recreations, on penalty of a fine of two hundred pounds of tobacco from the

---

[1] 1752, 1; 1790, 9; 1796, 67: Code of 1860, 66, 26.
[2] Council Proceedings, X, 211.

master. This fine afterwards became five dollars.[1] Any privileges of church-going which slaves might enjoy depended, much as with children, on the disposition of the masters. We have seen the prejudice that was widely spread at first, against the conversion of the blacks; but when men found that christianity did not work manumission, and after the earnest efforts made by the missionaries, such as Dr. Bray in Maryland, most masters seemed very willing for their slaves to worship. Some preferred that they should attend the churches of the whites, fearful of the teachings, perhaps, of preachers who were ignorant or, possibly, hostile to slavery. Others allowed their slaves to join societies of the blacks which were more or less under the supervision of regular church associations. It was customary for certain portions of churches to be set apart for colored persons. In an act for the erection of a church in St. Anne's parish in Annapolis, in 1774, there was stipulated the provision for a place, in addition to the public gallery, for those servants, and another for slaves, that might attend service.[2] Masters and slaves knelt at the same communion table. Of sixty-one communicants that belonged to one parish in Anne Arundel, in 1790, thirteen were entered as "Black Brethren;" and a piece of the church glebe next to the church yard, was given these, by their request, for a burial place for themselves and their descendants. We find an interesting vote of the vestry of another parish, in 1747, that the churchwardens prevent the negroes from going in among the white people to disturb them, as they frequently did, and from going in and out of church during service. But in this, we may add, the blacks had had the example set them by their betters; for ten years before, the sexton had been ordered to keep the vestry-house locked, as persons were in the habit of running in and out of church in cold weather,

---

[1] 1723, 16.
[2] 1774, 11.

to visit the fire that was kept in the vestry.[1] In the generation before the Civil War, many earnest workers were busied in the South in the religious instruction of the blacks. There was never anything in the laws of Maryland to prevent slaves from holding religious services quietly on their masters estates; but with the Southampton insurrection and the growth of abolitionism throughout the land, some restrictions were placed on religious and other associations of the blacks—free blacks as well as slaves.

Ordinarily, the constables and magistrates were looked to to enforce the laws concerning blacks as well as whites. But after 1820, any justice in Anne Arundel, Calvert, Charles, Prince George's and St. Mary's counties was empowered, on the application of three judicious persons, to call out patroling parties to search the neighborhood, for from four to eight hours, to see that the negroes were at home and orderly. These patroling parties were formed of citizens subject to the militia duty, were limited to fifteen in a party, and were to be commanded by discreet persons named by the justice. They received fifty cents a night when on duty. The commissioners of Frederick county were soon empowered to appoint justices to summon a patrol whenever necessary. And, after 1856, the commissioners of Kent county could appoint if they saw fit, a dozen or so special police to enforce the laws against the blacks.[2] But it was at times of excitement only—of rumors

---

[1] Colonial Church Life in Maryland.

[2] 1820, 200. Calvert county was added by 1822, 85. 1821, 148; 1826, 210; 1856, 177.

Slaves could not carry guns or "other offensive weapons" off their master's estates—a prohibition which seems to have been made in 1704, at a time when Romanists and negroes were looked on, as we saw, as possible enemies of the government. If they did so, they could be whipped and the guns be forfeited, if belonging to them. Before that time negroes and other

of runaways or uprisings—that the patrols were called out; and at such times, impromptu patroling parties helped to execute the laws everywhere. For instance, in the summer of 1835, a stranger who had been seen talking with the negroes and attending some of their meetings, in the neighborhood of Chestertown, was put in jail for examination. The town, wrote a gentleman to *Niles' Register*, was in an uproar for several days, and was guarded every night by armed men of the greatest respectability. At one time in the winter of 1857, the patrols were out nightly in Prince George's county—but the papers soon announced that the excitement had subsided, that the patrol had expired by limitation, and that people did not think that there had been any intention of a rising among the blacks. The slaveholders' convention of Worcester county in 1858, resolved to call on constables and magistrates to enforce the laws for watching the blacks. On the night after an alarm of insurrection in Somerset county, in 1859, a patrol was organized, and search was made, with guns and other weapons, in the houses of free blacks in the neighborhood. In a part of Montgomery county a meeting of citizens was held after John Brown's attack on Harper's Ferry, to denounce Brown and express sympathy for the Union; and a "protective committee" of twenty-four members was appointed, to call a meeting of citizens whenever the public safety was endangered, and to call out such of the volunteer companies as might then be needed to patrol the neighborhood. It is stated also, that the commissioners of St. Mary's county appointed a patrol in the autumn of 1860, in each district, to visit their neighborhood at least once a week at night, to disperse all negro meetings and arrest all abolitionists.[1] For patrols that were called out by the sheriffs

---

slaves had been exempted from training or any military service whatever (L.L. 3, 40, &c.; Code of 1860). White servants were enlisted on emergencies only (1715, 43). See Chapter on the Free Negro.

[1] See *Niles' Register*, Aug. 22d, 1835; Baltimore *Sun* (quoting the local papers often), Jan. 9th, 1857; Jan. 4th, 1860; Oct. 13th, 1860. See Chapter on the Free Negro.

in Allegany, Cecil, Frederick and Harford counties, after the attack on Harper's Ferry, the State paid some fifteen hundred dollars.[1]

But the patrol, like most of the laws which it was intended to enforce, was directed, in the latter days of slavery, as well against the free black as the slave.

One of the most interesting phases of our subject, as a study of historical development, is the growth of the slave code touching crimes and punishments.

It is notorious that the English criminal law, and the administration of justice under it, were exceedingly severe down to the present century. The sentences of the Court of Star Chamber are well known. In one case, in 1630, a Scottish divine; for writing a scurrilous attack on the bishops, was sentenced not only to be degraded from orders and to pay a large fine, but to be whipped, set in the pillory, to have one ear cut off, one side of his nose slit, and one cheek branded with S. S. (sower of sedition), to have these repeated a week later in another part of London, and then be imprisoned for life. These cases may be regarded as exceptional, but in all parts of England hanging was a common punishment for many offences. It is stated on the authority of a magistrate of Somersetshire, that in that county, in the year 1596, there were thirty-seven persons whipped, thirty-five burned in the hand, and forty executed; and many among the large number discharged, deserved, in his opinion, similar punishments. Two years later, in a neighboring county, there were seventy-four persons sentenced to be hanged in a year. More than one-half of these were condemned at quarter sessions; several of them for stealing sheep. Though the sentence of death was often commuted, as to branding, whipping, or transportation to

---

[1] 1861-2, Ch. 163.

the Colonies, the criminal law remained exceedingly severe during the eighteenth century. A woman who killed her husband, or a maid-servant who killed her master or mistress, could be burned to death, until 1790. Nor was this law obsolete, for there is mention of a woman burned in 1782 and of another in 1784, though they were probably strangled before the torch was applied. In 1752, it was enacted that persons convicted of murder should be executed with little delay, and that the bodies should in no case be buried, but either be hung in chains or given over for dissection; and such was the law until William IV. Inhabitants of London were accustomed, as late as 1745, to see heads and portions of human bodies nailed up on Temple Bar. The last heads were those of nine Jacobites, of the Revolution of '45, who had been hanged, cut down, disembowelled, beheaded, quartered, and their hearts thrown into a fire—all before the eyes of the public. The spikes which held the heads were not removed till this century. The pillory was not abolished in England till 1837; and whipping has remained the penalty for certain offences.[1]

It was as natural for the colonists to follow, largely, the customs of their old home as it was for them to continue to speak English. In Maryland, it was specially provided that justice was to be administered, where there was no special law or fixed usage of the Province, by English law and usage, in so far as this was deemed applicable by the courts.[2] Each county court was ordered to keep the usual branding irons, and the pillory and stocks without the court-house, and the ducking stool as near by as possible. The corporal punishments given, in those days, in all the colonies, are so well known as to make examples almost superfluous. When Capt. Josias Fendall was found guilty, in 1681, of speaking several seditious words against the government of Maryland, the Provin-

---

[1] See Pike's History of Crime, Stevens' Criminal Law, Wade's History of the Middle and Working Classes, &c.
[2] See Md. Arch., I, 147, 158, 192, &c.

cial Court showed great clemency in giving him only fine and banishment. This sentence, the Court said, was as favorable as could be expected; for an early law allowed not merely fine and imprisonment, but boring of the tongue, slitting the nose, cutting off one or both ears, whipping, branding with a red-hot iron—any one or more of these, as the court should think fit.[1] It was not treason and sedition, and such unusual crimes only, that were thus punished. The colonists were evidently much troubled by hog-stealers, and a law of 1666, declaring that previous acts had been insufficient, enacted that a hog-stealer should pay the treble damages, and also, for the first offence, have four hours in the pillory and his ears cropped; and for the second offence, be branded in the forehead with the letter H. A third offence could be punished with death.[2]

Some of the early laws reflected the class distinctions, so strongly felt in England. Treason was to be punished, in addition to forfeiture of all goods and franchises, by drawing, hanging and quartering of a man, and by drawing and burning of a woman,—except in case of the lord of a manor, who should be beheaded. Among the various penalties for burglary, house-burning, sorcery, &c., was service for a term of years—but this could not be inflicted on a gentleman. Another law, for rules of justice, prescribed that no corporal punishment be given a gentleman, except by virtue of statute law of the Province.[3] Of greater interest still is the law of 1723, which gave the stocks and whipping-post to blasphemers and drunkards who could not pay their fines—and who were not freeholders or other reputable persons.

The punishments provided by law of the Province especially for white servants, and incident largely to the custom of service, were very few. It was at first the law that servants who refused to perform the lawful orders of their masters were to be

---

[1] Md. Arch., V, 328, I, 248.
[2] Md. Arch., II, 140.
[3] Md. Arch., I, 71, 158, 184.

whipped or otherwise corrected by order of, and in the discretion of, a magistrate. On the other hand, a master who refused to carry out his covenant with a servant, or who denied him or her proper food and care, was to be imprisoned by the magistrate until surety were given for the performance of his duty.[1] It was the law for many years that a servant, if proven guilty of causing a servant-woman to be with child, should recompense the master of the woman for half his loss in her work. But the father, if a freeman, had to pay the whole loss, by servitude or otherwise. The case, whether of freeman or servant, came before the county court.[2] Any person who traded with an indentured servant, without license from the master, was liable to a fine, and the servant who purloined or traded with his master's goods, to a whipping. For a second offence, the servant was to be branded, in addition. These penalties were evidently given by a magistrate; but if the freeman trading with the servant was unable to pay his fine, he was bound over to the higher court, and could be there sentenced to a whipping, if found guilty. Later, all cases of petty thieving, not belonging to the Provincial Court or to special commissioners, were tried in the county courts, and the accused, freeman or servant, if proven guilty by one good evidence, was to restore fourfold, and to suffer the pillory and whipping. If a freeman had not goods, he paid his fine by a term of servitude, as did the servant. Nor was there any difference prescribed in the severer penalties for repeated offences.[3] Masters were accustomed to administer some justice, themselves; but the law forbade them after 1715, to give more than ten lashes for any one offence; providing that they might carry troublesome servants before a justice of peace, to be given such whipping, up to thirty-nine lashes, as he deemed fit, after hearing the complaint. The cases of

---

[1] Md. Arch., I, 53.
[2] Laws of 1662, 1674, 1715.
[3] Md. Arch., I, 501: Laws of 1704, 1715.

masters who might be accused of neglecting or abusing their servants had been changed from the jurisdiction of the magistrates in first offences to that of the county courts. Servants who absented themselves from their masters' service were adjudged before the county courts to renewed service, ten days for one absent day, at the expiration of their term. Persons entertaining such servants were fined; and after 1748, those who could not pay the fine could be whipped, and put under security for good behavior.[1] This custom of white service practically died out toward the close of the eighteenth century,—at the time when criminal law was being changed by the changes in public feeling.

We have seen already how careful and judicious the government of Maryland was in its relations with the Indians. It sometimes vied with the customs of those Indians who were at war, by offering a bounty for every ear of a dead Indian; and in a treaty with a tribe recently at war, is the stipulation that the colonists might shoot down any Indian found killing cattle or hogs.[2] But, in most of the treaties, it was expressly stated that all Indians who might kill Englishmen should be given up to the authorities, to be tried for murder as a white man would be. We find mention of a special commission of Oyer and Terminer for the trial of an Indian who had murdered a white servant.[3] A treaty with the Nanticokes in 1687, provided that an Indian who should commit any offence against the English,—be it murder or hog stealing or helping runaway servants and slaves,—should be tried by English law, and that any Englishman who might injure the Indians should be tried by the same law, also. At about the same time, a Pocomoke Indian was imprisoned for rape on an English woman, and the Council duly considered

---

[1] 1715, 44; 1748, 19.
[2] Md. Arch., III, 502, 530, 433, 486.
[3] Md. Arch., II, 195, V, 476. An Indian convicted of murdering a white was shot at St. Mary's, 1669.

in what manner he should be tried, and decided by the statute law. Thereupon several of the chiefs came before the Council and desired to be informed of the English law, which was duly expounded to them, and which they promised not to break in future. As it was found that the woman had willingly erred, the Indian was merely whipped, according to English law, and advised by the Court to be more circumspect. In 1648, four Patuxent Indians were brought before the Provincial Court, charged with stealing and killing hogs, and with other thieving, and it was stated to the Court that intolerable injuries had been suffered by the colonists at the hands of the neighboring Indians. The prisoners, brought to the bar, denied the charge, (there was evidently no objection to their testimony, be it noted), stating that a hammer which they had had on the day mentioned, had been purchased from another Indian two years before. And the plaintiff not being able to produce further evidence, the jury declared not guilty, and the Indians were discharged by the Governor. We find that two Indians were executed, by sentence of the Provincial Court, for the murder of two negroes.[1]

For three-quarters of a century after the settlement of Maryland, the negroes in the Province were few in number, and were nearly all, if not all, slaves. The punishments which were administered on the plantation were sometimes too severe, as we shall see, in the case of both white servants and slaves, though the laws early forbade excessive abuse or punishment to these alike. Whether justice was administered by magistrates and judges with greater rigor to the black than to the white, we cannot say; but during this long period, be it noted, there was no special provision by law for the trial and punishment of slaves for serious offences. For murder or burglary or any serious crime, any offender, white, black, or Indian, was brought before the Provincial Court, to receive, we presume, the same fair dispensation of justice. In 1700, there

---

[1] Md. Arch., IV, 409; V, 558. Davis' Day Star, 151.

were no more slaves, probably, in Maryland, than there were in Massachusetts at the time slavery was abolished there; and in Maryland then, as in Massachusetts always, there was no special code for the trial and punishment of slaves.[1]

But the slave trade was soon carried on with vigor, and the blacks grew to be a considerable part of the population of Maryland. White servants were then numerous, many of them mere adventurers and good-for-nothings. At the same time, transportation was made the penalty in England for various felonies, and English jails were in part emptied into the Colonies. Maryland had prohibited for some years the importation of these felons, and a further act was passed in 1723, to prevent the " great evils " arising therefrom, but the Lord Proprietor refused his assent. It was at this time that the law against petty thieving—of goods worth over twelve pence—gave the ordinary four-fold restitution, and branding or other corporal punishment, saving life, for a second offence; when blasphemers could be punished, in addition to fine, with boring of the tongue, and branding and even death for repeated offences; when prisoners " languishing " in jail for debt, were warned not to perjure themselves, at the risk of two hours in the pillory and the loss of their left ears; and when men were executed for burglary and jail-breaking. It was unfortunate for the community as well as the blacks, that these Africans—fresh from Africa, with much that was brutal, very ignorant and very imitative—should have been thrown so much with the worst elements of the whites. Then, as the

---

[1] We find mention of slaves tried for capital punishment in the Provincial Court, as all other persons were (as Council Record, Oct. 16th, 1688, &c).

In 1703, an Eastern Shore Indian came before the Council at Annapolis with the complaint that his cabin had been broken into, and various things stolen therefrom by a certain negro slave, and demanded in return sixty-nine dressed deer skins. On his agreement, finally, to take sixty good skins, the Council ordered that the master of the slave should pay these to him, and that the slave be whipped. Otherwise the slave was to be tried in the Provincial Court. (Council Records, X, 327.)

population was increasing, the plantations spread out more and more, making a sparsely settled country. One's neighbors were few and far between. The church may have been distant; the court house and the jail were probably miles away.

With the increase of the blacks we find—it may have been only because attention was thereby called to them as never before—a growing difference between the legal status of the black and of the white. The act of 1715 provided for the discharge of all persons held as suspected runaways and not claimed within six months—except negroes and mulattoes.[1] Constables had already been authorized to suppress with the ordinary whipping, of not over thirty-nine stripes, all frequent and noisy meetings of negroes and slaves.[2] In 1717, whereas, reads the law, negro and Indian slaves often commit misdemeanors or steal, and escape without punishment, or else the owners are put to expense by bringing them to the county courts,—there was enacted that any one justice might try slaves for small offences, and might order as many stripes as he deemed fit, not exceeding forty.[3] It was also found that some masters of slaves who had committed heinous offences, had concealed the crimes, thus hindering the execution of justice, rather than lose the slaves; so masters of slaves sentenced to death were paid three-fourths their loss. But masters were loath to lose, and the recompense was afterwards increased to the full value of the slave. It was at the same time that the testimony of Indians and negroes was declared

---

[1] 1715, 44. By the act of 1715, also, masters were forbidden to give over ten lashes or to abuse or overwork "any servant whatever." The earlier acts of 1692 and 1704 forbade the abuse or excessive punishment of English servants and slaves. From the way in which slaves, and servants and slaves together are expressly mentioned in the act of 1715 in other clauses, we presume that the expression, "any servant whatsoever," did not include slaves, who could be punished in the discretion of the master, unless, indeed, he was so harsh as to be prosecuted for cruelty. If so, this change in the law is very interesting.

[2] 1695, 6; 1723, 15, &c.

[3] 1717, 13.

invalid in all cases concerning whites—and Indians and blacks, too, where life or limb were involved. The act of 1723, enjoining constables to suppress noisy meetings of blacks, made any slave who should strike a white person at any time, liable to lose an ear by order of a magistrate. The owner of a plantation was authorized also to whip any slave who might be found thereon without proper business; and this act provided further, that slaves who might run away and remain out-lying in the woods, killing hogs and cattle, and who might resist capture, could be shot lawfully by their pursuers.[1] After 1729—as there was some doubt as to whether those who broke and entered buildings not connected with dwelling-houses, might not plead benefit of clergy—any person convicted of breaking into any store-house and of stealing from thence to the value of five shillings, was to be executed. And whereas, we read, several murders of masters and other cruel murders had been lately committed by negroes, which cruelties they were instigated to commit because they have no sense of shame or apprehension of future rewards or punishments, and as the manner of executing offenders as prescribed by the laws of England, is not sufficient to deter from such offences a people who consider only the severity of a punishment, any slave, continued the act, convicted by confession or verdict of jury, of murder or of wilfully burning a dwelling-house, may be punished, in the judgment of the court, by having his right hand cut off before being hanged. And the body, in such a case, might be beheaded and quartered, and set up in the most public places of the county where the crime was committed.[2] A few years later, benefit of clergy was taken away from all persons convicted of breaking into any tobacco-houses or other outhouses, reasonably built and secured, and stealing therefrom to the value of five shillings. And slaves found guilty in the county courts of rambling about at night or riding horses at daytime without leave, or of running

[1] 1723, 15.
[2] 1729, 4.

away, were to be whipped, cropped or branded, or otherwise punished, but so as not to endanger life or to render them unfit for labor.¹ A few years later, again, benefit of clergy was taken away from any person who might steal a horse or burn a boat of some size, or abet in these crimes. Servants and slaves who harbored or entertained their fellows, now became liable to whipping, by order of a magistrate.² In 1751, the testimony of imported convicts was declared valid against other such convicts in criminal cases; because, says the law, murders, burglaries and other offences had been very frequent, endangering the lives and property of the colonists,—offences generally committed by imported convicts and those whom they seduce to join them, which the convicts are encouraged to commit, as they know that they cannot be called on to testify against each other.³ Closely following, is an act for the more effectual punishment of slaves; because, says the preamble, the laws for that purpose are found insufficient to prevent great crimes, and to further the speedy administration of justice. Benefit of clergy, therefore, was taken away from any slave duly convicted of conspiring or attempting to raise insurrection, to murder or poison anyone, to commit rape on a white woman, or to burn any house or out-house containing any person or goods. Hitherto a slave, like his master or any white, would have been tried for a serious crime in the Provincial Court. Now, there was enacted that he should be tried for any offence which might be punished with death, at the next term of the county court. And he might be convicted on the testimony of other slaves, corroborated with such pregnant circumstances as should convince the jury of his guilt.⁴

---

[1] 1737, 2, 7.
[2] 1748, 19.
[3] 1751, 11.
[4] 1751, 14. If slaves testified, they were warned by the presiding judge to tell the truth, and were told the punishment they would incur by perjury—the cropping of one ear and a whipping, and, the next day, the cropping of the second ear and another whipping.

It was at this time that the killing of a slave who should resist arrest for any serious offence, was declared not punishable.

In the Council Records, about 1760, is a description of the judiciary of the Province. The Governor and Council formed the high Court of Appeals and Errors, and issued pardons where such were due. Besides the courts of chancery and vice-admiralty, there was the Provincial Court, held twice a year at Annapolis. Seven judges sat on this bench, having jurisdiction over civil cases of importance and all manner of criminal cases. Before them or special commissions, only, could white men be sentenced to loss of life or limb. County courts were held four times yearly by the justices of the peace of each county, to try certain civil matters, and all criminal cases not affecting life or limb, and even capital offenses when committed by negroes.[1]

By the close of the century, the courts and the jurisdiction of the courts had so changed that all persons, slave or free, were tried for serious offences before the same tribunal, as had been the case three generations before. The forms of punishment, too, had changed.[2] The Governor, in addition to the old power of pardon, could commute death sentences to other punishment—in the case of slaves, to transportation and sale. The courts could give the old penalties, or could sentence free males, male servants and apprentices, to labor on the roads for not over seven years, and free women, women servants and apprentices, to picking oakum, sewing, or other suitable labor, for not over the same time. The value of a servant's unexpired term was paid the master, and the county was reimbursed from the sale of the servant, at the expiration of his term of labor, for as long a time as was necessary. A slave

---

[1] Council Proc., 1753-1767, 323. There were also the magistrates, who exercised considerable power in the punishment of slaves and servants for petty offences. Commissions of Oyer and Terminer and Jail Delivery were often issued. We find one commission trying a slave, some twenty years earlier, for stealing £26. The jury acquitted him.

[2] See 1785, 87; 1787, 17; 1790, 50; 1793, 57; 1795, 82, &c.

convicted of a capital crime could be sentenced to death or to serve on the roads for not over fourteen years. In either case, he was bought by the State; but in the latter, as in case of transportation, the treasury could be somewhat repaid from the sale of him afterward. There was added, in 1808, that slaves in Baltimore county who might be convicted of manslaughter, could be whipped—or put to labor in the workhouse, if women,—in place of the other punishments.[1] In 1809, was enacted a general law on crimes and punishments. It gave such penalties, in general, as we are accustomed to, to-day—hanging for murder in the first degree; limited terms of imprisonment for murder in the second degree and manslaughter; indemnification for losses, and imprisonment for from three to ten years, for burglary; indemnification and at least a year's term, for stealing to the value of five dollars; imprisonment for not less than three months, for being a rogue or a vagabond, &c. The only distinction between white or black was that a negro or mulatto slave, not sentenced to be hung for any crime, under the act, might be punished by imprisonment, or, in the discretion of the court, by a whipping of not over a hundred lashes, and also by banishment, by transportation and sale into some foreign country.[2] This act on crimes, and the opening of the State penitentiary in 1811, finished and formulated the change which had been taking place in public sentiment. Experience evinces, states the old-fashioned preamble to the act, that the surest way of preventing the perpetration of crimes and of reforming offen-

---

[1] 1789, 44, &c.; 1808, 113.
[2] 1809, 138. The act gave the penalty of hanging for any person, white, free black or slave, convicted of raising insurrection of negroes; and imprisonment for between six and twenty years, for attempts so to do. The keeper of the Penitentiary was empowered to punish unruly or idle prisoners by short solitary confinement; the Board of Inspection could order more severe punishment, including whipping. For attempts to escape, the Court should give additional labor, confinement, and also corporal punishment.

ders, is by a mild and justly proportioned scale of punishments.

By act of 1817, any colored person who would, under the act of 1809, have been sent to the penitentiary for less than one year, was kept in jail, or fined or whipped, or both fined and whipped. After the next year, the courts were forbidden to send any slaves to the penitentiary; the punishments for them, for crime, being hanging, or not over forty lashes, or transportation and sale—not necessarily, now, into some foreign country, but anywhere except into the District of Columbia. By a supplement of the following year, these were narrowed to either hanging or transportation.[1] We find the case of one negro who was convicted of burglary and, being deemed a free man, was put into the penitentiary, of course. It was stated afterward that he was a slave; and so the Governor was authorized by the Assembly to order his sale out of Maryland, provided that it was first proven to a jury that he was a slave.

Whether these convict slaves sold out of the State found their lot any real punishment for their crimes, seems to have been a matter of some doubt. Certain it is that the blacks themselves attached a very unpleasant significance to the words "sold South." We cannot believe that convicts would have been purchased for any other purpose than the most rigorous field work.[2]

An act of 1833 allowed masters to sell out of Maryland any slaves for a term of years, who were proven, to the satisfaction of the courts, to be notoriously vicious. These were sold for their unexpired term of service only, and the courts required proof that they had been previously warned duly of such punishment as the result of misbehavior. Slaves who

---

[1] 1817, 72; 1818, 197; 1819, 159.

[2] We notice an advertisement in a Baltimore paper of 1851, of valuable slaves for sale, for whom good homes rather than high prices were desired. Also, such good servants would be "exchanged for servants *suitable for the South, with bad characters*."

gave much trouble by attempts to run away, might, under the same restrictions, be sold in or out of Maryland for their unexpired terms. The very next year, the committee of the House of Delegates on Colored Population was asked for leave to sell thus out of the State a negro girl eighteen years old, who was known to have run away several times from a previous owner and to have been in jail for other charges also. But the petition was denied, with the observation that the petitioner must have known the character of his purchase, and that the girl's subsequent conduct could not have disappointed his reasonable expectations. We refrain, continued the committee's report, from touching the moral obligations of the State not to send an unworthy and dangerous part of her population upon another community, uninformed of the character of the persons; and we think, also, that sale out of the State for a term of years would, in most cases, although the black was given his right to freedom in papers under the seal of court, amount to nothing short of slavery for life. Two years later, the House of Delegates urged the Senate to pass a bill allowing a certain woman to sell out of Maryland a slave who was notoriously vicious and incorrigible, but who had not been warned of the possibility of such sale. The policy of the law, said the House committee, is to permit the removal of slaves known for vicious habits or gross misconduct; and when these characteristics are shown so as to destroy all reasonable expectation of reform in conduct, the slave may justly be subjected to the punishment of immediate transportation. But no act seems to have been passed—although the slave was said to be so vicious as to be kept in jail, to protect his mistress.[1] In 1845, Governor Pratt called public attention to the fact that the only punishments of consequence for slaves were either hanging or sale from the State—that is, reads the executive message, the substitution for his master of another master living without the limits of Maryland,

---

[1] House Journals, 1834, 544, &c.; 1836, 381, 569. Acts of 1833, 224.

which would not be considered by the slave or the community as any punishment whatever. The penitentiary was closed to slaves, and transportation would only defeat the ends of justice. The attention of the Governor seems to have been especially drawn to the matter by the case of a slave who had just been sentenced to death by the court of Charles county, for insurrection, but who was deemed worthy of clemency by a large number of citizens of the county. In accordance with the suggestion, the law was so changed that slaves, convicted of any of the higher grade of offences, should be punished as other persons were. On the expiration of their terms of imprisonment they were sold at auction, to be carried out of the State.[1] Petty larceny, of which the negroes as a class are guilty in large numbers, was not included in these offences, it is interesting to note. The executive message of 1858, telling the Assembly that nearly half of the convicts in the penitentiary were negroes, suggested that the courts should again be given the power of selling out of the State slaves convicted of certain felonies. This, it said, would relieve the institution of a large class, unprofitable and not to be reformed by prison discipline. The law was soon changed so that no negroes were sent to the penitentiary. Slaves could be given not over forty lashes, or be sold out of the State.

The many acts which declared that "any person" or "all persons" who were guilty of specified offences were liable to punishment, were interpreted, as had evidently been intended, to include blacks as well as whites—slaves as well as free. The Court of Appeals affirmed this judgment, in 1859, when a slave woman tried to escape a sentence of a county court on the plea that an act forbidding "any person" to obtain goods under false pretences, did not affect slaves.[2] We have noticed, and shall notice further, in the course of our study, the general

---

[1] 1845, 340. Masters were paid, of course, for slaves transported. 1849, 124. Code of 1860, 30, 194.
[2] 14 Md., 135.

laws declaring offences and giving penalties, which concerned negroes and slaves peculiarly. It would be tedious and useless to give more than a few examples of the many local laws. Varying in purport and in the penalties given, they show no general public policy, and reflect often, like much special legislation the world over, the whims and bad rhetoric of the local "member." Yet they help to show us the customs of the times.[1] Thus, for selling provisions out of the market-house at Fredericktown, by act of 1770, a free man could be fined ten shillings, a servant or slave could be given not over fifteen lashes. Again, for destroying the gates which a certain resident of Dorchester county was allowed to keep across the road, in 1846, a free man could be fined a trifling sum, while a slave who injured it or left it open wilfully, could be given not over ten lashes. Such cases came before a justice, of course. Other acts did not let off so easily the master of an offending slave. A free person who evaded toll on certain toll roads, was to be fined twenty shillings, by act of 1801, while the master of a servant or slave who evaded it, was to pay half that sum, in addition to the ten lashes which were to be given the culprit himself. If a servant or slave bought provisions out of market in Chestertown, his owner was liable to pay twenty-five shillings, half the fine for a free man. If a citizen attempted to avoid toll on the turnpike road from Washington to Baltimore, a law of 1796 made him liable to fine of two dollars, and if his slave offended, he was liable to pay one dollar. We find similar provisions on certain toll roads sixty years later; in one case, the parent of a minor being made equally liable with the master of a steward or slave.[2] So, in Baltimore, by law of 1843, the parent of a minor or master of

---

[1] When in 1731 the "Charming Molly" appeared off Annapolis with small-pox on board, the rule was made that no one should go aboard her and return without license. If a freeman offended, he could be sued for one hundred pounds; if a servant or slave, he was to be given at least thirty-nine stripes on the bare back and be sent back at once on board.

[2] 1847, 220; 1860, 267.

a slave or apprentice who might steal rides on vehicles, had to pay half the ordinary fine. The overseers of roads in Somerset county were authorized in 1799 to call out all males for certain work on the roads. If a slave or servant were not sent when duly called for, or if, when sent, he refused to do reasonable work, the master became liable to pay one dollar, the same fine as for his own failure to appear. At the very next session, this was so changed as to empower the overseers to compel the proper service from the slaves instead of fining the masters— a system, says the supplement, which had been found to be oppressive and injurious.[1] It is interesting to note here that certain citizens from Baltimore county petitioned the House of Delegates in 1824, that slave owners should be made liable for theft and misdemeanors committed by their slaves. The report of the House committee was adverse. They thought it would conflict with the principles of justice to make the master responsible for any misdeeds done while the slave was not in the discharge of his duties as a servant. This was the doctrine, continued the committee, recognized by the law as to injuries of a civil nature by servants of any kind, and the same should certainly be applied to criminal cases. There were also many local laws which allowed the master to save his slave a sore back by paying a fine himself. Thus, by act of 1785, a free person convicted of wilfully destroying any lamp, sentry-box, &c., in Baltimore, was to be fined three pounds, and a parent or master was liable equally for damage done by his children or his bound servants or apprentices. A slave would be given not over thirty-nine lashes, unless the master chose to pay the fine or repair the damage. Afterward, according to the laws for the enforcement of the ordinances of Baltimore City, slaves found guilty by a magistrate of breaking any ordinance were to be whipped, unless the fines and costs were paid, and magistrates were prohibited from trying the slaves

---

[1] 1799, 38; 1800, 5.

until the masters had been duly notified.¹ So the authorities of Annapolis and Frederick were allowed to punish by whipping those slaves who might disregard the town ordinances, unless the masters redeemed them. In 1792, the House passed a bill to fine free men who might beat the waters of the Patuxent at certain spawning seasons, and to whip slaves duly convicted of the same, unless the master would pay half the ordinary fine. The Senate amended so that no slave should be punished if he acted by his employer's order, but that the employer should, in that case, pay the full fine. A somewhat similar provision was made in 1800, to protect fish in the Great Choptank, but we notice that forty years later the law gave a whipping without any exception. Early in the century, three acts were passed at intervals of a few years each, to prevent the erection of seines and weirs in three rivers in different counties. One act, to prevent obstructions to navigation, fixed a penalty of twenty-five dollars for free men, and not over twenty lashes for slaves, acting without their master's directions, provided always that the slave might be redeemed by anyone who would pay twenty-five dollars. Free man or slave, the case was tried before a magistrate. The second act—to prevent certain obstructions to the movement of fish—fixed a penalty of one hundred dollars for free men, and of not over thirty-nine lashes for slaves, provided that anyone might redeem a slave by payment of fifty dollars, and that a slave who had acted by order of his master should not be punished, but that the master, in such a case, should pay a hundred dollars. The third act—also to protect fish—gave a penalty of twenty dollars for a free man, and not over thirty-nine lashes for a slave, unless some one redeemed him by payment of thirty dollars. If the master ordered the slave to commit the offence, he was liable to the twenty dollars. Under this

---

¹ An exception seems to have been made in Baltimore, in that a slave convicted before the Criminal Court of cruelty to animals might be given a good whipping, if the court saw fit.

act, as under the preceding one, the free man would be tried before the county court, the slave by a single magistrate. Of these three acts, the first remained in force in 1860 unchanged; the penalties of the second had been changed to a smaller fine and fewer lashes; the third had been done away, the law forbidding simply any obstructions to be erected by any person under penalty of fine of not over fifty dollars. In all cases, of free man or slave, the trial was before a justice.[1]

To make any sweeping assertions as to the rigor or mildness with which this criminal code was enforced against the blacks, would be hazardous. Even if we had the records of all the courts, the few words of the docket entries would tell neither the circumstances of a case nor the fitness of a penalty. Yet we may hope to throw some light on the matter, to say the least.

Death sentences were referred, we remember, to the Governor and Council; so the Council records show us somewhat how the greatest offences were dealt with.[2] In the case of one negro woman sentenced to death in 1738, for attempting to poison her master, the Council recommended the warrant for execution. In the same year, in an adjoining county, a negro was found guilty of felony deserving death, but the reports sent the Council were not satisfactory, evidently, for the execution was suspended until the Attorney-General could thoroughly consider the indictment and the process in the case. Some weeks later, that officer reported that the proceedings were regular, and so the negro was executed—it appearing to the Council that he was "a notorious offender." Soon after

---

[1] 1801, 70; 1805, 31; 1808, 78; Code of 1860.

[2] The Council records seem to be quite complete during the interesting period from 1738–1770, when, as we have seen, the criminal code became most rigorous.

We note that in 1688, on the happy birth of the young Prince, the Council pardoned several negroes who had been lately condemned to death, and returned them to their masters, on payment of costs. (Council Book B., Oct. 16, 1688.)

this, a court of Oyer and Terminer and jail delivery, of three men, commissioned for Anne Arundel county, reported that they had passed sentence of death on a slave, Isaac, for burglary and robbery, on another slave for murder, and on a white man who had committed the burglary with Isaac. As it appeared to the Council that Isaac had borne "a good character and was a real object of compassion," he was recommended to the mercy of the Governor; but as the crime of the other slave was murder, and as the white man was a notorious offender, the Council advised that they be executed; and the Governor acted accordingly. On the receipt of the record from St. Mary's court of the conviction of two slaves for conspiring to poison the overseer, clerk and gardener of their master, warrants for execution were ordered. So, in the next year, two slaves of Anne Arundel were executed, one for burglary, the other for rape on a white woman; and the body of the second, who had been a notorious offender, was hung in chains at some distance from the gallows. In 1742, seven negroes condemned by the Provincial Court, "on clear evidence," of the murder of their master, were executed. The court of Charles county passed sentence of death on two negroes for felony, but also recommended that the men were objects of mercy. In this the Council agreed, as the men had never before been charged with any felony, and the Governor issued pardon. In the next year, two negroes murdered an Indian, and they were hung in chains; and two white men were hung for burglary and murder; while a white boy and a young mulatto slave, condemned for stealing, were pardoned as objects of mercy. In 1747, two negroes convicted of horse stealing were pardoned; while another of an adjoining county, was executed for the same offence, as he bore "a very ill character;" and a servant was executed for the murder of a mulatto slave. In 1754, a slave and a white man were sentenced to death for storebreaking and stealing, but were pardoned by the Governor at the request of several gentlemen, as they were both very young, and had never been convicted for offences before. Negroes Pompey, Sambo and Jack were condemned to death in Anne Arundel for entering a storehouse and stealing fifty pounds of bacon and ten gallons of rum. As Sambo was young, and might, in the opinion of the Council, have been influenced by his father Pompey, he and Jack were pardoned, but Pompey was hung. And a negro who murdered his overseer was hung in chains as near as possible to the scene of the murder. When, in 1761, the conviction of two negroes was sent to the Council without proper information, a letter was sent to the clerk of the county court, thus: "The Governor and Council upon hearing read the copy of the conviction of negro Tom for a felony and also of negro Nace for a felony in breaking open the meat-house of Catherine Price of your county, sent up by you without any Letter or Report from the Justices of the county who were present at the Tryals, how the circumstances appeared to them, you are therefore desired to enquire of them in Relation to the same, and transmit their answer to me by the first opportunity, in order to lay it before the Council at their next meeting." At their next meeting was read the report of the justices and a petition from several of them and a clergyman, recommending the offenders as objects of mercy. They were accordingly pardoned. A negress, "Bett Pone," convicted of an attempt to poison her overseer, was also recommended to the mercy of the Governor by the justices, and was accordingly pardoned. When three negroes were sentenced for attempt to poison, in Calvert county, in 1764, the county clerk evidently neglected to send the full particulars to the Council, for the papers were returned with orders that he procure from the justices a report of the behavior of the culprits. Their owners were also asked if they chose to transport the negroes from the Province; but they requested the execution of the sentence. There were at that time a number of cases of poisoning or attempts to poison. One slave murdered the wife and child of his master. Another slave was sentenced, in Prince George's county, for poisoning a fellow-slave; but a reprieve was issued, in answer to a petition from his master, on the condition that he should not stay in the county after five days from that date. In several cases, negroes were bound over to good behavior—instead of being hung.[1] In 1766, a negro was condemned for attempting to poison his master; convicted by confession and by testimony of a slave who was privy to his preparing a "Dose composed of Ground Poppies and other Ingredients which he supposed Poisonous." A young negress, slave of a citizen of Charles county, was convicted in 1766, of setting fire to a tobacco house, from which the dwelling house of her master was consumed. On asking information, the Council learned that the girl in the absence of her master, drew some cider and left the spigot open, for which her mistress threatened to tell her master and have her whipped. Several times the girl asked forgiveness of her mistress and begged that the fault might be concealed from her master. Then, in despair, she set fire to a tobacco house, and the dwelling house and offices were wholly consumed. After the trial, the mistress went to the house of one of the justices and begged him to apply to the Governor for pardon, saying that if the girl were executed, she never could forgive herself for obstinately persisting in her threats of punishment; that she knew not but that the girl might have been intoxicated with the liquor she drew, and that she had before behaved herself "as well as negroes in common do." The master expressed himself as willing to have the girl pardoned. One of the justices testified to the fact that the court had inquired into the girl's character, that she seemed but little sensible of her situation at the trial, and that her youth and her confession of the crime appeared to be the only circumstances in her favor. But the attention of the Council was called, also, to the fact that two other cases of burning of

---

[1] In 1762, a negro was condemned for a felony, in Charles county court; but a reprieve for a month was issued by the Governor, and the sheriff was ordered to set the fellow free and acquaint him that unless he behaved, he would be called to his former sentence.

tobacco houses had occurred in the same county during the preceding winter. The Council evidently hesitated, consideration of the case was put off for some days, and then the warrant for execution was issued. A slave was convicted in St. Mary's county, the same year, of breaking into his master's store. The master asked for his pardon, stating that the slave had himself confessed, and had not before offended; a friend seconded the request, adding that the negro was a very valuable slave; and in addition, one of the magistrates wrote: "I am not fond of having rogues escape punishment, but on the contrary should rather choose they should suffer as examples to others, particularly negroes, among whom villainy and roguery is but too common, yet on this occasion I must hope your Excellency will grant what is desired." So, the following year, the master of a negro convicted of breaking open a building, asked for his pardon, as the black was valuable and had had a tolerably good character; while the owner of the building wrote—the master having told him that his consent, as the person injured, would be required—that "if your Excellency is inclinable to extend your mercy unto the poor wretch, I humbly submit." Again, a year later, a petition of twenty-nine names was presented for the pardon of a negro sentenced for burglary, stating that the crime was committed through over-persuasion, youth and inexperience; that the master could not purchase so serviceable a slave, and notwithstanding the high value the court was pleased to put on him, would be a great sufferer at that time if the negro must suffer death; and that the petitioners would not fear for their property should the boy be pardoned—and again, a pardon was granted.

In 1770, three negroes were condemned for murder in Prince George's county, one as having given the blow and the other two as abettors; and the court stated that it seemed to be the opinion of many gentlemen of the county, as well as of the court, that it would be very proper to execute the law in its full rigor. Warrants were so issued, save that the two abettors were spared the part of the sentence which directed that the right hand be cut off before execution. This is the only case we find in the Council Records in which the law for the punishment of slaves for the highest crimes seems to have been executed to the letter.[1] During this period many culprits, white and black alike, met with no clemency. One of the planters, for instance, who was said indeed to be no good character, was executed for breaking and entering a store house attached to an inn, and stealing therefrom "two Pair of women's leather Pumps" of the value of fifteen shillings current money. The Governor was empowered, a few years later, to commute death sentences to other penalties. We find mention of thirteen negroes sentenced to death between 1786 and 1801. Of these, one slave was hung for rape; five, of whom at least three were slaves, were transported for rape, arson and other felonies; two slaves convicted of murder were put to work on the roads for fifty years, and two others for twenty years for other felonies; and the death sentences of three slaves were commuted without specified conditions.[2]

Anne Arundel county had a large slave population. We find five cases of slaves before the county court between 1760 and 1764—one for assault and rape on a woman, evidently a white; three for breaking and stealing; and one for firing a building. All threw themselves, as the old phrase went, on God and their country, that is were tried by jury, and all chanced to be acquitted and discharged. From 1768 to 1771 two negroes were tried. One, evidently a free negro, was found guilty of manslaughter for killing a negro, and was branded in the hand. The other, a slave, found guilty by a jury of stealing a coat valued at one hundred pounds of

---

[1] Act of 1751, ch. 14. By this, the criminal was to have his right hand cut off before execution, and his body quartered and exposed afterward. From this special mention of the execution of the law in its full rigor, we presume that slaves were ordinarily executed as others were.
[2] See Votes and Proceedings, and Resolutions of the Assemblies.

tobacco, was sentenced to be hanged. About the same time, two white laborers, one of whom had stolen a sheep worth eighty pounds of tobacco, and the other various goods to the value of two hundred and eighty pounds, were sentenced to return those things and make four-fold restitution, and to stand in the pillory for five minutes, and to have twenty-five lashes on the bare back at the public whipping post. Of eighty presentments at two terms in 1790, several were for dealing with negroes, and in one case, a free black paid thirty shillings for an assault, but there were no slaves; of thirty-nine at one term in 1794, one was a white for an assault on a negro and another was a slave woman for an assault, but both failed to appear; of fifty-three, four years later, one seems to have been the same woman, one was a negro presented for murder, and there was one slave, who was referred to a single magistrate. Among a multitude of civil suits and of bastardy cases, with an occasional assault or other criminal case, it is here and there only that we find a slave brought before the county courts.

Among the papers belonging to the city of Annapolis are several books of proceedings of the mayor's court, which had apparently much the same jurisdiction as single magistrates had in the counties, and which dispensed justice to all persons who disregarded the ordinances of that little city. The court consisted of the mayor, recorder and several aldermen, but the mayor seems to have been absent often. The cases before the court were not, it must be confessed, of a very serious nature. One citizen who allowed his chimney to get on fire, was fined forty shillings; another, who left broken bottles before his door, paid five shillings on submission, without trial. But when in 1720 a man had the temerity to utter four separate oaths, one after the other, he was put in the stocks for three hours, and fined for the first oath two shillings and sixpence, and five shillings for each of the others. At the January term of 1790, there were several cases of assault, and one white man was fined seven shillings sixpence and fees for assaulting another, and a fellow culprit, five shillings and fees for assaulting a negro. The most common offence under the city ordinances seems to have been the entertainment of, and sale of liquor to, apprentices, indentured servants and slaves. One person who ventured to sell a bottle of rum to a young Dutchman in the Governor's service, had to pay five shillings; and another, who sold a pint of liquor to a negro of Charles Carroll, Esq., without the required permission in writing from the master, atoned by forty shillings. This sum was the customary fine for thus selling without leave, or for keeping a disorderly house. We find one item of fines due in 1754, from a woman, to wit, to entertaining six slaves, two hundred pounds of tobacco each, or a total of five pounds sterling. At a session in 1765, the grand jury found indictments for entertaining and selling liquor to servants and slaves, to the number of sixty-five against one person, of forty-two each against two others, and some forty and more beside. The first mention of negro culprits is at a session of 1783, when of twenty presentments, five were slaves. One, for suffering hogs to go at large, does not appear to have been brought to trial. Two of them, women, appeared and confessed to carrying fire through the street, whereupon one was excused on payment of costs, and the other—probably because she had neither money nor indulgent master—received the only corporal punishment of which we find mention in these dockets, to wit, one lash on the bare back. She was handed over to the sheriff, who soon informed the court he had executed the judgment. The two others were men, who paid the court each ten shillings and costs for galloping on horseback through the streets. The negro boys seem to have taken great delight in fast driving and riding. Several years later, a free black accused of the same offence, plead not guilty, but was convicted by jury and paid the customary fines. One grand jury of this little court desired to be no respecter of persons, for they presented in 1813, for allowing his sleigh to be driven at improper speed, no less a personage than Charles Carroll of Carrollton; but the case was dismissed on motion of the prosecutor. Another citizen was presented, as his slave had over-driven or overworked a horse. Of nineteen presentments in 1785 one was a black; of twenty-three in 1789 two were blacks, but the cases were not brought up till the following year evidently. All three were accused of forcing horses; one case was declared off, and fines were paid in the others. Two of these were slaves. Of over two hundred cases mentioned between 1790 and 1805, twelve were of blacks. Of two, of free blacks, accused of keeping a disorderly house and of letting hogs go astray, we find no further notice. That of a slave for assaulting a man—a white apparently—was quashed. A free black paid ten shillings and costs for riding in a cart unlawfully, and the case of a slave accused of the same offence was declared off by the court. Two free blacks and two slaves were fined for forcing horses, while the indictments against three slaves for the same offence were quashed. In 1812, there is the mere mention of a negro accused of an assault. The next year, a certain white man was fined eight dollars for assaulting another, and was also found guilty by a jury of assault on a negro, and was fined one cent therefor. There is no mention of a case against a negro in the dockets from 1813 to 1818.[1]

With the abolition of capital punishment except in extreme cases, with the decay of the pillory and the stocks, and with the building of the penitentiary, we find the slaves convicted of serious offences in the circuit courts, ordinarily imprisoned or sold out of the State, and those convicted of minor offences, before these courts or a magistrate, receiving a whipping. Thus in Baltimore, in 1858, a white man was fined three dollars and thirty-three cents, and committed in default, by a justice, for pitching cents on Sunday; and a slave brought before the same justice for the same offence, was given fifteen lashes. Another slave, for throwing a brick, contrary to ordi-

---

[1] These docket books seem to cover very largely, if not wholly, the work of the mayor's court for the time.

nance of the city, got the same punishment; and another atoned by twenty lashes for a threat to shoot a colored lad. One slave who pleaded guilty to stealing a large quantity of iron, was given ten lashes, by request of his master, instead of being sold South. The case of two slaves of Prince George's county, charged with robbery, was dropped on condition that they be sold South. For more serious offences,—a slave boy was given ten years in the penitentiary for setting fire to a stable; while a young slave girl who tried twice to set fire to her employer's stable, in order, as she confessed, to see the fire engines come up, was released by order of the grand jury of Baltimore criminal court, as not being bright. A slave convicted in Talbot county court, in 1851, of a violent assault with a knife on a white man, was given five years in the penitentiary. A young slave girl presented in Caroline county, in 1855, for causing the death of her mistress by putting arsenic in her coffee, and found guilty of murder in the second degree, was sentenced to eighteen years imprisonment. And a slave of Queen Anne's county was given nearly the same time, for the murder, in the second degree, of a white man.[1]

We see that the letter of the law alone is not sufficient testimony to the customary administration of justice. But we

---

[1] The local paper adds that a mob was seen about the jail, and that the negro was at once taken to the penitentiary.

That part of the old act of 1723 (ch. 15) which allowed the cropping of the ear of a "negro or other slave," convicted before a magistrate of striking a white person or of certain other offences, was formally done away in 1821 (ch. 240). Whipping, limited to thirty-nine lashes, was substituted. *Niles' Register* for September, 1826, states that a white man had recently undertaken to chastise a black woman who was not his slave, and, when she resisted and whipped him, had had her arrested under the old law which provided cropping of the ear of a black who should make defence against the assault of a white. But the magistrate dismissed the case. "Several severe and very uncouth laws," added the report, "yet remain on

must remember that the court in which the slave was most liable to meet injustice was that of the local magistrate, who might be called away from business or pleasure, when drunk or sober, to give sentence within a few hours perhaps of the commission of the offence, while the injured neighbors were still angry. Of these courts there are no records; nor are there of those countless courts to which slaves were liable for their every-day conduct—the master or the overseer. Slavery used often to be spoken of by those who favored it, as a patriarchal institution, under which the slaves were subject to the master's judgment and guidance, somewhat as were his children. There is every reason to believe that the great majority of slaves in Maryland were properly and kindly treated. But as some parents seem to be devoid of that affection which is so common, and which is called natural, so not even the usual kindly feeling of men and their natural disinclination to injure their own property, were sufficient to keep masters occasionally from maltreating their slaves.

If the white servant was unjustly or abusively treated by anyone, he could enter complaint before the authorities, like any of the colonists. And he could testify in any case as freely, of course, as if he were free. In the records of the

---

our statute books in full force, being unrepealed, but unenforced, because of the ameliorated condition of society, and the changes that have taken place in public opinion." The writer evidently did not know that the law had been changed—we are by no means sure that the magistrate did!

In 1829 was repealed that part of an act of 1793 which allowed the sale at auction, for terms of service, of persons remaining in prison for a month, for non-payment of fines, unable to give recognizance. (1793, 57; 1829, 38.)

We notice the sale, as servants, of a white woman and her bastard mulatto child, in 1790; and of white women for having colored children, in 1793 and 1794. The punishment of such bastard children, for the sins of their parents, was abolished in 1796. (1796, 67.)

When the act for the punishment of criminals was before the House, in 1793, a motion to strike out the clause allowing female prisoners to be given not over fifteen stripes, for misbehavior, was carried by vote of 40 to 10. Males could be given thirty-nine stripes.

Provincial Court for 1658, for instance, there is mention of two such complaints. But the Council, a half century later, did not allow a servant, we remember, to have his master put under bonds to keep the peace, saying that such a custom would be inconvenient.

In 1692, the attention of the Assembly was called to the fact that a certain resident had "most barbarously" cut off the ears of a mulatto girl, a servant for a long term of years. A special act thereupon manumitted the girl, as a recompense for the injuries. And there was further enacted that the county court should thereafter set free at once any slave who should be dismembered or cauterized by the master, or by the overseer with the master's consent. And any master or overseer who should deny to any English servant or slave sufficient meat, drink, lodging and clothing, or should unreasonably burden them with overwork, or refuse to them necessary rest and sleep, should be fined for a first or second offence, in the judgment of the court; and on a third offence, the servant or slave should be freed. The fines were soon afterwards limited to not over one thousand pounds of tobacco, but there was added that servants and slaves should not be excessively beaten or abused. But the general act of 1715, which superseded earlier acts on servants and slaves, provided the fine of a thousand pounds of tobacco, and loss of the servant for a third offence, against any master, or overseer acting by the master's orders, who should fail to provide sufficient food, clothing and lodging for, or should unreasonably burden or abuse or keep from proper rest, or give more than ten lashes for any one offence to, "any servant whatsoever." If a master thought his servant deserved more punishment, he could take him before a magistrate, who could order thirty-nine lashes. This evidently applied to servants only.[1] But before and

---

[1] Acts of 1692, 1699, 1704, 1715, 44, on Servants and Slaves.
In some sections of the act of 1715, slaves only are mentioned; in others, both servants and slaves are expressly mentioned; other sections, still,

after these acts—whether or not the act of 1715 applied to slaves as well as servants—very cruel masters were liable to be brought before the courts.

We find notice of an inquest held by the court of Kent county in 1652, over the death of a Scotchman, a servant, with the verdict of the jury that his death was caused by fever, and that the stripes given him by his master, not long before his death, were " not material." Some six years later, a woman was tried in the Provincial Court for causing the death of her servant, and was found not guilty. A planter of some note was brought before the Provincial Court, about the same time, for causing the death of a slave who died under his correction. This case was tried at length, the accused being held over from one court to the next in the sum of one hundred thousand pounds of tobacco. The jury gave a verdict of ignoramus, the evidence not being found sufficient to convict.[1] If we turn to the latter days of slavery, we find that a resident of Talbot county, complained of to the grand jury by his neighbors, was fined a hundred dollars and heavy costs, for cruelty to a slave. When another report of cruelty came to another

---

mention, and apply evidently to, servants only. Herty's Digest of 1799 gives this section in question as applying to servants by indenture or otherwise. (Herty, 476.) By the Code of 1860, a master who did not provide his slave sufficient food, lodging and clothing, or who unreasonably overworked him or kept him from necessary rest, or excessively beat or abused him, was liable to a fine of twenty dollars for the first and second offences, and to the loss of the slave for the third. After 1793, the penalty for maliciously maiming or dismembering any one was hard labor for years, at least.

[1] See Hanson's Old Kent, 22, 223. Provincial Court Records, 1658-1662, 146, 161, 493. In the case of the planter we read, on the one hand, how the negro was put in chains by order of his mistress for some misdemeanor; how he refused then to work, and pretended to be in a fit; how he was whipped with a little switch, had hot lard poured down his back, and then, when he got up, was tied to a ladder. Still being stubborn, he was left tied; a cold wind arose, and he soon died. On the other hand, the overseer testified that the negro would not do even as much work as to get his own food, and had run away and lived by stealing, and was withal "an ugly, yelling, beast-like brute."

grand jury of the same county, an examination showed that the master, who had recently moved there, had been sold a number of troublesome negroes, that he had suspected one of setting fire to his barn, and had handled them rather roughly, attaching to one of them a ball and chain. The jury decided after careful consideration that there was no ground for prosecution. In 1843, there was some little excitement in Baltimore county over the case of a slave boy who was found hung after he had been whipped by his master. The coroner's jury found it to be a case of suicide; and the master recovered in a libel suit, by jury trial in the county court, the sum of one hundred dollars from one of the prominent Baltimore papers which had mentioned the matter, at first, with some slight suspicion as to the circumstances. In 1847, the attention of the Criminal Court in Baltimore was called to a negro boy who was held as an apprentice by one of the superintendents of chimneys there. He wore a strong iron collar riveted about his neck, which, the master said, had been put on some six months before, as the boy had run away. The boy himself did not complain of any bad treatment other than this collar. The court examined the indentures of apprenticeship, and found them wholly invalid, and so ordered the boy's discharge from servitude. Later, in the same court, a man was fined ten dollars and costs, amounting to nearly twenty dollars, for an excessive assault on a slave. Again, a colored chimney sweep, aged only ten, was thought by the coroner's jury to have died from exposure. The sweep-master was then brought before a justice and held over to answer the grand jury in the sum of five hundred dollars. He was tried a month later and found not guilty.[1] But there were other cases of cruelty than of white to black. In Howard county, in 1858, a man was fined one hundred dollars and costs, and given a keen rebuke besides, for abusing an apprentice boy. A colored

---

[1] Baltimore *Sun*, Feb. 21st, 1845; Oct. 20th, 1847; Oct. 29th, 1853; Feb. 10th, 1858; Sept. 25th, 1860.

woman of Baltimore was convicted of manslaughter in 1858, in causing the death of her niece, a colored girl, and was given imprisonment for over nine years—the full extent of the law. A white man of Baltimore was put in jail for three months and fined in all over seventy dollars, for severely whipping his daughter. We find here and there in the court records, those expressions of the brutal side of human nature which are to be seen the world over. But the presence of a servile class, of a race deemed far inferior to the whites, added temptations to the man who might be quick in temper, drunken in habit, or cruel in nature. And it was often impossible—however the best elements in the community may have desired it—to have cruelty punished with deserving rigor.[1]

---

[1] Leave was given in the House of Delegates, in 1818, to bring in a bill on assaults and batteries committed on slaves. All we know of it is that it was to apply to certain counties only, that it was reported by a committee, and that the matter then ended by its being referred back to the committee with instructions for a bill for the summary punishment of slaves using provoking and insolent language. (House Journal, 13, 36.)

Note.—As personal property, slaves were subject to sale at their masters' will. Many masters, as is well known, avoided any sale of their servants, especially faithful ones. In some cases—in the distribution of estates most likely—there was attached to the sale the condition that they should not be taken from the State. Thus we find in the Eastern Shore *Whig*, 1830, the notice of a trustee's sale of negroes, not to be sold to persons out of Maryland, or to those who would sell them out. Again, in the Baltimore *Sun*, 1858, a negro is advertised, sound, sold for no fault, and not to be taken out of the State. A certain resident of Baltimore had bought a girl for a term of years, on condition that she should not be sold away; but finding her vicious and of troublesome habits, he applied to the court, and got leave to sell her in or out of the State. A firm of slave dealers on the Eastern Shore advertised in the Easton *Gazette*, in 1845, under a large heading, Cash ! Cash ! "We have returned from the South, and are again in the market with a plentiful supply of the needful, which we will exchange for every description of negroes," but those who did not care to sell servants out of the State were assured that their wishes would be followed. The same firm offered for sale a woman, slave for a term of years, and two young children, on condition that they be not separated.

Of goods and chattels to be sold at sheriffs' or constables' sales, notice was to be given for ten days previous to sale, by posters in at least three public places, except for slaves, who, like lands and tenements, were to be posted for twenty days and published in a newspaper. (1816, 129, &c.)

A wife's property was not responsible for her husband's debts, unless acquired from him in prejudice of creditors. The control and management of slaves owned by a wife were in the husband, and at the death of the wife, the slaves and any increase born up to her death, went to her children, subject to the use of the husband during his life, without liability to his creditors. The increase of the slaves born during the survivorship of the husband were his in absolute right. If the wife died without leaving children or their descendants, the slaves went to the husband. (1842, 293. 17 Md., 352.)

Slaves had frequently to be sold or separated in the settlement of estates. The Provincial Court, in 1749, had decided that the issue of slaves born during the life of one who held the slaves for life only, passed with the slaves to the remainderman; but the Court of Appeals, three years after, held that the legatee for life was entitled to the increase born during the continuance of the life estate. This was on the principle that the bequest for life of the use of a female slave vested in the tenant for life a property in the issue born, as "a part of the use." Thus, in the case of an antenuptial contract by which the husband was to be entitled, on the death of the wife, to whatever profit or issue accrued to the wife's property during her married life, the Court of Appeals held that the slaves owned by the woman at marriage went to her representatives, but the children of the negroes, born during that time, belonged to the surviving husband, being "issues and profits." (1 H. & McH., 109; 7 H. & J., 194; 10 G. & J., 299; 10 Md., 251.) But a case which came before the Chancellor in 1850, in which land and negroes and other property were left in trust, the "income" to be applied to a certain person during life, was held to be different, and the increase of the negroes was deemed the property of the person for whom the estate was held in trust. "To separate the issue from the mother," added the Chancellor, "involves the necessity of determining at what age this may be done. The infant cannot be torn from its mother.... No one would buy, and humanity would cry out against it." Appeal was taken on this decision, the Court of Appeals was divided, and so it stood confirmed. (4 Md., 532). The general principle in such cases was as before stated. (4 Md. Chan., 162.)

In 1836, also, the Court of Appeals,—reversing a decree of the Court of Chancery,—decided that the issue of a mortgaged slave born after the title of the mortgagee had become absolute, although the slaves were in the possession of the mortgagor, was liable for the payment of the debt as well as the parent, and might be sold, in the process of law, with the parents. The mortgagee being legal owner of the parent must also own the offspring born during his title, subject to the equitable right of the mortgagor to redeem. "We are happy to find," said the Court, "that in this instance, the law of the land and the law of nature . . . . are in perfect harmony." (8 G. & J., 24.)

No slaves, the subjects of an action of replevin, could be sold during the action. The House of Delegates urged on the Senate the passage of the prohibition, as slaves had been replevied from their owners and sold at once out of the State. (1833, 274.) There is mention of a bill reported to the House in 1856, to prevent the sale of slaves at the suit of creditors, or for payment of the owner's debts.

It is not uninteresting to note that at the Assembly of 1671, a bill for the "Preservation of Orphans' Estates" was carefully considered. Objection was made to the provision that the guardian should deliver to the ward, on becoming of age, negroes of like ages and ability, "because no man can be sure hereafter to purchase any negroes," and guardians might also take or sell the negroes of the estate to their own use. So it was enacted that no negroes should be disposed of in any way as long as there were other goods of the estate sufficient to satisfy all just debts; but all slaves should be appraised to the guardians or administrators and employed to their benefit, and the like number and of like ability returned to the wards out of the increase; any deficit to be made good in money or tobacco, under the appraisement of the county courts. And if the guardians did not wish to accept the slaves on these terms, the courts should so let them out as to best preserve them and their increase, that the wards might have the original stock made good to them "in number, value and ability." (Md. Arch., II, 317, &c.) The act of 1729 (ch. 24), which was in force apparently to 1798, provided that no slaves should be sold by an executor or administrator, or reserved for his own use for payment of any private debt; nor should slaves be taken in execution for debt so long as there were other goods. We shall see, in the chapter on manumission, the protection that was given at law to slaves manumitted.

An act of 1662 declared as taxables, all male children born in the Province, at sixteen years of age; all male servants imported, at or before ten; and all slaves, male and female, at ten years. But the age was soon fixed at sixteen years and upwards for all males of the Province, all male servants imported, and all slaves whatsoever. After 1715, there were excepted all settled clergymen of the Church of England, all poor living at public cost, and all slaves too old or infirm for labor. In 1725, free negro women, and female mulattoes born of white women, were added. (Md. Arch., I, 449: II, 539. 1715, 15. 1725, 4.)

All slaves and servants, the young as well as the aged, had been taxed for the "muster master general's" fees, under the act of 1662; but as this was found to be a "real grievance," there was enacted, four years later, that no slaves whatever, nor any person under sixteen or over sixty or impotent, should be taxable for the fees.

Taxes on slaves were afterward regulated by law according to ages. At the end of the last century, and as late as 1812, male slaves who were tradesmen were to be valued according to their trade and proficiency. (1782, 4; 1812, 191.) In 1852, the general valuation on slaves was—

Males:
- −12 years...$ 75.00
- 12−21 "   ... 250.00
- 21−45 "   ... 400.00
- 45−60 "   ... 160.00

Females:
- −12 years...$ 50.00
- 12−21 "   ... 200.00
- 21−40 "   ... 300.00
- 40−60 "   ... 100.00

Those who were incapable from age or infirmity were exempt from taxation. (1852, 337.)

We may add, that we have looked with some interest, to see if the early legislation of Barbadoes may have influenced the slave code in Maryland. Apparently, it did not.

CHAPTER IV.

Manumission.

For a hundred years and more after the settlement of Maryland, there were no regulations by law for the manumission of slaves. There was simply the declaration that baptism did not give freedom. Some masters freed their slaves, and some slaves petitioned the courts for freedom; but such cases were few. The forms and solemnities by which freedom was vested in the negro depended, probably, on the legal ideas of the master or of the local magistrate, as was the case in some Northern States always, where the number of slaves remained insignificant. Claims for freedom were tried, as far as we know, in the Provincial Court or the General Court only, for many years. Thus, in 1693, the Provincial Court received the petition for freedom of a negro woman who had been born in New England and brought to Maryland, as she claimed, as a servant. But the jury found her a slave, and such she remained.[1] In 1747 a citizen of Queen Anne's county manumitted several slaves by his will and gave also to them and their heirs a tract of land. A hundred years after, the heirs sold a portion of this land, but doubts were expressed as to the validity of the title given, as the original bequests had been made at a time when manumission by will was not authorized by law. So a special act declared the will valid, and the heirs

---

[1] Court Records, Liber C, 162, 361. The provision of the act of 1715, that the Provincial and county courts could determine complaints between masters and servants by way of petition, may have brought petitions for freedom before the county courts. (See 2 H. & McH., 29; 4 Gill, 257.)

of the negroes free and in full possession of the land, so as to give a good title.¹ In 1752, when the slave population may have been forty thousand, was enacted the first law on manumission. Some masters had used their slaves as long as they were profitable, and had then turned them adrift to burden the community or to perish through want, to the great scandal of Christian society, as the act tells us. It was enacted, therefore, that all slaves unable to support themselves should be supported by their masters " in fitting food and clothing," and kept from begging. Delinquent masters could be put under bonds to do their duty. And slaves to be manumitted must be sound in body and mind, capable of labor and not over fifty years of age. And in order that there might be an uniform way of granting freedom, there was enacted further, that all manumissions must be in writing, under hand and seal, with two witnesses; the papers to be acknowledged and endorsed by a justice, and then to be recorded within six months in the clerk's office of the county. This need of two witnesses, said the Court of Appeals in 1835, was to surround grants of manumission with such form and solemnity that slaveholders might be guarded against hasty and inconsiderate action. And the grant of freedom to slaves was declared null and void, if by a will or deed or any order, during the last fatal illness of the master; inasmuch, says the law, as the right to give freedom by last will may be attended with many evils. Manumission was also declared illegal when it would operate in predjudice of creditors.² This act was entitled, an act to prevent disabled and superannuated slaves being set free, or the manumission of slaves by any last will or testament. It dates from the time when an interesting case was before the authorities at Annapolis. By the will of a certain citizen, made shortly before his death apparently, in 1747, nineteen slaves were freed and given also a great part of

---

¹ 1845, 327.
² 1752, 1; 7 G. & J., 183; 5 H. & J., 253.

his real and personal estate; but a niece of the testator began legal proceedings against the executors, to prove the will null and void. The executors, who made no claims to anything under the will, neglected to produce testimony or have witnesses examined in favor of the negroes, so a petition was presented on their behalf to the judge of probate, Daniel Dulaney, Esq., asking that they might be admitted defendants "to defend the said libel," and that they might have the witnesses to the will. In answer, though the petition was not shown until after depositions were in and the probation closed, they were allowed two months in which to have depositions taken, in order that all legal rights and advantages might be given them. Over a year later, in 1751, Mr. Dulaney gave the opinion that the will was the result of the influence of the slaves—rather the will of the slaves than of the master. Such a will, he said, was contrary to law, and to pass it would be the greatest encouragement to the slaves of a person in the situation of the testator, to compel their master to give his property to them in prejudice of his own relations. The will was therefore declared void. On the prayer of the negroes, a court of delegates was appointed by the Governor to review the decree of Mr. Dulaney; and this court closed its work some six months later, divided in opinion, two for and two against a confirmation. Finally, in 1752, another court of commissioners was appointed; the case was reviewed, the decree of Mr. Dulaney declared null and void, and the will established and freedom given, and all costs ordered to be paid from the testator's estate.[1] In 1786 a petition for freedom of several slaves came before the General Court. Their master had properly executed a deed of manumission, but it was done during his last illness, only eleven days before his death. Two weeks earlier he had spoken of manumission as desirable, but as an injury to the public; but he had since, he said,

---

[1] Record of Court of Delegates, Liber C. D., 186 pages.

changed his mind, and his conscience would not rest until he had freed the negroes. The magistrate testified to the manumittor's soundness of mind; but the General Court held that freedom could not be granted, and the Court of Appeals confirmed this.[1] In 1786, the question of a change in the law of 1752 was raised in the House of Delegates, but was defeated by forty-four votes to eleven. In 1787, there was presented an address on the same subject from the yearly meeting of the Society of Friends, but it was referred to the next Assembly. Then it was given a committee of seven members, three of them being from the large slave-holding counties Anne Arundel and Prince George's. The committee reported four days later, that the subject was well worthy the attention of the legislature. Experience had pointed out, they said, that such laws as that of 1752 were inadequate to the purpose intended, and were neither directed by policy nor warranted by justice, for it was improper and unjust that any person, influenced by motives of religion or of humanity, should be debarred the right of manumitting his slaves at any time, by deed or will. On the second reading of this report, two weeks later, motions to amend so that the last will, to free slaves, must be executed by a testator in perfect health, or at least three months before death, were lost. Then, the House refused to concur with the committee's report by a vote of thirty-nine to twenty-four. On reconsideration, the amendment that the will be executed at least four months before decease, was carried by two votes, and then further consideration of the report was left for the next Assembly.[2] There, in response to petitions from the Society of Friends and the Society for the Abolition of Slavery, a committee of seven members reported to the House that restrictions on voluntary emancipation were neither good policy nor just. It should be the wish of every free community, said the committee through

---

[1] 2 H. & McH., 127.
[2] House Journal, 1788, 22, 26, 41, &c.

Mr. Wm. Pinkney, to abolish civil slavery, and no opportunity should be neglected for reaching that end, by silent and gradual steps, with the slave-owners' consent. The House in so far concurred as to pass a bill relaxing the stringent act of 1752, but providing that no will should give freedom unless it were made three months before the testator's death. This clause was struck out by the Senate. The House insisted on retaining it by a plurality of one vote. The Senate, by two votes, refused to recede, and the House then voted, by twenty-six to twenty-one, to continue the act of 1752.[1] Again, at the next session of Assembly, the Society of Friends renewed their petitions, and again did the committee of the House urge the desired changes. This time the House concurred, and the amendment that the will be made three months before decease, was defeated there by eleven votes. The act of 1790 was passed by forty voices to twenty-three. It allowed manumission freely by deed, properly executed, as before, or by will at any time, saving only the rights of creditors, and provided that the slave be not over fifty years and be able to work, at the time that he was to be free.[2]

In 1791 the House committee on Grievances and Courts gave a lengthy report on the inconveniences and loss which certain citizens had received from the action of the Abolition Society in Baltimore, in legal proceedings over several petitions for freedom. Though one of the counsel for the society's agents acknowledged finally that the petitioners seemed to have no grounds for freedom, yet new petitions were filed. The court had advised the society to pay the costs of former trials, but found that payment could not be compelled. The House, after hearing the memorials of the society in its defence, and examining some witnesses, condemned its action, and provided by law that no petitions for freedom, except on appeal, could be tried a second time between the same parties,

---

[1] Ibid., 1789, 13, 78, 97, 103.
[2] Ibid., 1790, 11, 15, 23, &c. Acts of 1790, ch. 9.

unless the costs of the first suit, and all reasonable damages, were first paid or secured.[1]

During the last part of the eighteenth century, manumission became more common. The population of the State, at the same time, was spreading out more and more. In 1793 there was enacted that petitions for freedom, instead of coming before the General Court, should be tried in the counties where the petitioners lived; but either party could appeal to the General Court on matters of law, where the facts had been tried by a jury. And the county courts were authorized to compel, if necessary, the appearance of masters in such cases.[2] In 1796, the extreme age at which slaves could be manumitted was made forty-five instead of fifty. And there was added that in any case of petition for freedom thereafter in which the petition should be dismissed or judgment be given against the petitioner, all the legal costs of the case should be paid by the attorney prosecuting or appearing to the same, unless the court should deem that there had been a probable ground for supposing that the petitioner had a right to freedom. When the House was considering the bill, a motion to strike out this entire provision was lost by thirty-three votes to twenty-one.[3] Two years later a memorial to the House from sundry inhabitants of Charles county, that the time in which slaves could bring suit for freedom might be limited, was referred to a committee of seven, but without result.

By an act of 1804—made part of the State constitution in 1805—a party to any suit or action who could give reasonable evidence that a fair and impartial trial could not be had in the county court, could have the case removed to another

---

[1] House Journal, 1791, 82, 106; Acts of 1791, ch. 75. There was an unsuccessful attempt at further legislation on the matter the next year.

[2] 1793, 55. Either party could apply, of course, for trial by jury.

[3] House Journal, 1796, 82, &c.; Acts of 1796, 67. In 1844, in order to end some doubts which had been expressed, it was declared lawful for bodies politic or corporate to manumit under the act of 1796, and deeds already made were declared valid.

county. A few years later, a negro woman of Charles county, a petitioner for freedom, gave her affidavit, according to the law, to show that the trial could not probably be a fair one in that county. The court overruled her motion, but the Court of Appeals reversed this, holding that while a slave could not by law of testimony ordinarily make an affidavit, yet that an appeal for freedom was included in the act of 1804. And an act of 1810 allowed the transmission of record, in a case of petition for freedom or *homine replegiando*, before the trial was begun, to the county in which, as shown by competent testimony, a female ancestor of the petitioner had been held a slave at the time of the petitioner's birth, and where other material testimony could be had. Removal of the case was also allowed from the county in which the petition was filed to that in which the owner of the slave might live.[1] There was enacted in 1834, that all appeals from county courts on petitions for freedom should be heard and determined at the first term of the Court of Appeals after their entry.[2]

Slaves were frequently manumitted, to receive their freedom after a specified term of years, and questions arose as to the legal status of the offspring of these, born during those years of service. Such offspring certainly became slaves if there was no provision to the contrary in the deed or will manumitting the mother. An act of 1809 declared that persons who should manumit slaves, after January of the following year, to be free after some specified time or on the performance of certain conditions, might determine the condition of any issue which might be born meantime. Such issue, if there was no provi-

---

[1] 1804, 55; 1810, 63; 9 Gill, 120; 3 H. & J., 124. The residence of a slave, said the Court of Appeals, (in 9 Gill, 120) depends on the master's will; but if a master, on hearing that slaves were about to petition for freedom, should remove them in order to injure their claim, the court of the county in which they had lived would still have jurisdiction of the case.

[2] 1834, 248.

sion to the contrary, would be slaves. When this bill was considered in the House, an attempt was made to change it so that such issue should in all cases serve the owners of the mother, twenty-five years for males and twenty for females, and should then be free; but this was defeated by a large majority.[1]

As has been seen, no deed or will was valid to grant manumission to slaves who would be over forty-five years, or unable to gain a support, at the time of becoming free. The law, if carried out to the letter, would then operate to shut out not only the old or infirm, but also infants, who were plainly incapable of work. A certain young negress was manumitted by deed in 1803, to receive freedom when she became thirty years old, and any children born to her before that time were to be free at birth. A child of this woman, born during the term of service, was treated as a free person until she was nineteen years old. On her petition, Baltimore city court confirmed her right to freedom; but the Court of Appeals reversed the judgment, as no child was capable at birth of self-support, and hence of receiving freedom. Again, a certain negro woman and two children were manumitted by deed in 1825, when the children were very young. When, some ten years later, it was represented to the Assembly that those children might therefore be enslaved, and that their mother had supported them until they were able to support themselves, a special act was passed to ensure their freedom.[2]

---

[1] 1809, 171. 6 H. & J., 431.
[2] 4 H. & J., 199; 6 H. & J., 17; 8 G. & J., 19; 1834, ch. 246.
At the Assembly of 1808, the House received a petition for leave to manumit a slave who was above the age limited by law. A bill was passed, but was defeated in the Senate. In 1825, a special act allowed the manumission by deed of a slave above the age of forty-five, with the proviso that if the negro became unable to maintain himself, he should in no case come on the county for support, but should have the same claim on his old master or the master's estate, as if the act had not been passed. An act of 1827 also made valid a deed of manumission to a negress, as if she were under

A deed of manumission, in order to grant freedom, must not only be properly executed before a magistrate and witnessed by two witnesses, but be recorded within six months in the county court. In a case on a petition for freedom in Anne Arundel, in 1802, parol evidence was admitted to show that the two witnesses had been present when the deed of manumission was attested, though one only had signed; but the General Court and Court of Appeals reversed this, and the petition was lost. In 1810, a law declared valid all deeds of manumission acknowledged and recorded before that time, and invalid only in not being evidenced by two good witnesses—saving, of course, the rights of *bona fide* purchasers of slaves, and not freeing such as had already been adjudged slaves by any court. A similar bill was passed in 1826; not, however, to extend to cases of petitions for freedom then under litigation, and not to grant freedom to any slave who would have been over forty-five or under ten years, when entitled to it, and who had not been acting as free for seven years.[1] In one case, in 1832, deeds of manumission for three slaves, for some reason, not the fault of the slaves, were not recorded. Two years later they were recorded and made effectual by special act of Assembly; but one of the slaves had been twice sold meantime, and the county court and Court of Appeals both denied her petition for freedom. A deed of manumission not recorded according to law, said the higher court, does not change the relation of master and slave. Nor could the petitioner in the present case have her freedom, for by that her

---

forty-five and able to maintain herself; but before freedom could be granted, a bond must be given to the levy court of the county, with security, that the negress should receive $18.00 annually for her support from the family giving her freedom. (House Journal, 1808, 46, &c. 1825, 83. 1827, 158.)

It is interesting to note that in nearly all the Northern States, so long as slavery lasted, masters could not manumit without security to the town—in some cases, bonds in a goodly sum—that the freedman should not become a public charge.

[1] 2 H. & J., 151; 1810, 15; 1826, 235.

present owners would be deprived of their property. In one case, in 1814, the Court of Chancery had put on record, under authority of a law giving certain general powers to chancery, a deed of manumission made some years before; but the Court of Appeals held that deeds of manumission could not be so recorded as ordinary deeds. In no way could a master be compelled to have such a deed recorded.[1]

A certain citizen executed in 1812 a deed of manumission by which a negro boy of his was to be free in 1840. But he continued to hold the black—who had no idea of the deed or of any right to freedom—until his death in 1846. On being freed by his late master's executor, the black entered an action to recover the value of his services from 1840 to 1846; but his rights to any damages were denied in the county court and in the Court of Appeals.[2]

No second suit on a petition for freedom between the same parties could be tried, if the charges of the first suit were unpaid. About 1855 a case of petition for freedom, removed from Baltimore city, was called in Prince George's county, but was dismissed, as the petitioners did not appear, with judgment for the defendant for about twelve dollars costs. On the same day, a second petition was filed, whereupon the defendant

---

[1] 9 G. & J., 115; 4 H. & J., 249. In 1796 the House passed an act, in answer to a petition from three negroes, to make valid a deed of manumission to them, which had been recorded by mistake in the office of the general court instead of in the county court. On the rejection of the bill by the Senate, the House added a saving clause for rights that might have been already acquired, and urged the Senate to pass it. We are satisfied, said the House, that the principles of this bill have often influenced the Legislature: this case seems to require legislative aid especially, as the negroes never had control of the deed, and so no neglect can be imputed to them. The Senate reconsidered the matter, but refused to pass the bill. (House Journal, 1796, Nov., 13, 69, 73.) In 1836 a special act allowed a free negro to manumit his wife and children, whom he had purchased before 1831, but for whom he had executed by mistake, instead of a deed of manumission, a bill of sale to their former owner. (1836, 167.)

[2] 8 Gill, 322.

at once filed an affidavit of his costs and expenses, and a stay of proceedings was ordered. The charges stated by the defendant, including not only board and jail fees of the negroes but also cost of counsel, amounted to over seven hundred and fifty dollars. From this the petitioners appealed; but the second petition was finally dismissed, as costs had not been secured. The Court of Appeals, reversing this judgment, allowed the case to be carried on under the second petition. Such large fees were not included in reasonable damages, held the court, and to allow such, or any counsel expenses, would only be to clog the right of further petition which it had been intended should be secured. Three years later, the court held that no appeal could lie from an order of the circuit courts ascertaining the amount of such costs to be paid, if the ascertainment, when made, was within the limits of the court's discretion.[1]

But the will validly made and the deed properly executed and recorded could not still give the intended freedom, if it were shown that the rights of creditors would be injured thereby. Several interesting cases under this law were brought before the Court of Appeals. One slave was manumitted by will in 1808 to be free at the age of twenty-eight. The debts of the testator were paid from his personal estate, exclusive of his negroes; but his wife renounced the devises and bequests, and took her thirds of the estate as allowed by law, and this negro was allotted to her under order of the orphans' court. When he became twenty-eight he petitioned the county court for freedom in vain. The Court of Appeals sustained this judgment, holding that, if the personal estate of a slaveholder is not, after payment of debts, sufficient to give the widow her thirds, negroes bequeathed to be free may be allotted her as slaves for life. A certain citizen, a few years later, freed his slaves by will, declaring that if his personal estate was not enough, without the slaves, to pay his debts, his executor might sell some of his real property, so as

---

[1] 10 Md., 322; 14 Md., 64.

to leave his slaves free. The personal property alone was found insufficient, while the administrator admitted that real and personal together would be enough or more without the slaves. From the decision of the county court denying their petition, the slaves appealed. The three judges before whom the case was tried in the Court of Appeals, while differing somewhat in their reasoning, but agreeing in regrets that the wishes of the master could not be carried out, sustained the judgment of the lower court, on the ground that the question of the testator's real estate could not enter into the case, nor be dealt with by the executor, under the laws, without possible injury to the creditors—who were not parties to the case. But in another case, some eight years later, the Court of Appeals held that the inability to determine in a court of law as to whether the estate of the manumittor was sufficient to pay his creditors, could not be taken so as to bar petitioners of their rights to freedom. The law, in its true construction, said the court, charges the whole of a manumittor's property, real and personal, with the payment of his debts, in favor of his manumitted slaves. Nor is it incumbent on the slave to prove, as a condition precedent to his freedom, that the balance of his master's property was enough for all debts: the burden of proof rests on the creditor. And the proper remedy for a creditor is by a bill in equity, where the slaves and all parties may appear, and an account be taken of all property. If the assets are then found inadequate, the slaves may be decreed to be sold, as necessary to pay the debt, for life or a term of years.[1] All negroes, said the Court, again, thirteen years later, declared by will to be free at the death of the testator or at any time thereafter are held by the executor and regularly appraised at full value, as are slaves for life. And no court would award them freedom, and so release the executor, until the time had elapsed within which creditors were warned to present claims, and the executor was required to settle his accounts—nor then,

---

[1] 5 H. & J., 48; 2 H. & G., 1; 7 G. & J., 71.

unless the court is satisfied that no prejudice could be done to creditors. In case of deficiency of assets, the executor may hire out the slaves for a time or sell them, if necessary, by leave of the orphans' court; the proceedings of the court being open to investigation. And manumitted slaves are the proper parties, complainants, to proceed in equity to have a charge enforced on lands for the payment of creditors. Then, the legally manumitted slave, either with the executor's assent or by petition, may have his freedom secured by judgment in a court of law.[1] All the testator's property, said the Chancellor, the same year, will in equity be charged with payment of his debts, in favor of slaves manumitted; and in a judicial proceeding, to determine whether a deed is in prejudice of creditors, such slaves are entitled to the assistance of the heirs or persons holding the real estate, in taking the account of the amount of it.[2] The Court of Appeals, in 1858, assured to several negroes, who had filed a bill in equity, asking the court to marshal their master's assets, the right to an injunction, to restrain the prosecution of their petition for freedom, and any payment of legacies by the executor, until the proceedings in equity were settled. To the objection that negroes could not make a proper affidavit to verify the bill, the court replied that documentary evidence would be enough in such cases, to win the confidence of a court[3] A slave manumitted by will, who was sure that the master's estate, at the time of his death, was enough to pay all his debts thrice over, could not still be sure that he himself was free—until the executor's release had been given, and the official freedom papers secured at the county court. For the Court of Appeals held that if

---

[1] 6 Gill, 299. Also, 12 Md., 274; 17 Md., 508.

[2] Md. Chan., I, 296.

[3] As soon as these slaves had applied for such an injunction from the circuit court for the county, the executor had applied to the orphans' court for leave to sell them, to pay the testator's debts. The orphans' court had refused to allow the sale—in which it was sustained by the Court of Appeals. (12 Md., 274.)

in due course of administration, and by no fault of the administrator, an estate changed so as to become insufficient for the debts, the right of manumitted slaves to freedom became void; and, *vice versa*, slaves who might have been held by the executor for payment of debts, could not be resisted in their claim to freedom, if the estate increased sufficiently in value.[1] The Court of Appeals, reversing the judgment of the orphans' court of Howard district, declared in 1848, that the State was entitled to a tax of two and a half per cent. from executors on all negroes manumitted by will, under an act of 1844, taxing legacies. The bequest of freedom to a slave, said the court, is a legacy within the meaning of that act.[2]

Manumitted slaves were clothed with these powers in favor of freedom. In 1828, a certain resident of Washington county died, leaving the provision in her will that her executors were to free certain slaves, if of suitable age and condition, at such times as they, the executors, might deem expedient. For fourteen years the executors kept the negroes as their own slaves, though there was no legal hindrance to the desired freedom. The Court of Appeals, with one justice dissenting, held that the negroes could apply to a court of equity that the execution of the powers created by their mistress' will might be enforced. Though in general a slave is incapable, said the court, of instituting a suit in a court of law or of equity, yet he has been made capable by law of acquiring freedom by deed or will, and so his ability to assert that right is recognized. Chancery cannot grant freedom, but may direct the execution of deeds of manumission, and so enable slaves to assert their claims to freedom in a court of law.[3]

---

[1] 9 G. & J., 103 (1837).
[2] 6 Gill, 388. Act of 1844, ch. 237. Code of 1860, 81, 125. The Court of Appeals said, the next year, that there was no hardship or injustice in this tax; that the objects for which the great debt of Maryland had been contracted, the great public improvements, were believed to be beneficial to all property. (8 Gill, 316.)
[3] 4 Gill, 249.

Pending or during a case on petition for freedom, the petitioner was treated as a slave. In 1796, a slave entered an action of assault and battery and false imprisonment against his late master, for having held and imprisoned him for over two years, from the time when he filed his petition for freedom to the time when it was granted; but the General Court refused to give him damages.[1] It was usual, however, for the master of a petitioner to be required to satisfy the court that he would allow the slave to attend court when necessary. The General Court held on an appeal, in 1802, that a master, in order to retain the services of a slave, a petitioner, must enter into a recognizance to suffer him to prosecute his case, and to use him well; and that the master, further, should he appeal from a grant of freedom, must enter into bond with security to prosecute the appeal, in order to keep the black in his service pending the appeal.[2] We find an injunction served in Baltimore in 1857, on certain officers and slave dealers, to prevent the sale of a negro until his claims to freedom were determined. In a case in 1831, in which the punishment of a negro convicted of crime would depend on his status as slave or free, we find counsel assigned the prisoner, and the right of appeal further assured him, by order of the Assembly. There was enacted in 1856, that when proceedings should be entered into, for declaring void a deed of manumission, on the ground of fraud or prejudice of creditors, and for the sale of negroes for payment of debt, it should not be necessary as usual to summon the slaves before the court, but a guardian *ad litem* should be appointed. The guardian, who should be "some gentleman learned in

---

[1] 3 H. & McH., 255. This case and that in 8 Gill (322) seem to be the only cases in which actions were brought by freedmen to recover damages for false imprisonment, &c.

[2] See Report to House of Delegates on the Baltimore Abolition Soc., 1791, 1 H. & J., 208. A bill was introduced in the House of Delegates in 1795, to prevent the removal from the State of those who had petitioned or might petition for freedom, but it was defeated by eleven voices.

the law," should defend his wards as they might defend themselves, if free, and the court on full hearing should pass such judgment as would be given if all the parties to the case were free men. And all costs, including a fee of twenty or thirty dollars to the guardian, in discretion of the court, should fall on the complainant.[1]

When a certain petition for freedom came before Baltimore county court, in 1848, there was stated to the court that the petition was in the slave's name but was filed without his authority. The slave, on examination, stated that he did not wish to have the case pursued; that his only hope of freedom lay in his mother's effort to purchase him. So the case was dismissed. In the same court, the next year, it was suggested by counsel that the free parent of a petitioner for freedom who seemed to be under age and whose petition was about to be dismissed, might have interests which would allow her to maintain the petition, but the court held that the right to freedom was strictly a personal one. And in another case, in which a father petitioned in behalf of his children, a new petition had to be filed, in the name of the parties asking freedom, by their next friend.

The cost for recording a deed of manumission was the ordinary trivial fee for record. And a certified copy of a deed was always deemed good evidence of freedom. A bill was passed in 1805 to prevent, as we read, the great mischiefs which had arisen from slaves who had gotten possession of certificates of free blacks, and had so passed as free. Certificates of freedom were to be granted only by clerks of the county courts and registers of wills, and were to contain the particulars for identification of the negroes and statements of the time at which

---

[1] 1856, 140. We notice that in two cases, county officers were ordered by the Assembly to pay jailors for taking care of and feeding several petitioners for freedom. It is mentioned in one case that they belonged to an insolvent estate. Experience has fully shown, said the Court of Appeals, that negroes before the courts as petitioners for freedom have never lost their rights from the want of generous professional aid. (8 Gill, 331.)

freedom had been acquired. No other person could give a certificate, under penalty of five hundred dollars, and clerks and registers were liable to the same amount if they issued any illegally. A negro applying for a certificate must prove that he was the person manumitted, and no second paper would be given unless he took oath or proved by some credible and disinterested witness that the original was lost. Another act, two years later, provided that papers could be given only in the counties where the deeds or wills had been recorded. In 1831, the records of St. Mary's county, and, a few years later, those of Worcester, were destroyed by fire. In the acts of the Assembly allowing documents to be recorded over again, and the existence of rights and possessions to be established, there is no special mention of certificates of manumission. But an act of 1852, after the burning of Dorchester court-house, required the commissioner appointed to re-establish all records and legal documents, to take all testimony as in other cases, in regard to the rights of such free negroes as might apply to him in writing, and to report this evidence to the circuit court, which should decide on the validity thereof. From this judgment the negro could appeal, as in cases of petition for freedom.[1]

From time to time, petitions for further legislation, mostly to restrict manumission, were received in the House of Delegates and referred to committees without further result. Thus, in 1823, from sundry residents of Dorchester, to prevent emancipation by will; and five years later, to restrict all emancipation to certain conditions. A bill, in 1823, to compel all slaves thereafter manumitted to leave the State, was

---

[1] A certain negro woman was manumitted in 1823, and a few years after bought several acres of land, the deed for which was properly executed and recorded. Years after she lost her deed of manumission, which, as was then ascertained, had never been properly recorded. She was then too old to get a new deed from the heirs of her old master. So a special act, in 1847, vested the land in her, as if she were still possessed of her freedom papers. (1847, 206.)

referred to a day of the following summer—when the Assembly would not be in session—by a vote of fifty-one to twelve. During these years a number of petitions were presented to the House of Delegates, from slaves, that some defective manumission might be declared valid. All were considered, and at almost every session, a special act or two gave the desired freedom to some petitioners.[1] Just before the Assembly of 1831, the Southampton insurrection occurred in Virginia. Maryland had for some years encouraged the work of the American Colonization Society, but now the plan of colonization in Africa was adopted as a State policy. The act of 1831 ordered the Governor and Council to appoint, as soon as convenient, a board of three managers, members of the Maryland Colonization Society, whose duty should be, in short, to have removed from Maryland all blacks then free who might be willing to leave, and all those who might be freed thereafter, willing or not. And the State pledged its credit for this purpose to the sum of not over two hundred thousand dollars. Every county clerk who should receive a deed of manumission for record, and every register of wills, on the admission to probate of a will by which any slave was given freedom, was ordered to send the State board of managers, within five days, an extract from deed or will, with the names and age of every slave manumitted. The board should at once notify the American or State Colonization Society, that the freedmen might be taken to Liberia. Should the Society refuse to remove them, or should they refuse to go, the board was authorized to remove them to such proper place out of Maryland as they would be willing to go to, and to give them some reasonable assistance there, until

---

[1] Thus, 1821, ch. 117; 1823, 170; 1824, 39 & 78; 1827, 48. In 1829 a resident of Kent county petitioned for a special act to release to him any claims of the State to the personal estate of a late relative. On the other hand, a number of residents of Kent and vicinity asked that certain slaves of the estate might be freed. The Committee on Grievances could not decide the case, and the House voted in favor of the petitioner by two votes. (House Journal, 1829, 49, 328. Acts of 1829, 182.)

they should be able to help themselves. And if any person manumitted should refuse to leave Maryland, and persist in remaining, the sheriff should be called on by the board, and he was thereupon required to arrest and transport such person. All slaves, of any age, could be freed. In case any slaves manumitted could not be removed without separating a family, it was provided that slaves might if they desired, renounce freedom, before the court, and remain at home as slaves. The board of managers could hire out manumitted persons whom they might have to remove, to pay the expenses of removal. But to all this there was the important proviso, that the orphans' courts might grant annual permits to remain in the State to such manumitted persons as were deserving from good character.[1] On consideration of the bill in the House, it was moved in vain to amend this, so as to allow manumitted slaves to remain, on condition of giving bond for good behavior, to the amount of one hundred dollars, with security. The bill was passed by thirty-seven votes to twenty-three. The Senate added the amendment that manumittors should, as before, be liable for the support of those freedmen who might become burdens to the public by age or inability. At the next session, was added that a sheriff who should neglect to remove a freedman within a month after receiving notification from the board of managers, became liable to fifty dollars fine. But while the Assembly furnished these stringent means for the reduction of the free black population, public sentiment neglected to call for their enforcement. In but a single instance was a sheriff called on, under the law of 1831, to remove a manumitted slave from the State. "The harshness that prompted the above legislation," says a gentleman prominent in the colonization work, "soon gave way to the kindly feeling that had always influenced the people of Maryland towards the colored population."[2] Colonization was carried

---

[1] Those who were entitled to freedom under deeds already recorded or wills already probated, were exempt from the operations of the act.

[2] 1831, 281. "Maryland in Liberia," J. H. B. Latrobe, 16.

on by some earnest workers, with the encouragement of the State, but manumitted slaves were not carried away against their will. The number of manumissions reported to the board of managers from 1831 to 1845 was some twenty-three hundred and fifty. Of these, eleven hundred were freed forthwith; one hundred and seventy were manumitted to be free on some condition, such as emigrating to Africa; the rest, after service for stated terms. From 1845 to 1850, some eighteen hundred and fifty more manumissions were reported.[1] Some negroes, freed by will without mention by name, probably were not reported. To what extent manumitted slaves received annual permits of residence from the orphans' courts, would not be easy to ascertain. There was a favorable report from the House committee, in 1844, for a bill to abolish the power of the court to issue them, in Calvert county; and, next year, a bill to the same purport for Charles county—another large slave-holding county—was passed by the House. But if manumitted slaves were not forced to leave against their will, it is obvious that such permits would be needed only to secure legal, not actual, residence.

The Assembly of 1832 enacted that all deeds of manumission which might have been executed but not recorded before the act of 1831, could be recorded then within six months without making the freedmen liable to that act. And deeds of manumission recorded before 1831, but attested by only one witness, were declared valid. And, further, any slave who could satisfy the orphans' court that he—or some one for him—had an understanding for the purchase of his freedom, on which part payment had been made before 1831, was made exempt, on becoming free, from the act of '31. In 1833 a further supplement made valid other defective papers of manumission—entitled, as the act reads, to the same consideration and protection. From time to time, also, special acts

---

[1] Reports of Committees to Assembly of 1846 and to Constitutional Convention of 1850.

were passed, to make valid ineffectual grants of freedom—dating from both before and after 1831—or to allow manumission. By two acts in 1833, certain manumitted slaves were expressly exempted from any effect of the act of 1831. At least fourteen petitions for special acts were presented the House, in 1834. Five were reported unfavorably, bills in favor of two passed the House but were rejected in the Senate, and seven bills were passed. These acts varied in principle—according to the wont of special legislation. In 1835, a free negro was empowered to manumit his wife and four children, whom he had purchased but could not free, owing to the act of 1831.[1] When a certain free black died, in 1834, without manumitting as he had planned to do, his wife and two children, whom he had purchased, the Assembly declared them free, capable of holding property, and heirs of each other. Another freeman had bought his wife and three children from an administrator, and the wife, having borne him five other children, died without having been freed. The father then died without freeing his eight children—but these also were declared free, heirs of their father and of each other. A certain free black of Worcester county asked leave to free his children, in 1835. A bill in his favor, introduced by the committee on Colored Population, passed the House, but was rejected by the Senate. Three years latter, he tried again, and again the Senate objected, but finally passed the bill. One freedman left at his death several hundred dollars, and a slave—his only son. The children of his old master petitioned that the slave might be bought with the money and freed. This was granted—on condition that he be subject to all the laws then, or thereafter to be, in force against free blacks residing in the State. This was in 1845. A free negro who

---

[1] On being freed, they became entitled to all the legal privileges of free blacks—any law to the contrary notwithstanding. As a slave owner could free his slaves subject to the act of 1831, it is obvious that such acts as these were to secure legal residence and a good title to property.

owned his wife and children, died intestate without legal relatives within the fifth degree, so that his personal estate, after payment of debts, devolved on the State. An act of 1846, ordered the administrator to free the slaves, to be subject to the act of 1831. In two other cases, in 1853 and 1856, the wife and children and nephew and niece of deceased free negroes, were similarly disposed of. But when the attention of the Assembly—or more properly speaking, probably, of the House committee—was called in 1841 to the case of a free negro who had died suddenly without freeing, as he had intended to do, his wife and children and grandchildren, a special act freed the entire family, with the proviso that they leave Maryland within a year, never to return. In 1852, two slaves, the sons of a free black who had died without will and near legal relation, were ordered to be put to service, under the orphans' court, until they became twenty-one years of age. If they then agreed to remove from Maryland within a year, they would be free, otherwise they would remain slaves; though, if they became free, the orphans' court might give them annual permits of residence, if it saw fit.[1]

The intentions of some manumittors, in freeing slaves with the condition attached that they should emigrate to Africa or elsewhere, were frustrated by decisions of the Court of Appeals. The will of a certain slave owner, dated 1831, declared that all his negroes should be free at thirty-eight years of age, provided they should leave Maryland within thirty days after reaching that age, and should not return to reside. If they so returned, they should be slaves to his heirs. One of the blacks reached that age in 1845, and received a certificate of freedom from the register of wills. He then went at large as a freeman and remained in Maryland. Four years later, the second husband of his old mistress notified him that he must give security or leave the State,

---

[1] See 1833, 97, 231; 1834, 245; 1835, 68, 266; 1838, 385; 1841, 232; 1845, 314; 1846, 144; 1852, 207; 1853, 413; 1856, 72.

under penalty of being sold, as he had stayed longer than allowed by the will which gave him freedom. Of this he took no notice; but was forced to protect himself by applying for freedom. Both Baltimore county court and the Court of Appeals held him to be free. A testator, said the higher court, may prescribe the period when freedom may begin, but he cannot put an end to a state of freedom. That the petitioner in this case was to be free at thirty-eight years is shown by the conditions attached, for the performance of these would require that the black be free. Such conditions were wholly subsequent to the grant of freedom, and were not authorized by law. A petition for freedom was filed, in 1856, in Calvert county, by a certain negro woman, Lucinda, for herself and her seven children. The will under which freedom was claimed, which had been executed and probated in 1840, gave the woman to a certain person until she became twenty-seven, when, reads the will, she shall be free to go to Africa at the end of her term, and carry with her any child or children she may then have, under the age of five years. The judgment of the circuit court was that the mother was free. The Court of Appeals also confirmed her freedom, holding that the words "to go to Africa" did not affect it. So, in another case, negroes who were devised to be free, to go to Africa, but to be slaves if they refused to leave, were deemed absolutely free.[1]

The circuit court in the case of Lucinda, had adjudged that the children were not free. The Court of Appeals held that all children born after she reached the age of twenty-seven were free, as she was, but that such children as were under five at that time were not entitled to freedom, as she had not removed to Africa. A master, said the court, may limit the time at which freedom is to begin, and if this is fixed by a contingent event, and the event does not occur, the negro remains a slave. Certain negroes were left in 1837 to an

---

[1] See 8 Gill, 314; 3 Md., 119; 14 Md., 109 & 115.

executor in trust, to be hired out until all debts of the estate were paid, when the executor might, if he chose, take to Kentucky or elsewhere such as were willing to go, and should there manumit them. Twelve negroes, petitioners under this will, were granted freedom in 1859, by the circuit court of St. Mary's county, but the Court of Appeals reversed this judgment. The will ordered that any of the slaves who should refuse to leave Maryland could be sold, and such a choice, said the court, is not inconsistent with a state of slavery: the very act of 1831 allowed manumitted slaves to renounce, if they chose, the freedom about to be secured them. And, in this case, the removal of the blacks by their consent was a condition precedent to manumission.[1]

There was enacted in 1858, that no slave thereafter manumitted by deed or will upon condition of leaving the State or any other contingency or condition, should be entitled to freedom until the condition had been performed.[2] And no slave could be manumitted who was not at the time of manumission over ten and under forty-five years, and able to earn a living by labor. In 1860, manumission was totally prohibited, and free blacks over eighteen years of age were empowered, if they chose, to get permission from the courts to renounce freedom and choose masters.[3] The prohibition of manumission was anticipated largely in some parts of the State. There were said to have been one hundred and thirty-six slaves freed in Frederick county during three months. In Baltimore county, during the last few weeks—and mostly during the last few days—before the new act went into force, eighty-one slaves were manumitted.

---

[1] 14 Md., 109; 17 Md., 413.
[2] We find that a bill to require all negroes to leave the State, who had been or might be freed on that condition, was passed by the House in 1854, by a vote of 49 to 5. It was probably the same bill as, or a precursor to, 1858, 307.
[3] 1860, 323. The right to manumit was granted again in 1864, some six months before slavery was abolished.

About 1784, a certain citizen of Anne Arundel county was known to possess two negro women, Dinah and her daughter Livinia. But a dozen or more years later, these negroes were going at large as free women, renting small tenements, owning property, and in every way living as freemen in the neighborhood of, and to the knowledge of their old master. He died in 1805, leaving all his property to his wife, with remainder after her death to his children. She settled the estate and died in 1824. None of the children made any claim to Dinah, to Livinia or her brothers and sisters, or to the children of Livinia, until in 1832 an heir took out letters of administration on the estate, and seized on the issue of Livinia as slaves for life. The county court decided that there was presumption that Dinah had been legally manumitted, and the Court of Appeals, two years after, affirmed this judgment. A negro in Maryland, said the higher court, was presumed to be a slave, and on petition for freedom must bear the burden of proof of free ancestor or of manumission. Yet, to quiet possession, the court, upon a proper foundation being laid for it, will in certain cases direct the jury to presume the existence of a deed of manumission, as in the case of other deeds and patents. The presumption of a deed of manumission must be founded on acts of the petitioner or his ancestors, inconsistent with a state of slavery, acts known to the owner, and which could only be accounted for rationally on a supposition that he had intended to free his slave. If the exercise of apparent freedom were without the owner's knowledge, or began only shortly before his death, no such presumption could be drawn. In 1836, a negro woman who had been living as a free woman in Baltimore for six years, was put into jail as a runaway. She petitioned for freedom, but the defendant showed that she had been born a slave, had belonged to a late resident of Queen Anne's county, and was included in the inventory of the estate, and that he as administrator had received an order from the orphans' court, in reply to his application, to sell her. The petition was denied in Baltimore city court; but the Court of Appeals held that while the fact of the negro's living as free was not evidence that all debts of her master had been paid, as there was no proof that her whereabouts were known to his representatives, yet, on the other hand, the order for sale from the orphans' court was not sufficient evidence of the insufficiency of the estate, in opposition to a claim for freedom. Sent back to the city court, the petition was granted.[1] Abandonment of a slave by the owner, said the Court of Appeals in another case in 1850, is not a legitimate mode of manumission, nor even in itself a sufficient foundation for the presumption of a deed of manumission. Nor is the presumption of a deed authorized, as a matter of law to be declared by the court, or of fact to be found by a jury, on the ground of acting as free with the master's knowledge, unless the negro has so acted uninterruptedly for a period of at least twenty years. A negro woman was allowed by her mistress, in 1831, to live with her reputed husband, with the understanding that he should have her free forever, if he would raise for her mistress two of her children then young. The woman accordingly went at large, and was not molested by her old mistress, who lived until 1846 and who knew of her whereabouts, nor by the heirs of her mistress. Four children born to her after 1831, petitioned for and received freedom in 1851, and the Court of Appeals affirmed the judgment, on the presumption that the mother was legally manumitted when she went at large.[2] But the act of 1860, prohibiting manumission, declared that the fact that a negro went at large and acted as free, or was not claimed by any owner, should not be deemed evidence of the execution previously of any deed or will granting freedom, nor be taken as a ground for presuming freedom.[3]

---

[1] 6 G. & J., 86; 8 do., 102.
[2] 9 Gill, 120; do., 483.
[3] A bill was reported by a committee to the House of Delegates, in 1821, for an act of limitations, to prevent slave owners from reclaiming female slaves and their posterity, after having allowed them to marry free men and live as free; but it was referred without result to the next Assembly.

A certain negro woman who had been given certain lands by will of her deceased master, was granted a certificate of freedom by Prince George's county court, which was confirmed by the Court of Appeals, in 1821, on the ground that a devise of property, real or personal, to a slave by his owner entitles him also to freedom, by implication. A certain resident of Charles county devised by his will, probated in 1857, that a negro woman and her four children "shall work for themselves, by paying my executors, annually, one cent per year hire." The balance of his property was left to certain parties, by a residuary clause. The executors claimed the freedom of the negroes, the residuary legatees opposed, and the circuit court, in equity, gave them to the legatees. The Court of Appeals affirmed this judgment, as the intent of the testator was evidently that the negroes should be discharged from servitude, and be free in fact but not in law—a state entirely contrary to the policy of the law, and in plain violation of the act of 1831 touching manumitted slaves, and of that of 1817 prohibiting owners of slaves to allow them to go at large and hire themselves out.[1]

---

[1] 5 H. & J., 151; 17 Md., 23. The negroes here (17 Md.) were not deemed parties to the proceedings, being dealt with by the courts as property.

CHAPTER V.

THE FREE NEGRO.

To end a study of African slavery with manumission would be neither thorough nor just. For the status of the freedman shows most clearly the distinction that was felt, aside from the relation of master and slave, between Anglo-Saxon and African; and the growth of the free black population affected more and more all questions of slavery and emancipation. If we find, on the one hand, slaveholders anxious for the repression or banishment of the free-black, as dangerous to their interests, we find also many zealous opponents of slavery unable to believe that the whites and blacks could live together in freedom and in peace. We have left those laws which affected all negroes, free and slave alike, to be noticed under the head of the free negro, to emphasize the better this race distinction.[1]

The number of free colored persons was small and there was little mention of them, until the close of the eighteenth century. The population of Baltimore county—including the later Harford county—in 1752, was given as over eleven thousand free whites, nearly a thousand white servants, between five and six hundred convicts—the imported felons, one hundred and sixteen mulatto slaves, one hundred and ninety-six free mulattoes, and four thousand and twenty-seven

---

[1] The subject can be studied to great advantage in Maryland. In several of the lower counties there were more slaves than whites, while the total free black population was larger than that of any other slave State.

negro slaves and eight free negroes.[1] In the lower counties, the proportion must have been less. The census of 1790 gives about eight thousand free colored persons in the State. Some of these, or their ancestors, had come as freemen, most had been manumitted.[2] From this time on, the number increased with surprising rapidity. In January, 1807, was begun the permanent policy of forbidding the removal of free negroes or mulattoes into Maryland. The bill passed the House by a vote of forty-three to eight. No free black coming in, except sailors, wagon drivers and messengers in the actual service of a non-resident, could stay over two weeks, under penalty of ten dollars a week. And those failing, on conviction, to pay the fines or give satisfactory security for departure within two weeks, were to be sold by the sheriff for a term sufficient to pay fines and costs. No one could employ or harbor a non-resident free black without liability to a fine of five dollars a day.[3] But the blacks continued to come. In 1814 and 1816, bills for further legislation passed the House, the second by the casting vote of the Speaker, and were defeated in the Senate. In 1822, sundry inhabitants of Worcester county petitioned that the free blacks coming into their county from Virginia might be fined or whipped. The next year, a supplementary act declared that no length of residence would exempt from punishment, and that those who might return or remain after being punished, should be again arrested, and ordered the magistrates and officers of nine counties to enforce the law.[4] Officers could be fined ten dollars for neglect. The Senate at first rejected this bill, but yielded to the representation of the House that the evils against which the

---

[1] Griffith's Annals of Baltimore, 33. The distinction between negroes and mulattoes is interesting.

[2] We find the mere mention of the reading in the House of Delegates, in 1802, of a petition from the freeborn people of color in Maryland.

[3] 1806, 56.

[4] 1823, 161. The counties named were Allegany, Anne Arundel, Calvert, Charles, Kent, Montgomery, Prince George's, Somerset and Worcester.

act of 1806 had been directed, had increased in ten-fold ratio in the counties on the Virginia line. We find mention of petitions for residence on behalf of some twenty negroes, between 1806 and 1831, but eight of these only were favored. One fellow, for example, from Virginia was given legal residence, as it appeared that he had lived in Maryland for some time, usefully employed in boating, and had proven his good character. In 1824, the House passed a bill in favor of a certain black who had moved from Virginia into Charles county, but it was rejected in the Senate. The man seems to have then moved into another county and to have renewed his petition at the next session of Assembly, but with the same result. A colored woman of Pennsylvania asked leave to move to Maryland in vain,—the House refusing, on reconsideration of the bill, to admit her on condition that she should procure a bond of fifty dollars, conditioned for her good behavior. The next year, 1829, leave was refused for a bill to allow a member of the House to import a free black to work at his forge. Later in the session, the bill was again brought in, but so amended as to limit the residence to five years; and was then defeated. On the other hand, several free blacks were allowed to bring in their wives.

More stringent legislation followed the Nat Turner insurrection, in 1831. The fine for remaining in the State after ten days was fifty dollars a week—half to the informer—on conviction before a justice; and sale, as before, in default. For harboring or employing the black, the fine was raised to twenty dollars a day after the expiration of four days—half to the informer—to be recovered before a justice, with the right of appeal to the court. And any negro who might leave Maryland and remain away over thirty days, would be deemed a non-resident and liable to the law, unless before leaving he should deposit with the county clerk a written statement of his plans, or on returning, could prove by certificate that he had been detained by sickness or coercion. Wagoners, hired servants with their masters, and sailors on vessels having white officers, were exempted, as were those who might enter the State and be prevented from leaving by sickness or accident. And, to encourage colonization, persons might go and come at will between Maryland and Liberia. Each Assembly received some half dozen petitions for residence. One bill, to allow a black to bring in his wife, passed the House and was thrown out in the Senate; while, several years later, a black of Washington county was allowed to bring in his wife, on condition that she should not leave that county. One negro was allowed, in 1833, to move into Charles county from Virginia, on paying fifty dollars to the State, and giving bond with two securities, citizens of that county, in the sum of two hundred and fifty dollars, for his good behavior for a year. Another was given residence, in 1837, on payment of fifty dollars for the State Colonization Society, and a bond of two thousand dollars. Out of six applications for residence, in 1835, one only was granted. Four petitions were rejected the next year. And the next year, again, seven were rejected and one granted. Some were signed not only by the negroes but by friendly citizens.

In 1836, petitions were presented in the House of Delegates from sundry residents of Baltimore and Harford counties, and one, two years later, from Queen Anne's county, for more stringent laws. A motion to inquire into the expediency of allowing free blacks to enter the State for the shad and herring fisheries, was lost by one vote. In 1839, there was enacted that no free black belonging in any other State, could enter Maryland, except servants with their masters, under penalty of twenty dollars for the first offence, to be given as a reward to the taker-up, and of five hundred dollars for a second offence—half to the taker-up or informer, half to the Colonization Society. All cases came before the county or orphans' courts. In default of payment of these fines and costs, the blacks would be sold as slaves to the highest bidder, whether a resident of Maryland or not. If a black who had paid the fine for the first offence did not remove within five days, he would be deemed liable to punishment for a second offence. But it was made lawful, by another act of the same session, to encourage emigration, for free blacks to visit, and return from, Trinidad or British Guiana, with view to possible colonization there, provided they could first satisfy the courts of their sincerity of purpose, and obtain licenses to go and come, and that they return within eighteen months, unless detained by a reasonable cause. Free blacks of Maryland could, as we have seen, remain out of the State for less than thirty days, at will, and for a longer time by permit. In 1844, this privilege of a longer absence was limited to the period between the first of May and November yearly, and the permits were given in the discretion of the orphans' courts, on the written recommendation of three well known citizens.[1] The act of 1839 had forbidden the entrance of any blacks belonging to any "State," and as much annoyance was said to have been caused by blacks coming from the District of Columbia, the words "district or territory" were added, in 1845. In 1840, the answer to a petition of ninety-five citizens of Caroline county, against this strict legislation, had been leave to withdraw. In 1847, sundry citizens of Kent asked for such action as would wholly prevent free blacks from going and coming. The committee on Colored Population was divided. The majority deemed the existing laws sufficient. The minority said it was very necessary for the protection of the slaveholders bordering on the free States, that all communication should cease between the free blacks of Maryland and of those States. If the former were allowed to go and come, there was great danger of a coalition being formed which might result in most alarming consequences to slaveholders. This minority report was accepted, but the bill introduced accordingly was not then passed. Two years later, there was enacted that any free black of Cecil, Kent or Queen Anne's counties who might cross the

---

[1] 1839, 38; 1844, 283. Part of 1831, 323, repealed by 1844, 16.

State line would be deemed a non-resident and liable to the act of 1839. This evidently bore hard on farmers and other residents near the boundary. Two hundred and thirty citizens of Cecil petitioned, in 1853, for its repeal. Though a bill to this effect was unfavorably reported and refused engrossment, the petitioners were favored in so far that free blacks in the employ of any white resident of Cecil county were free to return after an absence of not over twenty-four hours, for transacting business for their employers. And, three years later, the time of absence was lengthened to ten days, to all in regular employ in Cecil and Kent.[1] So the law remained.

Attempts to secure admission or residence by special acts, met with varying results. One man tried in vain for leave to work in Maryland between April and November. The fishermen of Cecil could not take the free blacks in their employ beyond the State lines during fishing seasons. A respectable colored minister of Annapolis—who paid taxes on property assessed at over five thousand dollars—asked in 1846 for an act to allow his children to visit him from time to time, and again in 1861, to allow his sons to return to Maryland, but both petitions seem to have remained with the committee. On the other hand, legal residence in Cecil county was given in 1846 to a family of nine blacks, on the representation of a number of citizens of the county, that the father, ignorant of the laws of Maryland, had removed to Pennsylvania to seek employment, and being unsuccessful wished to return to his old home. But each of the family had to give bond to the State in one hundred dollars, with surety, that they would not leave Cecil county—if found elsewhere, any justice could have the bond collected, half to the informer, half to the county. The steward of the Naval School at Annapolis, who had been for over twenty years in the naval service, asked to be allowed, in 1847, to bring to Annapolis from Philadelphia his wife and children. Permission was given—as he had always maintained,

---

[1] 1849, 538; 1853, 177; 1856, 161.

we read, a high character for subordination and faithfulness in his various duties—on condition that the family should not reside out of Annapolis, and should remain so long only as the father should be steward at the school. A free negro of the District of Columbia obtained permission to visit his wife, a slave of Prince George's county, by giving bond with security in fifty dollars that he would not come there for employment, that he would not stay over four days at a time, barring illness, and that he would behave well. A Washington firm, which had a hotel and health resort in St. Mary's county, was allowed to import their free negro servants, who had, however, to restrict their movements to the grounds of the establishment, and to leave at the close of the season. Two others of these occasional special acts are interesting in pointing out reasons for the general legislation.[1] A colored family was allowed in 1856 to return to its old home in Maryland, if the orphans' court of the county should be satisfied, on examination, that the parents were of good character and able to support their children. A free negro of Prince George's county had appointed by will as his executor his son, a resident of the District of Columbia, and leave was given the son to enter that county freely during the settlement of the estate, for a disposition was felt, we read, among the citizens of the county, from the good character the family had always borne, to extend such privileges to them as would not materially interfere with the policy of the State. The plain policy of the State was to free itself of the black population.

These laws against the entrance of free blacks seem to have been enforced with some strictness. Early in 1842, a justice of Anne Arundel county sentenced five blacks, who had come there from Virginia five years before, to pay fifty dollars a week apiece for the two hundred and fifty and more weeks of their residence there, or be sold in default of fine and costs,

---

[1] See 1846, 65; 1847, 103; 1849, 381; 1854, 66; 1856, 37, 229, 271; 1858, 364.

under the act of 1831. Appeal was taken to the county court, which quashed the writ of *certiorari* and remanded the case to the justice; but the Court of Appeals—stating that the writ of *certiorari* should not have been quashed—held that the act of 1839 superseded that of 1831, where it covered the same ground and gave penalties for the same offence, and thus all such cases should be tried before the courts and not before magistrates.[1] In this case, too, the blacks were not liable under the act of 1839, having come into Maryland before that time; nor, as the court pointed out, could the informer sue for the fines, as an old law required such suits in general to be begun within a year from the date of the offence. We find mention in the Baltimore papers, between 1850 and 1860, of ten arrests for entering the State. One of these was a respectable and well-to-do barber of Baltimore, who had been away for several months, chiefly on account of his health, and was then brought before a justice under the act of 1831, to be dismissed in accordance with the opinion of the Court of Appeals. But within a week after this, another justice of Baltimore sentenced a free black woman to pay two hundred and fifty dollars for five weeks' stay in Maryland, and to be sold for the necessary term in default, evidently under the act of 1831.[2] We notice the case of one negro fined twenty dollars by the court, by the act of 1839; and another black, committed to Cecil county jail to await court, left the State without fine or other hindrance—by climbing the jail wall. When it was represented to the Assembly in 1854, that efforts were about to be made to arrest a free negro who had formerly worked on a Virginia wood-boat plying to Talbot county, but had lived for several years in that county in the employ of a number of citizens who testified to his good character, a

---

[1] 12 G. & J., p. 329.
[2] Baltimore *Sun*, Jan. 4th and 10th, 1856. We notice that there was a black in Baltimore jail in 1832, and another in 1838, for entering the State contrary to law.

special act was passed to give him legal residence and exemption from the act of 1831. It is to be feared that some free blacks, who did not secure able counsel, suffered from ignorance on the part of magistrates of the decisions of the Court of Appeals. The act of 1839, in so far as it imposed a penalty of twenty dollars only for a first offence, was indeed, as the chief judge stated in 1842, a merciful modification of the old law of 1831.[1]

Within the State, an orderly free black would be master of his movements without hindrance, in the communities where he was known, but beyond these he might be liable to annoyance and possibly to arrest and delay. Color created the presumption that a man was a slave, and the burden of proof of freedom, by certificate of freedom or otherwise, rested on the black. We read in the Baltimore papers of one negro who was chased as a runaway, roughly handled and struck by officers, but was found to be free on examination at the police station; and, again, how a man brought to Baltimore, and tried to sell to slave dealers, a good looking colored boy whom he found at Annapolis Junction and presumed to be a runaway, and how the boy spoiled the sale by taking to his heels, by being caught, being heard by a magistrate and discharged as free.[2] Suspected runaways were taken before magistrates to be discharged at once if found to be free—to be locked up and duly advertised otherwise for a reasonable time, at the end of which, if there were no reasons for presuming them to be

---

[1] The majority report of the committee in the slaveholders' convention of 1858 stated that it was believed that the general act against the return of free blacks to Maryland had not been enforced and was wholly inefficient, but that the special and stringent law for Cecil, Kent and Queen Anne's counties had recently been enforced.

[2] Baltimore *Sun*, May 23rd, 1853; June 2nd, 1859. The boy then got work through the interest of the policeman who had caught him.

slaves, they would be discharged by a judge of the circuit or orphans' courts, and all fees would be paid by the county. While fears of such arrest or of kidnappers could not have troubled most free blacks, it is certain that, especially in times when insurrections were talked of and patrollers were more or less about, the customary salutation of a white to any strange and suspicious looking black: "Well, boy, whom do you belong to!" sometimes ended in an unpleasant delay in the business or pleasure of a free Nace or Pompey. The act of 1838 forbidding the transportation of slaves without passes, made all colored persons liable to examination by officers of railways and steamers. Thus, a colored woman on one of the West River steamers, without a pass or certificate of freedom, was arrested on suspicion at the instance of the captain, and committed, as it could not be shown that she was not a slave. Again, a colored boy on a Baltimore and Philadelphia train, who did not make satisfactory answers to the conductor, was brought back and delivered to a magistrate.[1]

One of the objects of the Maryland Abolition Society of 1789, and of the philanthropic work of the Society of Friends, was the prevention of kidnapping. In 1790, the penalty of three hundred pounds fine was provided for fraudulently carrying, or causing to be carried, from Maryland any black known to be free. The Friends, the Abolition Society, and sundry citizens of Kent and Caroline counties—which bordered on Delaware—asked for still more stringent laws, but the House committee replied, that if offences were not always detected the fault was not in the law. After 1796, the penalty for the importation and sale of free blacks was fixed at eight hundred dollars, or in default, labor on the roads, afterwards imprisonment, for not over five years. There was the same penalty for

---

[1] Baltimore *Sun*, June 3rd, 1856; Sept. 9th, 1858.

transporting them fraudulently from the State until 1809, when the act on crimes gave imprisonment between two and ten years for transporting or arresting with intent to transport a black known to be free. We find the Society of Friends and others asking for further legislation, in 1815, and again in 1816, when the grand jury of Baltimore county presented a memorial to the Assembly to the same effect. These efforts seem to have been directed against the transportation both of free negroes and of those to be free after a term of service. A lengthy bill was introduced in the House in 1816, to forbid the purchase of any slaves for transportation, except under certain forms and conditions. Also, it ordered magistrates to hold for the courts all parties suspected of fraudulent purchase, and to require the defendent to give special bail, should the black file a petition for freedom and institute a suit for false imprisonment. And, further, as there was represented that negroes committed as runaways were sometimes free persons, and were prevented by imprisonment from procuring evidence of freedom, it provided that all negroes held as runaways and duly advertised, and held then for a limited time after the notification of the reputed owners, should not be sold as heretofore, but should be set free, all costs being paid by the public. This bill practically failed to pass the House then, for these two vital clauses were lopped off; but the next Assembly passed a bill embodying its essential features, *except* the mention of suits for false imprisonment. Three memorials were read at that session against kidnapping. The Senate passed the bill with one opposing vote only, but there was considerable opposition in the House, directed probably against the discharge of unclaimed runaways. The preamble to the bill states that servants and slaves had been sometimes removed by fraud from the State, and the children of free negroes sometimes kidnapped and sold as slaves for life in distant places.[1] In 1824, the penalty of death was

---

[1] See House Journals. Journal of 1816, 97, &c. Act of 1817, 112. See Runaways and Sale of Slaves.

prescribed for the murder of any person known to be free or entitled to freedom, committed in arresting such with the intention of transportation beyond the State. There were several motions for further legislation, with no result; and a bill to repeal the act of 1817 was left on the table.[1] The files of *Niles' Register* and of the Baltimore papers, show what we might expect, that the laws and the stronger public opinion of all good citizens were not able to prevent kidnapping entirely. Niles says, in 1821, after the notice of a kidnapper just sent to the penitentiary for five years, that "this infernal business" was carried on to a great extent, owing, in his opinion, to ineffective laws; and again, in 1826, that a number of colored children had been stolen.[2] This most abominable of all trades, he adds, had revived with scarcity of money. We find notice of several suspected kidnappers given over to the police by slave dealers in Baltimore. In 1860, when the Baltimore police were making special efforts to execute the law, there were ten arrests at least for kidnapping. In several of these cases, the blacks kidnapped were of those who had been sentenced to service for limited times by the courts—a punishment which increased, surely, the opportunities for abuses.[3]

By the Constitution of 1776 the right of suffrage was given to all freemen of age who held a certain amount of property. It is certain that some free negroes voted in the early years of the State. For instance, evidence was given in Baltimore

---

[1] House Journals, 1822, 127; 1825, 260; 1845, 465; 1826, 355.
[2] See *Niles' Register*, 13, 80; 15, 110; 20, 303; 29, 419.
[3] See Baltimore *Sun*, 1849, March 28th, June 21st; 1858, June 25th; 1860, May 17th, 21st, &c. One case mentioned by Niles is that of a free black who had kidnapped, and probably sold as slaves, three free blacks. He was given a fine of £300, and 3 years at hard labor. (*Niles' Register*, October, 1818.)

county court, about 1810, that a certain free black of that county had voted at elections, and had been allowed to give evidence in a case in which white persons were concerned.[1] But it was enacted in 1783 that no colored person freed thereafter, nor the issue of such, should be allowed to vote, or to hold any office, or to give evidence against any white, or to enjoy any other rights of a freeman than the possession of property and redress at law or equity for injury to person or property. An amendment to the Constitution, adopted in 1810, limited the right of suffrage to whites. Free blacks enjoyed fully the right, ascribed to everyone by the Declaration of Rights, of petitioning the Legislature in an orderly manner for the redress of grievances. Most of the special acts passed in their favor were in answer to petitions, presented usually by the members from their counties, and there is every reason to believe from the Assembly journals, that the committees on Colored Population gave due attention to these petitions. The Declaration of 1851 repeated the words of the Declaration of 1776, that no freeman should be deprived of life, liberty, or property, but by judgment of his peers or the law of the land—but added that this should not be construed to prevent the Legislature from passing such laws as it might deem fit, for the government and disposition of the free colored population.[2]

---

[1] 3 H. & J., 71. We hear of another free black who was also in the habit of voting, and did not know of the law of 1810 until his vote was refused at the polls in Baltimore county, that year. It is said that when his vote was refused, he addressed the crowd about the polls "in a strain of true and passionate eloquence," which kept his audience in breathless attention.

See the valuable memoir of Benj. Banneker, by J. H. B. Latrobe, Esq. (Md. Hist. Soc. publications, 1845.)

[2] It is interesting to note that the House committee on Grievances, &c., reported to the House, in 1798, that they had found in the jail of Anne

Many free negroes owned small houses and pieces of land, and some of the most industrious not a little personal property. The acts of incorporation of some savings banks limited depositors to white persons, others could receive from any persons. In Annapolis, for instance, several free blacks were depositors at the savings bank, and one at least owned shares of the bank stock. The act of 1852, allowing the formation of homestead or building, and of other associations, to promote economy and frugality among the people and an increase of the taxable property, expressly excluded free blacks. There were evidently doubts as to whether real estate could be held legally by blacks, or the descendants of blacks, manumitted after the act of 1831. In 1848, the chancellor held as void a devise of certain real estate to several negroes, by the will under which they were freed, as such freedmen could not remain in the State on terms compatible with sure and unrestricted enjoyment of the property. Ten years later, however, the Court of Appeals affirmed the judgment of the circuit court for St. Mary's county, that the taking of real estate in trust for the benefit of manumitted blacks was not inconsistent with the policy of the State. A devise of land, added the court, might promote this, indeed, by giving negroes the means to emigrate, if called on to do so by officers of the law; nor would it give any rights not enjoyed by other free blacks.[1] The act of 1831, as we know, was not executed. When a certain negro petitioned in 1835 for leave to dispose of real estate to his

---

Arundel county a negro claiming to be free, who had been committed by a justice of peace by an order not under seal and which did not specify the offence—in short, without those forms and solemnities which warrants should have, by the law, "to have the effect of depriving a citizen of his personal liberty." The committee advised the passage of a resolution, to order the black to be brought by writ of *habeas corpus* before a judge of the General Court, to be discharged or remanded, according to law. This was adopted by a vote of 25–21. Note act on *habeas corpus*, 1798, 106. (House Journal, January 18th and 20th, 1799.)

[1] Md. Chancery, I, 355; 12 Md., 87. We find property held in trust for negroes; 1860, 180, 206.

children, the House committee on Grievances answered that the laws did not prevent free blacks from holding real estate, or from transmitting it to their legitimate issue. In 1836, when it must have been plain to many that voluntary emigration was not likely to succeed, a member of the House moved an inquiry by the committee as to the expediency of forbidding free blacks to acquire or hold real estate, with the suggestion that two years at the utmost would be time for those already holding real estate to dispose of it. This was laid on the table. Two years later, a motion to the same effect was evidently allowed in the Senate, but we find no further mention of the matter. A petition presented in 1849 by seventy-six citizens of Caroline county, for a law to allow free blacks to inherit and hold property, may have been signed as a protest against the recent decision of the chancellor, or else for exemption for freedmen from the law of descent, which hindered transmission of property to children not born in lawful wedlock. The fact that the marriage of a slave was not recognized at law, as well as the looseness of the marriage tie among the free blacks, would have caused the estates of some negroes to have devolved to the State. There are a dozen or more acts in the statute books, relinquishing the rights of the State in favor of colored families. For instance, a certain freeman died about 1832, leaving a house and land in Frederick county, and some personal property. His reputed and acknowledged wife, unable to furnish legal proof of marriage, was freed by special act from danger of having this forfeited, to the school fund of the county, in default of heirs. One act allowed eight colored families to inherit and enjoy the property of their respective fathers. By another, the property of a free negro was allowed to descend to his only child, subject to right of dower of the wife.[1]

---

[1] 1832, 204; 1834, 183, 187; 1849, 475; 1856, 337; 1858, 75, 296, 351, &c. There was a favorable report in the House, in 1860, on making the law giving certain allowances to widows, apply to free negroes as to whites. A

We have seen in the chapter on manumission that free negroes not infrequently owned as slaves their wives and children—whom they feared, perhaps, to manumit, lest the right to residence might be questioned. It would seem, also, that other free negroes owned and hired slaves, as did their white neighbors. We hear of one free black, of Dorchester county, receiving payment for a slave, whom he had bought for a term of years, and who was sold out of the State for crime by the court. In 1827, a member for the same county had introduced a bill to forbid anyone owning slaves for life or a term of years, from hiring such to a free negro there. Kent and Somerset were added to Dorchester and, later, Worcester and Anne Arundel were added, and Kent struck out; and then the committee on Grievances, ordered to inquire into the expediency of preventing free blacks from purchasing slaves under any circumstances, reported that any legislation on the subject was inexpedient.[1]

The law of evidence in the Code of 1860 was very simple, and based strictly on the color line; colored persons, free or slave, could testify for or against colored, but not in any case

---

regular marriage between free negroes was duly recognized, of course. We find two cases in which colored men were brought before Baltimore city criminal court for bigamy, but were dismissed from lack of proof of second marriage. (Baltimore *Sun*, February 5th, 1856; August 11th, 1860.) On the other hand, an indictment against a black for bastardy was quashed in Baltimore county circuit court, the judge holding, after consultation with the Court of Appeals, that the act of 1781, 13, against fornication, and other similar acts, did not apply to negroes. (Baltimore *Sun*, January 18th, 1853.) We find mention of a marriage license for blacks; and of an application by a colored woman for divorce, to the city circuit court.

[1] 1852, 114; House Journal, 1827, 11, 73, 358, 382. Persons having free black apprentices were forbidden by 1846, 355, to allow them to remain in the employment or custody of free blacks. This may have been to prevent their remaining at home with their parents.

in which a white person was concerned. But the law had not always been so simple, and the history of its growth is most significant. In 1717, there was enacted that no Indian or negro, slave or free, nor mulatto slave should be admitted as evidence before court or magistrate in any case in which a *Christian* white person was concerned. This was at a time when ship-load after ship-load of the rudest Africans were imported yearly, and it must have been long before many of them learned even the English language. But the law was not to protect the whites only, for these Indians and negroes were not allowed to testify against their fellows except—where other evidence was lacking—in petty cases not punished by loss of life or member. Nor, apparently, could a slave testify against a free black. And further, while the child of a white man and a mulatto slave would be during life incapable of witnessing against a white, the child of a black man and a white woman—there were not a few cases of such offspring —would be so disqualified during the limited term, only, for which he was put to service. A free mulatto was good evidence against a white person. In short, the status was not dependent on color only. In 1751, as heinous felonies had been committed, the testimony of slaves was allowed against slaves accused of capital crimes, where there were pregnant circumstances to confirm it, in the judgment of the court. And slaves were always to be warned by the court of the severe corporal punishment to be given them, if they perjured themselves. The imported convicts, mostly felons from England, were at the same time declared good evidence against one another; as they had been encouraged to wickednesses, we read, by the fact that they were not legal witnesses. In 1792, the House of Delegates considered a bill to prevent stealing by free negroes, which provided, among other things, that any slave over fifteen years of age might testify to convict a free negro of illegal dealings with a slave; as there had been great inducements for slaves to steal and dispose of the goods to free negroes, who could be convicted by the testimony of white persons only, who were seldom privy to such dealings. This clause was struck out by a vote of thirty to twenty-seven. But nine years later, slaves were declared good evidence for or against any colored person on trial for stealing or for dealing in stolen goods. A few years later, in 1808, the grand jury of Queen Anne's county asked the attention of the Assembly to inconveniences which had arisen from the inability of a free negro to testify against another free negro in capital cases; and it was therefore enacted that in all criminal cases any negro or mulatto, slave or free, could testify for or against any negro or mulatto, slave or free.[1] To the House bill for the general act on negroes, of 1796, the Senate offered the amendment that no free colored person, free as descended from a free ancestor, nor the descendants of such freeman, should be allowed to testify in favor of any slave petitioning for freedom. This amendment the House rejected by a vote of thirty to sixteen, and requested the Senate to give up, as it would operate, said the message, to affect the competency of witnesses born of free ancestors and entitled to the privileges of citizens; and the credibility of such persons should rest with the jury. The Senate receded, but the act forbade persons manumitted since 1783 to testify for petitioners for freedom. Since 1783, no new freedman could testify against a white person.[2] Mulattoes, free as descending from free ancestors, were still good witnesses. The Court of Appeals, in 1810, sustained Baltimore county court—in its just ruling under the act of 1717—in refusing to allow a free black woman to testify in a case in which a Christian white was concerned, although it was shown that her brother, a free black of that county, had once been allowed to testify, with-

---

[1] House Journal, 1792, 80, 98—this bill did not pass. 1801, ch. 109; 1808, 81. In 1815, the act of 1728 was abolished, which gave to free mulatto women and to their offspring by negro slaves, the same penalties given to white women and to their offspring by negroes. After 1796, colored children of white women were no longer punished for their mother's crime.

[2] See page 187.

out objection, in some similar case. But in 1814, the Court sustained Frederick county court, in a case on petition for freedom—in which a white was concerned to a considerable sum of course—in allowing the evidence of a free mulatto, whose mother, though a colored woman, was descended from a white woman.[1] In 1846, the religious distinction of the old act of 1717, in favor of Christians, was wiped out; and all colored persons were disqualified in cases where whites were concerned. In 1856 and again in 1860, there were favorable reports from House committees for admitting " in certain cases" the testimony of blacks against whites. These cases were probably embodied in the provisions of a bill which, according to the newspapers, was advocated at the session of 1860, to admit the testimony of negroes, subject to ordinary rules of evidence, when whites were tried for enticing or aiding slaves to abscond, or for circulating "inflammatory" documents; and to allow the jury to convict on such evidence, when accompanied by proof of additional circumstances tending to confirm it.[2]

In the trial of a white man for the manslaughter of a black, before the circuit court for Baltimore county, in 1856, a witness was about to give the declarations of the black after the assault, when the counsel for the prisoner objected to such testimony, as being virtually that of a black against a white. The court held that the declarations of a negro, when part of the *res gestae* of a case, were admissible as evidence, that it would be a most unjust theory, that the exclamation of any man when assaulted must be debarred from notice. Nor was the question a new one, for it was stated that the court for Baltimore county had in two previous cases admitted statements of negroes when part of the *res gestae*.[3]

The Court of Appeals held, in 1820, in an appeal over a petition for freedom, that declarations of a colored person

---

[1] House Journal, 1796, 102, 110; act of 1796, 67; 3 H. & J., 71, 379.
[2] Baltimore *Sun*, Feb. 10th, 1860.
[3] Baltimore *Sun*, Dec. 18th and 19th, 1856.

from whom the petitioner derived his title to freedom, might be used as evidence against the petitioner. The case in question, said the Court, sustaining the ruling of the county court, did not come within either the letter or spirit of the act of 1717 on evidence.[1] That law of evidence was evidently to prevent possible injury from incompetent or dangerous testimony, to the whites above all others.

A free black of Somerset county asked leave of the Assembly, in 1823, to prove accounts against white persons; but the House committee deemed the prayer unreasonable. A free black of Anne Arundel, for instance, an industrious carpenter, who had undertaken large repairs on the farm buildings of a neighbor, found himself unable, when the neighbor died, to prove the accounts to the executor, and had to enlist the interest of a white man, who knew of the work done, to testify to his statements.[2]

There seems to have been some doubt as to whether a free negro could maintain an action at law without first stating in his pleadings, and proving, the fact of his freedom. When a colored man entered an action, in Baltimore city court of Common Pleas, in 1855, to recover wages as a seaman, and the defendant raised the question of his status, the court held that as he was colored, he could not maintain the action without showing that he was a freeman. The Court of Appeals declared in 1858, that the words "free negro" were not essential in the averments of the pleadings, for an action to be maintained, except in case of a petition for freedom; the word

---

[1] 5 H. & J., 41.

[2] Petitioners for freedom were not allowed to make regular affidavits to remove their cases. Nor could manumitted negroes, as we have seen, make affidavits, in calling on the courts to marshall assets of their masters' estates. (3 H. & J., 124; 12 Md. 274; Md. Chan. I, 296.)

"negro" being enough to notify the opposite party of the fact of color, and thus to afford him "an opportunity to show the condition of slavery, if such be the case, by pleading that disability." The question, added the Court, is one of great practical importance, and all doubt should be removed. There are but two cases in which, at law, a negro suffers a disqualification because of the presumption arising from his color— when brought forward as a witness in a case in which a white is concerned; and where the question is his freedom *vel non*, when he must bear the burden of proof. From the earliest history of Maryland, free negroes have been allowed to sue in courts, as well as to hold both real and personal property; and as long as they remain there could be no greater incentive to thrift and respectability than the protection of their earnings.[1] The Court of Appeals also refused to allow a man who had treated a negro as a freeman in a lower court, to turn about and try to prove him a slave, on an appeal, so as to deprive him of a legal status in the higher court.[2]

Some of the English serving women imported early into the Colony, married negro slaves, and a law of 1664 gave penalties for "such shameful matches." The marriage of such women with free negroes was also soon forbidden—as soon probably as attention was called to the presence of free negroes. The master who allowed the marriage, and the minister or

---

[1] Baltimore *Sun*, July 9th, 1855; 12 Md., 450. This decision confirmed the judgment of the circuit court for Dorchester.

[2] 7 Gill, 211, (1848). In a case (8 G. & J. 53) involving the status of a colored man, in an appeal from an orphans' court, in 1836, the Court of Appeals held that however it might be urged that the man was from his color presumably a slave, the facts that he had not been claimed by an owner, that he had engaged on a voyage at sea as a sailor and recovered wages in his own name, were sufficient to repel that presumption so far as to justify the courts in granting an administration.

magistrate who performed it, could each be fined ten thousand pounds of tobacco. This heavy fine dates from about—if not immediately after—the time of the marriage of an Irish servant, brought over by the Calvert family, to a negro slave. After 1715 there was a fine of half that amount for the minister or magistrate who should marry with a white person any negro whatever or a mulatto slave. But a law of 1717 provided that any white who should marry any colored person should serve for seven years, and that a free negro or mulatto inter-marrying with a white should become a slave for life—except mulattoes born of white women, who should serve seven years only. The fact that this old law is found in the Code of 1860, with this distinction in favor of certain mulattoes, and with the disposal of white culprits as servants for the benefit of the public schools, shows that public attention could have been seldom, if ever, called to it in the nineteenth century.[1]

The militia act of 1777, like all previous acts, confined the service to whites. In the next few years, there were urgent demands for more troops for State and Continental service but recruits seem to have come forward slowly. In 1780, all males, those previously exempt included, were made liable to draft, and able-bodied slaves were received as recruits with their own and their masters' consent. The following year, when one-fifth only of certain quotas called for months before for the Continental service had been raised, two extra

---

[1] 1681; 1692; 1715, ch. 44; 1717, 13; Code of 1860, Art. 30. The status of the free mulatto under these laws is very interesting. We note that by the acts of 1692 and 1715, a white man who became the father of a colored child was liable to service for seven years, if the mother was any slave or a free negro. There were afterwards penalties only for white women allowing themselves to be with child by colored persons, and for colored persons getting white women with child—the same penalties for slaves and free colored persons.

battalions were ordered to be added to the militia by the enlistment of volunteers and the conscription of all vagrants— free males over sixteen years, idle and without family or apparent means of support. Free blacks could certainly have been enlisted under the act of 1780, but now we find them specially included—all freemen, not conscripted as vagrants, being enrolled in the militia and liable to draft, though negroes and mulattoes.[1] A gentleman at Annapolis, at that time, wrote to Washington of the plan to raise seven hundred and fifty negroes, to be incorporated with the other troops; but it is not probable that such large numbers were enlisted. An official return of negroes in parts of the Continental army, in 1778, gave sixty as belonging to the second Maryland Brigade, of whom one-fourth were sick or absent.[2] The militia act of 1793 limits the service again to whites.

The education of free negroes and of slaves was not forbidden by law in Maryland, but the black was indebted for what he got to the interest of individuals or of such societies as the Society of Friends. Nevertheless, he was obliged, if he had property, to give his share of the assessments necessary, over and above the school fund of the State, for the support of the common school for white children. In 1860, there seems to have been one exception to this rule, Carroll county, where these taxes were levied on the parents or guardians of school children.[3] For some time, earlier, the free colored people of Cecil and Montgomery counties, too, had been specially exempted from school taxes. Sundry citizens of a district in Caroline county petitioned, in 1843, for exemption for the

---

[1] 1715, 43; Oct., 1780; May, 1781.
[2] Sparks' Correspondence of the Revolution, June, 1781. Document quoted in Williams' Negro Race in America, I, 362.
[3] After 1852.

free blacks of their district, and a bill in answer was passed by the House, but was defeated in the Senate. The chairman of the House committee on Education reported a bill two years later, to exempt a certain free black of the same county, but this was rejected by the House.[1]

The act of 1818, empowering the orphans' courts to bind out as apprentices those free black children who might be neglected or not usefully employed by their parents, provided that the courts might require as a condition in any indenture that the child should be taught to read or write, or in lieu thereof that a sum of not over thirty dollars should be given in addition to the ordinary freedom dues. The Code of 1860 stated that it should not be necessary in binding out colored children, by the orphans' court or trustees of poor, to require that any education should be given them. A petition of thirty-two citizens of Frederick county, in 1858, for a law to prohibit free blacks from holding schools, was referred to a committee, without result. Schools were held, from the African Institute, with its hundred or more scholars, on Saratoga street, Baltimore, to the half dozen urchins learning their words under the counter of the little tobacco shop in Annapolis. The census of 1860 stated that thirteen hundred and fifty-five free black children were attending school, in the State.[2]

---

[1] 1838, 327; 1849, 221; House Journal, 1843, 401, 411, 446; do., 1845, 224, 253, 254. In several counties, free blacks who did not pay taxes to any amount or were not hired out regularly to a taxpayer, had to do some extra labor on the roads. Thus, for two days, in Anne Arundel, Charles, Kent, Montgomery and Prince George's counties; for one day more than unassessed whites in Worcester, &c.

[2] The census gives the number of adults (over 20) who cannot read and write, as 15,819 whites and 21,699 free blacks. The total white population was over half a million; the total free black was some 84,000.

It is said on the best authority that in Annapolis, early in this century, a free colored woman kept a little school, attended by some of the young white children.

Tumultuous meetings of slaves had early been forbidden, as we have seen; one object being to guard against the spread of any possible spirit of disaffection or rebellion. By the act of 1806, any free negroes found by constables at noisy or suspicious meetings of blacks, were to be taken before a magistrate, to be committed to jail unless they could give recognizance for good behavior and appearance at next court. If convicted then of breaking the laws of good order, they were to be fined or imprisoned.[1] Sixteen years after, a committee was appointed in the House of Delegates, to consider the propriety of further legislation against undesirable meetings, but nothing seems to have been done. Three years later, again, the Governor's message spoke of the "pernicious tendency" of meetings of bodies of blacks for dissipation and riot; and again the matter was referred to a committee without result. In 1827, a committee was appointed in the House, to bring in a bill to restrain blacks from roaming abroad or meeting in numbers on Sundays; but the matter was referred to the next Assembly. The act of 1806, mild in its provisions and milder still in its results, might have remained long on the statute books, had not the work of Nat. Turner and his handful of followers in Virginia cast suspicions over the movements of the blacks far and wide. By the act of 1831, all colored persons were forbidden to assemble or attend meetings for religious purposes which were not conducted by a white licensed clergyman or by some respectable white of the neighborhood authorized by the clergyman. The white person had to be present to the close of the meeting, and any meeting held otherwise would be deemed tumultuous and might be broken up by a constable. If a constable of the neighborhood knew of such a meeting and did not disperse it, he could be fined from

---

[1] Any slave taken at a meeting and not belonging to the owner of the place, got a good whipping. See 1806, 81. Leave was given in 1809 to bring in a bill to prevent free blacks and slaves from attending musters or drills.

five to twenty dollars. But the act did not interfere with religious exercises held by slaves at home, with their masters' consent; while in Annapolis and Baltimore—and the growing free black population in Baltimore made this an important exception—negroes could hold their services by themselves, up to the hour of ten at night, with written leave of a white licensed preacher.[1] In 1841, leave was given the committee to introduce a bill to prevent secret societies of colored persons. The next year, the judges of Baltimore city court communicated to the Assembly the presentment by the grand jury of a number of associations of blacks in Baltimore for secret purposes. The grand jury of Baltimore county had similarly called the attention of the county court to such societies, professing to be Masonic. There was enacted accordingly that any free colored person convicted of becoming, or of continuing to be, a member of any secret society whatever, whether it held its meetings in Maryland or without, should be deemed a felon, and be fined not less than fifty dollars—half to the informer, half to the State—or, in default, be sold for a term of service sufficient to pay the fine. For a second offence, the penalty was sale out of the State as a slave for life, the proceeds to be divided as before, between the informer and the State. A slave would be sold out of the State, or given thirty-nine stripes on bare back. For forming or attempting to form any such society, or association of blacks and whites, or for trying to induce any black to join such, or for allowing any societies to meet on one's premises, there were the same fines or sale for a free black. A white man who allowed a society to meet on his premises, was liable to fine of not less than five hundred dollars or imprisonment for between five and ten years; while for taking part in the formation of them, there was the long term of imprisonment only. And all persons

---

[1] 1831, 323, 7. A number of citizens of Frederick county petitioned, in 1840 and again in 1845, for a repeal of the restrictions on religious meetings; but with no results.

were authorized to disperse any assemblage of blacks whose proceedings and objects were not lawful, and to carry participators before a magistrate, and peace officers could summon as large posses as were necessary. Any officer who neglected his duty could be fined not less than one hundred dollars, and any citizens who refused to serve on a posse, between twenty and a hundred dollars.[1] In 1844, the committee on Colored Population was ordered to enquire into the need of imposing still heavier penalties than those provided for constables who neglected to disperse unlawful meetings. In 1845, negro camp-meetings and other protracted out-door meetings were forbidden, as being deemed nuisances to the public. In addition, all meetings of blacks for religious purposes, except those held at regular houses of worship under the provisions of 1831, were forbidden — including evidently Baltimore city and Annapolis; but this was repealed at the next session. Negroes were still allowed, of course, to attend regular camp-meetings held by the whites.[2] In most of the incorporated towns, free negroes wandering about the streets after certain hours of night—as, for instance, nine in winter and ten in summer—were liable, as slaves were, to be taken up and given a moderate whipping or be shut up till morning, by the constables, by virtue of local ordinances. But in Baltimore, free blacks were evidently subject in their movements, as whites were, to the single police rule of orderly behavior.[3]

It is easy to see here, again, that the demand for stringent laws was often a very local matter, and that the strictness with which they were executed depended much on variable public feeling. A goodly number of citizens of a certain district of Prince George's county petitioned the Assembly of 1828 for the correction of evils arising from frequent assem-

---

[1] 1842. 281. These acts were in force in 1860.
[2] 1845, 94; 1846, 166.
[3] See, for example, the law for Easton, 1790, 14; the ordinances for Annapolis; and the powers of bailiffs in various towns, in Code of 1860.

blages there, for the apparent purpose of religious worship, in a meeting-house used exclusively by negroes. They stated that the meetings were a nuisance to the neighborhood and tended to demoralize the slaves. The House committee on Grievances, to which this was referred, reported that the complaints were strictly local and had best be left to the members from Prince George's. A bill was accordingly introduced by a special committee, and finally passed, having first been rejected by the Senate. Thus, after 1828,[1] no colored persons could meet anywhere in that one district, under the pretext of or for the purpose of public worship—other than at services attended by white citizens—except between the hours of seven in the morning and five in the afternoon, on Sundays, Christmas days, Easter Mondays and Whit-Mondays. For meeting illegally, slaves were liable to be whipped, and free blacks fined in moderate sums—for the benefit of Sunday-schools of the district. The fact that in 1853 the State's attorney for Baltimore county instructed the sheriff to summons a force sufficient to arrest all slaves and free negroes who might thereafter be found at camp-meetings of blacks in that county, creates the presumption that the act of 1845 had not been strictly enforced there.[2] When the rumors were abroad in Talbot county, in April, 1855, that the negroes of the neighborhood planned a movement during the approaching Easter holidays, one object of the large and respectable meeting held at Easton was to take precautionary measures—in particular, for suppressing effectually the schools and meetings illegally held by blacks without supervision of whites. These meetings, says the Easton *Gazette*, have been held in Easton until they have become an annoyance, and it is time to have the laws enforced. Although, adds the report, there was probably no truth in the rumors, it was deemed best to adopt a resolution asking the citizens to keep their servants at home during the

---

[1] 1828, 151; Code of 1860.
[2] Baltimore *Sun*, August 29th, 1853.

holidays.[1] A certain justice of Baltimore county was called on, early in 1859, to try nine blacks for fighting at services in a colored church. He dismissed them, after a severe reprimand and the explanation to them and the witnesses, some thirty blacks, of the laws forbidding blacks both to hold meetings for worship without the presence of a white, and to carry firearms.[2] According to the papers of Montgomery county, a thousand or more negroes met together there, one Sunday in July, 1860, for religious services, apparently, but the meeting was broken up by the sheriff. Such meetings, we read, were at one time quite frequent in that county, and were not looked on with much disfavor, but the work of abolitionists had become so dangerous to slave interests, that meetings of negroes for any purpose had come to be opposed by almost everybody.[3]

The act of 1842 forbidding all societies of blacks had been in force only three years, when a bill passed the Senate to modify it for Baltimore city, on the representation of a large number of highly respectable citizens that it had operated with much hardship on many honest and industrious blacks, in keeping them from forming beneficial societies for the relief of the destitute of their race. The plan was that free blacks who bore good characters, and who paid taxes to the amount of five dollars, could form charitable societies, with written permits from the Mayor, given annually, with the proviso that all meetings should be inspected by police officers, to be sent by the Mayor. This bill, though favorably reported by the committee on Colored Population, and supported by the members from Baltimore city—only five in number, however—was rejected by the House by a vote of thirty-nine to nineteen; but was afterwards reconsidered and passed by thirty-seven to twenty-nine. We should note here—what will be entered into

---

[1] Easton *Gazette*, April 7th, 1855.
[2] Baltimore *Sun*, January 20th and 28th, 1859.
[3] Rockville *Sentinel*, quoted in Baltimore *Sun*, August 6th, 1860.

at length, later—that at this time the city of Baltimore was represented in the legislature by only one senator and not over six members, though it contained nearly a third of all the whites and of all the free blacks in the State.[1]

It came to be the custom for negroes of Baltimore who wished to have any assembly or entertainment at their houses, to procure from the Mayor's office a permit therefor, to be shown any policeman who might visit the scene of festivity. The daily papers show that negro meetings, "cake-walks" and balls frequently ended in noise and disorder. On one occasion, in answer sent to a police station at three o'clock in the morning by peace-loving neighbors, thirteen policemen arrested thirty-three colored men and women engaged in a row at a dance. Again, we find thirty-six noisy dancers taken up, of whom eighteen were bailed and the rest committed. One colored man was fined ten dollars by a justice for giving a ball without leave. On the other hand, this police regulation might sometimes be an annoyance to peaceable persons. One large gathering for entertainment at a colored church was broken up by the police, who thought the proceedings noisy, and thirty or more blacks were taken to the station house.

---

[1] *Niles' Register* for 1835 (vol. XLIX, 72) prints a letter from three of the colored clergy of Baltimore, representing their congregations. It pledges their support to the cause of good order among the blacks and of friendly relations with the whites, and states that they have no sympathy with anything which tended to disturb those relations. It states, also, that the free blacks of Baltimore had then 35 or 40 benevolent societies, numbering each from 35 to 150 members, whose funds were largely in the savings banks. There were many week-day and Sunday schools, and ten churches. Many of the blacks had purchased houses and land, horses and wagons, and other property, and the letter bore witness, also, to the respect shown to the "orderly and discreet" blacks by captains of boats and owners of public conveyances. The colored people, it said, always feel the greatest pressure from anything that disturbed the peace.

Another letter, from the trustees of a colored church society of Baltimore, deplored the efforts that were being made by abolitionists—efforts which make more precarious the position of the free blacks and "rivet the fetter still more closely on the slave."

But the permit from the Mayor was produced, and they were discharged as not guilty of any offence. There is need, added the paper, next day, of the exercise of a little more care and discretion by the police.[1] There should be added that in respect to behavior at entertainments, as in many other ways, the lower classes of whites in Baltimore set no good example to the negroes. A certain colored man gave at his house, in the summer of 1858, a tea and fruit party, which was said to be orderly. Soon after midnight the police called to see his permit from the Mayor's office, and finding this without the counter-signature of the captain of the watch, put him in the watch-house, together with many of his guests. Released next morning by a magistrate on payment of fees, he brought suit against the city for thirty dollars damages, claiming that he had been told at the Mayor's office that the counter-signature was not necessary. From a judgment in his favor by a magistrate's court the city appealed, but the court of Common Pleas held that the arrest of the black was illegal, as there was no law forbidding such meetings as the one in question or requiring permits for them, and custom could not allow the police to place restrictions on them. Within a few months the city government passed an ordinance forbidding any number of colored persons to meet for any purpose, other than religious worship or as beneficial societies, under the State laws, without written permission from the Mayor, and the presence, in addition, of at least one white person. A black present at any meeting illegally held, could be fined between five and ten dollars.[2]

There were many churches for the blacks throughout the State, some of them under white pastors, others under blacks

---

[1] See Baltimore *Sun*, May 11th, 1859; October 3rd, 1860; January 1st, 1857; March 10th, 1854, &c.

[2] Common Pleas, February, 1859; Baltimore *Sun*, September 4th and 6th, 1858, and February, 1859; city ordinance, 1860, 39. The black mentioned was awarded $1.00 and costs, over $8.00.

licensed by the regular religious bodies, and some evidently independent. Conferences of some of the colored church members were held, and the Baltimore paper speaks of one of these, which met in that city for a week in 1855, as a model of decorum, even for similar assemblages of those who made higher pretensions. There were in Baltimore in 1847, at least thirteen colored church societies, ten of which were Methodist. The membership of the Protestant colored bodies there in 1859, was nearly six thousand four hundred—about a quarter of the total free black population of the city.[1]

Most occupations, from the small farmer, or livery or innkeeper, to the vendor of cakes in the markets, were followed by free blacks. But there were two which were forbidden them in the latter days of slaveholding—they could not be licensed as pedlars, nor run any vessel of any size. In 1833, a bill was introduced in the House, to prevent owners of vessels from allowing them to be navigated by negroes only. This was amended so as to except scows or lighters used on rivers or creeks, and was rejected by the Senate, in answer perhaps to a certain black commanding a vessel in the Bay trade, who had petitioned for leave to pursue his occupation. Two years later the matter was again under inquiry in the House. At the next session, 1836, was enacted that any vessel of the size required by government laws to be registered, worked in the waters of Maryland without a white captain

---

[1] See reports of the various societies. African conference of the M. E. Church, May, 1855 (*Sun*, of May 8th, &c.). When an address of an incendiary nature was announced to be given at Zion's Independent Church in Baltimore, a magistrate and several police attended and dispersed the meeting, under authority of the act of 1831, as the church was not under the control of, nor the preachers licensed by, any regular conference or religious body, and the exercises were conducted mostly by blacks (Baltimore *Sun*, July 26th, 1858).

over eighteen years of age, would be forfeited—half to the informer, half to the State. On information under oath, a justice might seize the boat, summon the parties and try the case, and sell the boat at auction, unless the owner appealed. The preamble to the act declared that great inconvenience and injury had resulted from the navigation of vessels entirely by negroes, by which a clandestine trade was carried on and slaves had found facilities for running away.[1] It is interesting in this connection to note that the House, in 1787, had struck out from a bill under consideration the provision that no slave, except pilots, should be allowed to manage any boat, over twenty feet keel, conveying goods which belonged to any one but the owner of the boat. In 1838 a free black asked leave to sail his own boat, but the House committee reported unfavorably. But, the year before, citizens of Baltimore and Anne Arundel counties had been specially exempted from the act of 1836, and so able to navigate their vessels by their slaves or by hired blacks only. A bill to repeal this exemption was passed by the House in 1844, but defeated by the Senate; and not till nine years later still was it done away with.[2] In 1856, a bill passed the Senate, without opposition, to allow two free blacks of Harford county to run their own vessel to and fro between Baltimore city and the Bush and Gunpowder rivers, but the House threw it out by a vote of forty-four to five; and the petition of another black, two years later, to run a vessel without a white on board, was left on the table.[3] In May, 1854, the Baltimore *Sun*, under the heading "Novel Action," stated that a schooner was condemned under the law of '36, and that the owner had appealed. And there is mention, in October, 1859, of the trial before a justice of a colored captain.

---

[1] 1836, 150.

[2] 1837, 23; Journal of 1844; 1853, 446. A bill was reported, the next year, to allow owners of vessels to employ colored men as captains in certain cases, but was not evidently considered.

[3] House Journal, 1856, 358, 445; 1858, 35.

A bill was passed, in 1858, in answer to a petition from sundry citizens of Charles county, forbidding any colored person in Charles or Prince George's counties to keep or use any boat on the Potomac, without license,—from a master to a slave, from a justice of peace to a free black. To obtain such a license, a free black must get a written certificate of good character from two respectable landholders of the neighborhood; and if any two landholders of the Potomac shore requested in writing the suppression of the license, the justice was bound to summon the black and hear the matter fairly. No license could be renewed when once forfeited. The penalty for using a boat without leave was a fine of from five to fifty dollars and costs, and loss of the boat, on conviction before a magistrate. A slave who crossed the Potomac or took a trip to the District of Columbia, without leave, could be given from ten to twenty lashes by order of the magistrate; and his boat was forfeited, unless the owner was a white citizen, and ignorant of its use.[1]

Free negroes could sell liquors and fermented drinks, with the customary license. But after 1831, licenses were granted to them by order of the courts only, not by clerks of court, as in the case of whites. The act of '31 urged the courts to exercise a sound discretion as to the continuance or withdrawal of licenses, and empowered them to require, if advisable, satisfactory securities from the blacks. In 1852,—in answer to several local petitions, one of which was signed by as many as one hundred and twenty-four citizens,—was passed, with little opposition in the House and none in the Senate, a bill by which free blacks of Somerset, Worcester and Anne Arundel counties were forbidden to sell ardent spirits, and were required to obtain licenses for the sale of all merchandise. Licenses were to be gotten only by special order of the courts, on the recommendation of not less than twelve respectable freeholders in the neighborhood in which the black proposed

---

[1] 1858, 356.

to do business. Beside, no white person in partnership with a black could get any license, nor could a white employ a free black as a clerk in any business, under penalty of five hundred dollars.[1] In Annapolis, the thrifty black found no trouble in getting his recommendations, nor is it likely that one lacked friends, elsewhere. In May, 1860, a resident of Baltimore was indicted, under the act of '52, for employing as his clerk in a retail store in Annapolis a colored man of that city. On pleading guilty, before Anne Arundel circuit court, he was fined the five hundred dollars and costs—for the payment of which, the father of the clerk, a prosperous and respected mulatto of Annapolis, became his surety.[2]

At the session of 1827, a memorial was presented the House from sundry citizens of Baltimore, for such legislation as would forbid colored persons there from obtaining licenses to keep hacks, carts or drays, as well as from driving such vehicles. The very next day was presented a counter-memorial from sundry merchants and citizens of Baltimore. The committee, consisting of the two members from Baltimore and one from Allegany, reported that such matters should be left to the city government, which would know best the special wants and interests of the city. And a considerable source of city revenue might be affected by any such prohibition, suggested the committee. In 1836, the committee on Colored Population was ordered to inquire into the expediency of requiring additional security from the blacks licensed as

---

[1] 1831, 323; 1852, 288. House Journal, 1852, 92, 141, 318, 553, 619. The petition from Anne Arundel, with forty-four signatures, speaks of the serious injury inflicted on the honest industry of a large portion of our white fellow citizens by the presence of the free blacks, and of the utter destitution in which thousands of this anomalous class are plunged by idle habits and vicious propensities. The idle should be hired out and the children apprenticed to learn useful arts and avocations before emigrating to Africa.

[2] Baltimore *Sun*, May 5th, 1860. An act of 1827, to protect public worship more effectually, forbade any negro to sell liquor or beer or cider within a mile of a camp-meeting, under penalty of a whipping, on conviction by a justice. The whipping could not be given also within the mile circle.

traders and inn-keepers, or of withholding licenses from them altogether. A stringent bill, evidently to prohibit licenses, which passed the House, four years later, was twice rejected by the Senate.[1] In 1837, the committee was ordered, on motion of a member from Prince George's county, to consider the expediency of forbidding free negroes to pursue for a livelihood any business, mechanic art or trade, in order to encourage them to emigrate. Later in the session, the committee reported, through the same member, a bill entitled an act to encourage the emigration of free negroes and to advance the interests of tradesmen, mechanics and other laboring persons. After some amendment, the bill was killed by striking out the enacting clause—though by a vote of thirty-eight to twenty-four only.[2] In 1840, a member from Baltimore obtained leave to bring in a bill to prevent the employment of negroes in the State tobacco warehouses at Baltimore, but the bill, reported at the next session, was left on the table. In 1844, two petitions came from divers citizens of Prince George's county—one to prohibit free black carpenters from working there, the other to impose a tax on free black mechanics; but the House committee reported adversely. Three years later, a memorial from a number of citizens of Baltimore for a law to prevent free blacks from huckstering hay or straw was referred, without result, to the committee on Ways and Means; and no better fate seems to have met the petitions of a large number of citizens of Baltimore, in 1860, that free blacks of that city be barred from pursuing any mechanical branch of trade.[3] The signers were said to be—what we should expect—white mechanics!

---

[1] House Journal, 1827, 119, 125, 410; Senate Journal, 1840, 68, 147.

[2] House Journal, 1837, 25, 447, 527.

[3] House Journal, 1844, 259, 261, 379; 1860, 309. The colored ship caulkers of Baltimore seem to have met with much injustice at the hands of their white rivals, in 1858, the police being required to keep the peace. But the paper adds that the same disposition was shown the German caulkers who succeeded some of the blacks. See Baltimore *Sun*, 1858, May 18th,

Those of the free blacks who went into business and were unfortunate, or otherwise got into hopeless debt, had apparently the benefit of the insolvent laws as fully as their white neighbors. Several citizens of Caroline county petitioned in 1829, for a law to prevent negroes from taking those benefits, but in vain; and the petition of some citizens of Dorchester, in 1858, for sale of free blacks for debts of their own making, was as ineffectual. Two years later, when a similar petition was received from Anne Arundel, leave was given the committee on Colored Population to bring in a bill for the sale of free blacks for debt in certain cases, but no further action seems to have been taken.[1]

As early as 1792 an attempt was made to pass a bill to prevent free blacks from stealing and selling stolen goods. In 1805, a bill to prevent them from selling corn, wheat, tobacco or other articles, without a license for the purpose from a justice, passed the House, after an attempt to refer it to the next Assembly, by a margin of three votes only. As finally amended, evidently by the Senate, it required a certificate of good character, under hand and seal of a justice of the county, for the sale of any corn, wheat and tobacco only. Such a license should be good for one year, and the black who sold these articles without it, was liable to a fine of five dollars. Any purchaser became liable to twice that sum. The preamble to the act states that much inconvenience had been felt from the sale by free blacks, as the product of their labor, of corn, wheat and tobacco received from slaves. Two years later a

---

June 9th, July 5th and 22nd; 1859, June 28th. We may note, in passing, that an act of 1811 (ch. 100) on county surveyors, required chain and pole carriers to be free white males over 21 years. And the sale of lottery tickets was forbidden (1856, 195) to colored persons or minors, doubtless to protect them against fraud.

[1] House Journals, 1829, 487; 1860, 44, 192; Acts of 1822, ch. 185. The Commissioners of Insolvency discharged in 1834, for instance, 140 whites and 17 free blacks; in 1835, 134 whites and 30 blacks, &c. See Baltimore Jail Reports.

supplementary and more stringent bill was brought in; providing, in part, that the certificate from the justice should specify the quantities of corn, wheat and tobacco which might be sold—as estimated from a written statement of two respectable neighbors of the black, of the probable amount which his lands could produce during the year—and that every purchaser should endorse on the certificate the quantity of his purchase, under penalty of five dollars. This bill, after consideration, was defeated by thirty-three to twenty.[1] In 1825, there was enacted that no one, under penalty of one hundred dollars, should buy of any free black any quantity of tobacco in transfer or parcels, unless the black produced at the time a certificate from a justice of the county giving the quantity and quality of the tobacco. And a certificate could be gotten only on proof of a respectable citizen of the neighborhood that the black had come honestly by the goods, and on payment of twenty-five cents.[2] The act of 1831, which was permanent in this respect, provided that no one should purchase from any colored person any bacon, pork, beef, mutton, corn, wheat, tobacco, rye or oats, unless the blacks had a permit—in case of a free black, from a justice or from three respectable persons of his neighborhood, that he was believed to have acquired the goods honestly. The penalty was a fine from the purchaser of five dollars or a sum equal to the value of the goods, should they be worth more —half to the informer and half to the county.[3] By act of 1842, a free black convicted of dealing in stolen goods should be sold out of the State for not less than five nor more than ten years' service, and be forbidden ever to return, under penalty of the law. Half the proceeds of the sale went to the informer.[4]

---

[1] House Journal, 1805, 17, 64, 80, 98, ch. 80; 1807, 19, 28, 36.

[2] 1825, 199.

[3] 1831, 323, 9. Slaves had to have a permit from their masters or overseers. The question was raised without result in the House in 1844, as to whether free blacks should be forbidden to ship on vessels any produce without permits from justices.

[4] A slave was sold out for life. 1842, 279. This act appears to have been in force until 1860. See Crimes and Punishments of Free Blacks.

The act of 1831 forbade also, under the same penalty, the sale by anyone of ardent spirits to any black who had not a permit—in the case of a free black, from a justice of peace of the county in which the black lived, and directed to the seller. At the session of 1832, the statement was made by a member from Dorchester county, which had a large free black as well as slave population, that this provision of the law had been in its practical effect, as was manifest to every person who had given the slightest attention to it, "a complete and entire failure." His motion for an inquiry into the matter and for further measures was adopted; but nothing was reported then. A bill to repeal that provision of the act of '31, reported at the following session, was left on the table.[1]

The Assembly of 1817 passed a bill entitled, an act for the better protection of slaveholders in Calvert, Anne Arundel and St. Mary's counties. Its provisions applied to those counties only, and exempted travelers and blacks employed as wagoners. No retailer or distiller of liquors was to allow any colored person, except servants or slaves with proper permits, to be on the premises where liquors were sold, between sunset and sunrise. The penalty was fifty dollars, half to the informer, and imprisonment for not over three months, in default. And the fact that a black was on the premises after sunset was sufficient to convict the proprietor, unless he could prove ignorance of it on the part of himself or his agent, or that all possible means had been taken to eject the black. And no one could receive any goods whatever from any black who did not hold a permit from a justice, under the same penalty of fifty dollars fine or the jail.[2] This bill had first been rejected by the House, but was passed on reconsideration. At the next session came a vigorous appeal from the citizens of Annapolis, seconded by the members of the House from Anne

---

[1] House Journal, 1832, 55; 1833, 110, 197.
[2] This is evidently the meaning of Section 5 (1817, 227), the permit to be under 1805, afterwards 1831.

Arundel, to exempt Annapolis from the act. A bill for that purpose quickly passed the House, but was rejected by the Senate. Two weeks later, the House requested the Senate to reconsider its action, stating that the bill was desired by the citizens of Annapolis "with an unanimity of voice seldom equalled;" but the Upper House not only adhered to its first decision, but refused to appoint a committee of conference on the matter.[1] But at the same session, the act was extended to Prince George's, Somerset, Dorchester, Charles and Talbot counties, with the addition that no liquor should be sold either on Sunday or after sunset, to any free black, or to any slave without leave from his employer.[2] The next year, another petition was received from Annapolis, and a bill was finally passed to exempt that city from the restrictions as to harboring blacks, so that retailers and distillers should be governed in that respect by city ordinances only, but keeping the fine of fifty dollars or the jail for buying unlawfully from a black. The entire act had already been repealed, early in the session, for Talbot and Dorchester counties. Four years later it was re-enacted for Dorchester, only to be done away at the next session, in answer to a protest from sundry citizens. A bill to repeal it for Prince George's county, in 1824, was defeated. It is to be found in the Code of 1860, in force in the other counties mentioned, except Somerset.[3] More rigorous provisions still against the harboring of blacks by liquor dealers, were enacted in 1854 for Anne Arundel, Calvert, Charles, Howard, Prince George's, Saint Mary's and Somerset counties, but were repealed two years later.[4] A bill was introduced in the House, in 1827, by a committee of two members

---

[1] The chances of this bill may have been injured by a slight passage at arms between the two Houses, the House having reminded the Senate that the bill had been kept in the Senate for a month before being considered. House Journal, 1818, 28, 60, 82, 85, &c.

[2] 1818, 184. The act of 1817 simply forebade the harboring of blacks.

[3] 1819, 77, 18; 1823, 15; 1824, 57. House Journal, 1824, 141.

[4] 1854, 194; 1856, 99.

from Anne Arundel county and one from Annapolis, to regulate marketing by blacks in that county and city, which provided a penalty of five dollars only against persons dealing with blacks without the proper license. This passed the House by thirty-six to twenty one—seven members calling for the yeas and nays—but was unfavorably reported and rejected in the Senate.¹ For some time, by an act of 1818, it was not lawful for anyone in Kent county to sell liquor to, or trade in any goods with, any black, between sunset and sunrise, unless the black had a permit—if a free black, a certificate of good character and special permit from two justices of the county. Such permits were to be recorded and were valid for a year. A person who dealt with a black otherwise was liable to forty dollars fine or, in default, not over three months in jail, and a freeman who counterfeited a certificate was liable to six months. Innkeepers could still entertain blacks who were passing through the county, and dealings in markets at the lawful hours were not included.² After 1858, all persons, whether licensed or not, were forbidden to sell or give any liquor, within the city of Annapolis or its neighborhood, to any minor or slave without a permit from the parent or owner, or to any free black who did not have a written order from a physician or a certificate from three respectable freeholders of the city, stating that he was of good habits. The penalty for a first offence was from fifty to two hundred dollars, and double that for a second—half to the informer, half to the State. And permits must be dated, and were good only for two days from the date.³ The license system of the act of 1831, by which the free black must get a permit from a justice in order to buy liquor, may or may not have been a complete and utter failure, as the member from Dorchester said it was, in the counties; but it certainly proved to be such

---

¹ House Journal, 1827, 78, 252.
² 1818, 170.
³ 1858, 55. In default, there was the jail.

in Baltimore, the courts holding that the act did not apply to the city, through lack of precision in wording. Several liquor dealers were fined by justices, in 1855, for violating the act, but the court of common pleas stated, on appeal, that the act had been held to be inapplicable to the city, that all action under it had been suppressed, and that to try to enforce it would be as unjust as *ex post facto* legislation.[1]

The House of Delegates, in 1805, referred to a committee a petition from some residents of Harford county for a law to limit the number of dogs which any family could keep, and to forbid all negroes to keep any dogs. The next session, came another petition from Harford, that negroes might be barred from keeping dogs and guns. A bill was accordingly passed—Allegany county being first exempted and then included, by amendments—allowing a free black to keep one dog only, by a yearly license from a justice, and making any free black who should go abroad with any fire-arm, liable to forfeit the same to an informer, and to pay all costs, unless he had a certificate from a justice, renewable yearly, that he was an orderly and peaceable person. Slaves could not keep dogs; and they had long been forbidden to carry fire-arms off their master's estate without leave.[2] Efforts for further and evi-

---

[1] The city counsellor also stated, on inquiry from the council, that the corporation had no power, under the existing laws, to prohibit the sale of liquor to free negroes. Court of common pleas, reported in the Baltimore *Sun*, March 29th and 30th, 1855.

The courts were empowered to revoke any licenses, ordinarily, when complaints were made against the holders by the grand jury. But acts of 1841 (273) and 1845 (131, 281) empowered the courts for Anne Arundel, Calvert, Howard and Prince George's, to examine into the case of anyone holding a license, on complaint of one inhabitant of Maryland—except in Calvert, where three residents must complain—and to revoke the license, if the accused were found guilty of dealing unlawfully with blacks.

[2] 1806, 81; 1715, 44.

dently more stringent legislation were made from time to time, and in 1824, free blacks were absolutely forbidden to carry fire-arms. The next year, in answer to a petition from Kent, to restore the privileges under certain conditions to the free blacks of that county, the House committee reported that they had been under the impression for some time, as these intelligent and respectable petitioners then were, that such privileges might be allowed under careful provisions, but had concluded that action was not then advisable. Several years later the House concurred again in a similar unfavorable report from the committee on Grievances.[1] The restrictions were evidently directed chiefly against injury to sheep and other farm property. By the act of 1831, free blacks could carry fire-arms, if they could obtain licenses from the courts. These licenses were to be renewed yearly, and could be withdrawn at any time by the court or by any one judge. The right to carry powder or lead was included; and a black who might be convicted by a justice of carrying arms or ammunition without leave, had to forfeit such to the informer and pay costs; and for a second offence, to be subject to punishment for a felony, or be whipped. And the sale of gunpowder or shot or lead to a free black was prohibited, under fine, unless he had a permit from a justice, directed specially to the seller.[2] At the next session, there was added that any fire-arms taken already and not forfeited to the informer, should be sold by the officers, and the proceeds, after expenses, be given the blacks. We find mention in the paper in March, 1859, of the arrest for examination of two blacks, coming to Baltimore in a Philadelphia train, with a gun. After the John Brown attack on Harper's Ferry, the courts in several of the lower counties, with large slave populations, withdrew

---

[1] 1824, 203; House Journal, 1825, 241; 1830, 198, 222.
[2] 1831, 323. A slave had to have a permit from his employer. This provision, like that against the sale of liquor to blacks, could not have been enforced in Baltimore city. See above.

all licenses for arms. In many places, search was made for fire-arms on the premises of blacks.[1] In 1838 and again in 1852, petitions were sent the Assembly, in vain, from Somerset county—one bearing the names of one hundred and one voters—to protect the inhabitants thereof from the evil consequences of allowing negroes to keep dogs,—but the orderly black still kept his one dog, if he had a justice's license. A white could keep as many dogs as he wished, but those dogs who were complained of for killing sheep, had to be killed.[2]

By the act of 1796 on negroes, "any free negro, mulatto or other person," found by a magistrate, on examination, to be living idly, without visible means of support, could be put under bond of not over thirty dollars for good behavior, or in default, be ordered to leave Maryland within five days. For refusing to go, or returning within six months, the vagrant could be committed to jail. In this case, if prison charges were not paid within twenty days, he could be sold by the sheriff, with the approval of any two justices of the county, to serve for not over six months, the balance of proceeds, after charges were paid, to go to the county.[3] These provisions are repeated in the act of 1825—but for vagrant free colored persons *only;* and fifteen days instead of five were

---

[1] Baltimore *Sun*, Dec. 12th, 17th and 23rd, 1859. Executive messages.

[2] House Journal, 1838, 223. See Code of 1860, article on sheep. An act of 1854, to protect sheep, put a tax on all dogs in Kent county, outside of the towns, and forbade negroes to keep any bitches there.

[3] See acts of 1796, 30, and 1797, 56, giving powers to Annapolis and Georgetown to suppress vagrants. In Annapolis, by a by-law of 1797, *any person* who could not give good account of himself and of his means of livelihood could be put under bond, or committed in default; and then, in lack of means to pay prison fees, might be sold in the same way for not over four months, in the discretion of the mayor.

given, before banishment, with the important proviso that the black should not be compelled to go if, within that time, he hired himself for not less than three months to some responsible citizen. He might also appeal from the decision of the justice to the county court, on giving reasonable security for appearance and prosecution. Old and infirm free blacks who could not labor for a living were to be cared for by the counties. Constables were ordered to take special oath to take up vagrant blacks and their neglected children. By the act of 1839, the magistrate courts,—or where there were none, the orphans' courts,—were to summon all necessary witnesses for the examination of any free black arrested as a vagrant. If found to be without the necessary means of support and not of good and industrious habits, he, or she, would be sold at auction as a slave for the current year. A bond, with security, was then given the black for the payment to him, at the end of his service, of the price paid, less certain fixed charges. The purchaser was also ordered to give him good and sufficient food, lodging and clothing. But if, within ten days from the end of the term, the black did not leave Maryland, or hire himself out to some respectable white, to serve as a slave for a year, he would be again sold by the courts, and so on, yearly.[1] So the law remained, save that after 1842 jurisdiction under the act was given also to justices of peace.

The children of lazy and worthless or vagrant free negroes could be bound out as apprentices in the same way that the children of pauper or vagrant whites were bound. In 1818, a bill to empower the orphans' courts to bind out, in their discretion, those free black children who were not at service or not learning a trade, passed the House of Delegates by a small majority, and was amended by the Senate so as to exempt those also who were employed in the services of their parents.

---

[1] 1796, 67, (20); 1825, 161; 1839, 38; 1842, 231.
[2] 1793, 45, and 1808, 54; 1818, 189, House Journal, 109, 110; 1839, 35.

The terms and conditions provided for the idle and neglected who were bound out, were those in use for whites, save that a female might be bound to eighteen instead of sixteen years, and that the courts might require, in place of the customary instruction in reading and writing, an extra freedom due of not over thirty dollars. As with whites, the wishes of the parents were to be consulted in the choice of the masters, as far as possible. After 1839, the orphans' courts could bind out any free black children whose parents had not the means to support them and were not willing to care for them and keep them honestly employed, so as to learn habits of industry. As to masters, the choice of the parents—or of the children, if orphans—was to be consulted as far as possible. An apprentice could be transferred to another master, if in the same county, and if the court approved. And runaway apprentices might be adjudged to serve additional time, as was done with whites, or might be sold for the balance of the term to anyone in the State, if the courts were satisfied that they had not been induced to run away by ill-treatment or fraud on the master's part. A special act for Harford county, —which creates the presumption that in that county, at least, the law had been ill enforced,—made any constable or magistrate who failed to execute the law, when called on, liable to be turned out of office and fined. Persons holding apprentices were forbidden to allow them to remain in the custody or employment of free blacks. Throughout the State, constables were entitled to a fee of two dollars from the master to whom a black child was bound, for bringing the child before the court. In several counties, after 1856, the courts were empowered, in their discretion, to require masters to give additional freedom dues to black apprentices and to secure reasonable sums also to their parents, as—so reads the preamble—free black children were sometimes bound out while those who raised them were left in poverty, and as it was but just that the services of black apprentices, who had become valuable to farmers and others, should be compensated in certain cases.[1] White children, of course, were frequently bound out, especially orphans, children of paupers, and those committed to the House of Refuge and other institutions.

We find mention in the papers of several sales of vagrant free blacks in the counties. One constable, in Caroline county, was reported to have brought thirteen before the orphans' court, of whom several were sold for the rest of the year, and the children were bound out.[2] The punishment for vagrant and vagabond whites was usually a short term in the almshouse or jail. In Baltimore city, by authority of special acts, "any person" found to be idle, without visible means of support, a vagrant, a beggar or disorderly person, was to be bound out, or put in the House of Refuge, or to be sent to the almshouse—after 1854, for not over two months for the first offence, and never for more than six months. The number of vagrants thus committed by magistrates to the almshouse of Baltimore city and county in 1853, for instance, was two hundred and thirty whites and thirty-seven blacks; in 1854, two hundred and sixty-nine whites and thirty-nine blacks. After greater efforts had been made to put down rowdyism and vagabondism in Baltimore, the number of white vagrants rose, in 1857, to over four hundred, and in 1858, to over five hundred, while that of the blacks remained under fifty. The total number of blacks—vagrants, paupers, sick—in the almshouse in January, 1853, was one hundred and thirty-two to five hundred and eighty-five whites; in January, 1854, one hundred and twenty-two to six hundred and forty-eight whites; in January, 1857 and 1858, the proportion of blacks was less —it may have been on the average, for several years, about one black to five whites. In Baltimore city and county

---

[1] 1846, 355. 1856, 87, for Caroline, Kent, Somerset and Worcester. There were some differences in the different counties in the binding out of apprentices, but the orphans' courts had general oversight, everywhere. In Worcester and Somerset counties, free black apprentices might be hired out, by leave of the courts, for not less than a year. 1856, 78; 1860, 75.

[2] Denton *Journal*, quoted in the Baltimore *Sun*, July 31st, 1855.

together there was, in the same round numbers, about one free black to seven whites.[1]

In 1836, the inquiry was made—evidently without answer—in the Senate, as to the expediency of compelling free blacks of the laboring class to hire themselves out by the year. The House committee reported, the next year, in reply to the suggestion of a member from Calvert county that all free blacks be forced to labor by the year, that such a measure would be at war with all preconceived opinions of propriety, as it would bring the free blacks in direct contact with the slaves—a state of things to be carefully avoided.[2] In 1845, a bill was introduced in the House, to compel the free blacks of Prince George's County, capable of labor, to hire out by the year. Calvert, Charles and St. Mary's, all large slaveholding counties, were added, but the bill was rejected by the Senate. Two years later, leave was given for a bill to better the condition of the free blacks in Prince George's, but we know nothing of the plans proposed. In 1852, the House committee was ordered to report a bill to enforce the provisions of the several acts of Assembly for the suppression of vagrancy among the blacks. There is mention, at that session, of a bill for "the government, regulation and disposition" of the free

---

[1] The almshouse was for the city and county.

We presume that idle or vagrant free blacks were not—certainly not as a rule—sold in Baltimore under the act of 1839, from the fact of these commitments under the acts of 1818, 169, and 1854, 116, for Baltimore, and as we have not seen mention of any sale in the daily papers from 1850–1860. The change in proportion between white and black inmates of the almshouse, and between whites and blacks committed to it as vagrants, may be due to the fact that efforts were made to enforce the laws, and—if we may believe all reports of that time—the vast majority of the rowdies and disorderly persons in Baltimore were whites. See the papers, the messages of the mayor, as in 1850 and 1858, and the reports of the marshal of police. Thus, of 1003 persons arrested for violations of law in May, 1859, 907 were white and 116 colored. Of 537 police "lodgers," the next month, only 48 were black.

[2] House Journal, 1837, 108, 173.

blacks, which was referred to the next Assembly. It seems, from what is said of its contents, to have given means for the stricter binding out of free blacks, and to have forbidden manumission except on condition of emigration to Africa. Brought up in the House, at the next session accordingly, it was three times rejected.[1] At the same session, a bill to furnish a remedy against free blacks who might quit service after hiring out, was first rejected by thirty-six to eight, was reconsidered and passed by forty to ten, and then finally rejected again. At the next session, 1854, the same or a similar bill was rejected by twenty-six to nineteen, was then reconsidered and rejected by twenty-eight to twenty, and was finally passed by forty-one to nineteen. In the Senate, it was first rejected by eight to four, and afterwards passed without opposition. This act declared guilty of misdemeanor any free black who might leave without proper cause, before the expiration of the time agreed, the service of one to whom he had hired himself. The black could be arrested on a warrant, and judgment on the case was to be given by the magistrate according to equity, each party having the right to produce witnesses. The oath of the employer and the evidence of some other person that the black had engaged in such service, was declared *prima facie* evidence of the contract; but the justice must be satisfied that the wages were reasonably secure to the black, and that he had not left service from improper treatment or other good cause. If convicted, he had to fulfil his agreement, compensate for lost time, and pay costs. If duly convicted of a second offence, he might be put in jail for not over a week, and be treated as a free negro apprentice. If a black were convicted of having agreed in writing, or by supplement of two years later, of receiving wages in advance on a verbal agreement, to hire out, and of having then hired out to another without cause for breaking his agreement, the first employer could sue to recover two-fifths of the wages agreed on. But

---

[1] House Journal, 1853; Feb. 5th—May.

it was specially provided that nothing in the act should be construed to debar any free black from prosecuting any action for cruel treatment or improper usage on the part of his employer.[1]

In 1850, the Kent county *News* had complained that laborers were scarcer than ever before, and attributed the fact to the refusal of free negroes to hire out on the farms as they used to do. In the winter of '55, there were complaints in the counties of scarcity of labor. Likely negroes were bringing high wages, and several farmers of Queen Anne's, according to the Centreville *Sentinel*, had gotten apprentices from the Phildelphia house of refuge. There were the same complaints the following summer. The Cambridge *Democrat* says that some farmers of Dorchester had called a meeting to consider what wages should be paid, as high rates were expected. Another local paper wisely regretted, the next year, that the farmers could not get hold of the able-bodied men who were loafing about the cities.[2]

It was during the winter of 1829–30 that Mr. William Lloyd Garrison was editing in Baltimore the *Genius of Universal Emancipation*, declaring that to hold slaves longer in bondage was both unnecessary and tyrannical, that justice demanded their liberation, and that to recompense slave owners for emancipation would be paying a thief for giving up stolen property.[3] But the press was free, and for such

---

[1] 1854, 273; 1856, 252. There were also penalties against those who might knowingly employ free blacks convicted under the act, within a limited time after conviction. The first employer would have a lien on the earnings of the black.

[2] See Baltimore *Sun*, 1850, Jan. 15th; 1855, Jan. 3rd, Feb. 16th, June 16th; 1856, Jan. 7th, &c.

[3] Life of Garrison, Vol. II, 143, 151. The indictment under which Mr. Garrison was imprisoned in Baltimore Jail, in 1830, was for libel against certain persons. He left Baltimore some weeks after his release.

general statements, however displeasing they may have been, there was no redress at law. In 1835, a supplement to the act of 1831 declared it to be a high offence, to be punished by imprisonment for from ten to twenty years, for any person whatever to take any part, knowingly, in the preparation or circulation of any printed or written matter having a tendency to create discontent among the colored people, or to stir them to insurrection. In 1841, a further supplement prescribed the same penalty for any free colored person who should, knowingly, call for or receive at any postoffice, or receive or have in his or her possession, any abolition hand-bill, pamphlet, newspaper, pictorial representation or other paper of an inflammatory character. And it was declared the duty of everyone, under penalty for neglect of a fine of not less than five hundred dollars or of not less than two months in jail, to inform against any free black who might be, or might have been, in possession of any such papers. And grand juries were ordered to have summoned before them at every term of court, for due examination, all the postmasters, deputies and agents, in their jurisdictions. This bill passed the House without roll-call or special mention, but was first defeated by the Senate, and passed on reconsideration.[1] The next year, the act was so modified that postmasters need not be summoned before the juries unless it were deemed necessary, and there was added that on the complaint to a justice of anyone, under oath, that a free black was thought to be having or circulating or furnishing to slaves, any abolition or "free papers," a constable and not less than three respectable citizens should be empowered to search the premises of the black, using as little violence to his feelings as might be compatible with a diligent search.

At the April term, 1857, of the circuit court for Dorchester county, a free black was tried—before the court by his choice—on two indictments. On one he was found not guilty, but

---

[1] See 1835, 325; 1841, 272; 1842, 163.

on the other, for knowingly having in his possession "Uncle Tom's Cabin," he was given the minimum term of ten years.[1] The courts may, of course, have regularly charged the grand juries with these acts at each term, as they were bidden to do, without any mention being made of it in the Baltimore papers, but in the spring and summer of 1860, after the John Brown invasion, we find special mention of charges to the juries by the courts for Baltimore, Frederick, Harford, Howard, Kent and Queen Anne's counties. The "Helper Book" and the *New York Tribune* seem to have given the most uneasiness. A free black was arrested in Harford county in February, 1860, but the indictment was quashed at the spring term of court. The incendiary document in this case was said in the papers to be the *New York Tribune*. In November following, a white man was tried in Dorchester for circulating *Helper's Impending Crisis*, but the jury found not guilty.[2]

The act of 1809—which, with the building of the penitentiary, marks most prominently the era of new ideas of crimes

---

[1] This negro was pardoned by the Governor of Maryland in 1862, on condition of his leaving the State, on the representation of a prominent citizen of Baltimore that he had been innocent of any attempt at violation of the law. It was said that the book had been left in his house by people who wished to get him into trouble.

[2] We find mention of the arrest of two other whites in the spring of 1860. See Baltimore *Sun*, for May 3rd and May 24th. The Chestertown *News* says that the grand jury of Kent thought it the duty of postmasters to read everything in papers received, but the judge said the general character of a paper was sufficient. See Baltimore *Sun*, April 24th, 1860. It is interesting to note that the Baltimore city Police Commissioners were not allowed to employ on the police any "black Republican" or endorser of the "Helper Book." See Code of 1860, Local Laws. In 1835 (*Niles' Register*, Vol. XLIX, 7) fourteen ministers of the annual conference of the Methodist Episcopal church, while approving of gradual emancipation, begged abolitionists to desist from spreading inflammatory papers, which could only embarrass the blacks, slave and free. In 1847, the House of Delegates laid on the table petitions from the citizens of Cecil county, both to allow and to prevent abolition lectures in Maryland.

and punishments—provided that slaves convicted of crimes for which the penalty was not hanging, might, in the discretion of the court, be whipped and banished by sale into some "foreign country"; but there was no line drawn between freemen, white and black. In 1817 there was enacted that no colored person should thereafter be sentenced to the penitentiary for less than one year; and that in all cases where the term prescribed was less than a year, or where the court, in the exercise of its discretion, might deem so long a punishment as a year unjust, the black should be whipped, fined or imprisoned in jail, as the court might adjudge. The next year the penitentiary was closed entirely to slaves who, in non-capital cases, were to be whipped or banished from Maryland. In 1821 a bill was introduced in the House to forbid also the punishment of free blacks by imprisonment in the penitentiary, but it was referred to the next Assembly. The question does not seem to have come up again until 1825, when a bill for that purpose was passed, after some opposition. No person was to be sent to the penitentiary for less than two years, and no free black for any term. For any crime not punished by hanging, a free black would be sentenced, in the discretion of the court, to not over forty lashes on the bare back—a slave could be given up to one hundred, by the act of 1809—or to banishment from Maryland and sale as a slave for the same number of years that a white would be imprisoned. The convict was given an official copy of the judgment. The proceeds of the sale paid for expenses, indemnified any injured parties, and the balance went into the county or city treasury.[1] Within a few days of the beginning of the next session, a resolution was offered to refer the operation of this new law to the committee on Grievances, to report amendments, if desirable; as it was obvious that great abuses would prevail under it, inasmuch as—the record of judgment being liable to be

---

[1] 1809, 138 (9); 1817, 72; 1818, 197; 1825, 93. The District of Columbia was excepted in the acts of 1818 and 1825.

destroyed by the purchasers—it was feared that in most cases the sentence of sale for a year would in effect amount to sale for life. This resolution was adopted after two readings; but when the mover asked leave, two months later, to introduce a bill to repeal or modify the act of 1825, the House voted against him by forty to thirty-two, seven members calling for the ayes and nays, and the committee was discharged from further consideration of the matter. Later in the session, however, the law was so changed that a free black was again imprisoned for crime, as a white man was, but on discharge from the penitentiary, whether by the expiration of the term or by pardon, he was given not over thirty dollars, from the results of his labor, and was banished the State within sixty days— under penalty of being sold as a slave for a term equal to the original sentence, for the benefit of anyone who might find him and could prove the facts of the case to a judge or two justices of the county.[1] The act of 1831 allowed the courts, in their discretion, to punish free blacks for offences not capital by the ordinary penalties, or by banishment "by transportation into some foreign country." It does not seem probable that many were banished under this provision, for we find numbers of them sent to the penitentiary in the following years. From November, 1832, to November, 1835, one hundred and forty-nine were sent from Baltimore city and county, as against one hundred and four whites. The act of '31, also, we remember, made free negroes liable to the same treatment and penalties as were given slaves, if they were convicted of taking part with slaves in any misdemeanor for which slaves were punished by a justice. For many petty offences, notably under local laws, free blacks could be whipped where whites would be put in jail.[2] The next important general law was

---

[1] 1826, 229; House Journal, 47, 422.
[2] 1831, 323, 8. Thus by 1852, 57, any negro who took oysters unlawfully in Worcester county, and who could not pay the fine, might be given not over thirty-nine lashes. In Baltimore jail, under act of 1831, 58, prisoners

that of 1835, which ordered the criminal courts to examine every free black convicted before them, and empowered them if they found that he, or she, had been previously sentenced to the penitentiary for any crime, to have him sold for a term of years without the State. The proceeds of such sales, after paying the expenses of prosecution, went to the public treasury. Three years later this was changed so as to pay one-fourth the net proceeds as a reward to the officer who apprehended and prosecuted the black.[1] In 1842, as we saw, the penalty for any free black convicted of dealing in any stolen goods was fixed at banishment and sale as a slave for from five to ten years, and that for a second offence in taking part in unlawful societies, was sale for life. Also, by act of 1849, the penalty for a second conviction of certain frauds on the revenue, might be sale out of the State. In 1836, leave had been given for the introduction of a bill, to punish by sale as slaves for life out of Maryland, free blacks convicted of felony in general— the old act of '25 revived with greater harshness. The committee on Colored Population was opposed to the plan, but

---

were worked with their own consent, but vagrants, slaves and free negroes had to work without option, if ordered. By 1837, 228, the penalty for injuring certain gates on public roads in Charles and Prince George's counties, was fine of not over ten dollars, or not over thirty-nine lashes for a slave, on conviction before a magistrate, and "any white person" aggrieved could appeal to the county court.

By many town ordinances, free blacks as well as slaves could be whipped for roaming about at night, &c.

[1] 1835, 200; 1838, 69. This must have been intended to reënforce the act of 1826, which had banished from Maryland all free blacks discharged from the penitentiary, under penalty of sale for the benefit of the finder. A petition from sundry citizens of Caroline, for a repeal of this provision of the act of 1826, was presented the House in 1838; but it is found in the Code of 1860, art. 30, 99. In a case before Baltimore county court, in 1841, the counsel for the negro claimed that the identity of a negro punished under the act of 1835, was a question for a jury to decide; but the court held that the act was merely for the regulation of the court in inflicting punishment, and raised no new issue. (See *Niles' Register*, Vol. LXI, 217.)

advised its reference to the committee on Crimes. This committee reported favorably, but the matter was postponed. In 1842, some one suggested, to no result, an inquiry into the plan of banishing to Africa all free blacks liable to imprisonment, and in 1845, certain citizens of Charles county asked for whipping and transportation for them; but the committee on Crimes did not evidently approve of any change. In 1853 there were two requests for enquiries into the wisdom of changing the laws so as to sell free black convicts for the benefit of the counties, instead of supporting them in the penitentiary. In 1856, a bill was introduced, to sell out of Maryland for the balance of their terms, all the free negroes then in that institution, the proceeds to go to the State treasury; and to sell the slaves for life, the proceeds to go to the counties which had already paid the masters.[1] Baltimore city and county had sent to the penitentiary, in 1852, twenty-nine whites and eighteen blacks, slave and free; in '53, forty-seven whites to twenty-one blacks; in '54, sixty to nineteen; in '56, thirty-eight to ten; in '57, twenty-eight to nineteen. A number of blacks were sold out of the State, most of them as having been already prison-birds, probably. At one term of Baltimore criminal court, in 1853, nine were sold; at another, two. The next year, two were sold at one term, four at another, and one at another. At the following winter term, four were sold. The number of blacks committed to the penitentiary had not increased in proportion to the whites, though slaves had been again imprisoned for serious offences after 1845, but the accommodations of the institution were insufficient for the total number of inmates. The executive message of 1854 called attention to the fact that for twenty years, with three exceptions, the annual expenditures were in excess of the receipts from labor. At the next Assembly, the bad condition

---

[1] House Journal, 1836, 198; 1842, 39; 1845, 27; 1853, 27, 285; 1856, 618, 683.

of the buildings was carefully pointed out. The message of 1858 declared the institution in great financial embarrassment, one wing of the building having been burned, in addition to the usual deficit, and advised a change of the law so that slaves might be transported, as before 1845, in order to reduce the four hundred and more inmates, of whom from a third to a half were negroes. A special House committee reported at the same session the need of fifty thousand dollars, and declared boldly that the over-crowded buildings were almost a "pest house." Something must be done, and a change in the punishment of petty larceny was suggested.[1] The Assembly chose to change radically the punishment of the free blacks. For stealing any goods under the value of five dollars, or for breaking into any store, barn or outbuilding and stealing goods under the value of one dollar, or for simple larceny above five dollars, the penalty for a free black was sale as a slave for from two to five years.[2] For wounding or killing wilfully a horse or mule not trespassing on his land, from two to four years. For stealing any horse or mule, sale for from two to fourteen years; for stealing a vessel or a slave, from three to twelve years; for persuading or aiding any slave or black apprentice to run away, for not less than five years—in all three cases, either within or beyond the State. For arson, instead of hanging or not over twenty years' imprisonment, a free black must be hung or sold as a slave for life, within or beyond the State. In cases of robbery, only, the choice was left to the courts between the ordinary imprisonment in the

---

[1] 1858, Doc. O. "Should a contagion," added the committee, "visit the prison, which may God in his mercy avert, no prediction can be made as to its consequences, not only as to the prison, but to the city in general." If the solution of the problem was to be the reduction on a large scale of the inmates, it is obvious that the Governor's suggestion would be insufficient, for the larger part of the negroes were freemen convicted of larceny.—an offence for which slaves were not imprisoned.

[2] The minimum term for which anyone could be sentenced to the penitentiary had been fixed at eighteen months (1839, 37). Imprisonment for enticing or aiding a slave to escape was from two to five years (1844, 80).

penitentiary for from three to ten years, or sale for ten years. The proceeds of the sale of any black paid for the expenses of prosecution and any just claims for damages, and any balance was given the county or city for the use and maintenance of any indigent child or wife he might leave. Not only was the convict furnished with a certified copy of the judgment, but the sheriff was ordered to give notice in the paper of the neighborhood where he had been convicted—or by posters in each election district of the county, if there was no paper published there—of the coming expiration of the term of service, for three successive weeks preceding the expiration. There was provided also the penalty of not less than one hundred dollars fine, or not over two months in jail, for a sheriff or clerk of court neglecting wilfully the duties of the act. And anyone who sold a convict for a longer time than his term, or in anyway deprived him of freedom, when it was due, was liable to be fined double the sum paid for the black, and in default, to be imprisoned for from thirty to ninety days, or to be fined and imprisoned.

During the two years following the passage of this act, eighty-nine free blacks in all were sold, twenty-four by the courts of Baltimore city, eleven in Baltimore county, eight in Harford, seven, each, in Dorchester, Frederick and Talbot, &c. Four of these were sold for life; but the average term was between four and five years. The crime seems to have been invariably larceny of some degree. Without the act of 1858, said the committee on Colored Population in their report to the House, the number of free blacks in the penitentiary would have been two hundred and ten instead of one hundred and twenty-one. The number of slaves imprisoned was only thirteen.[1] During the year 1860, sixteen men and ten

---

[1] Report of House committee, Feb. 7th, 1860. Baltimore jail had twenty-one free blacks and two slaves. In 1861, there were seventeen blacks sold and one black and thirty-seven whites sent to the penitentiary from Baltimore jail.

women were sold from Baltimore jail, and one negro only sent thence to the penitentiary—against fifty-three whites. It is obvious that the objections raised in 1826, that the sale of free blacks for a term of years out of the State amounted often, to say the least, to sale for life, were equally patent against this act of 1858.[1] For larceny and two other offences, the act of 1858 ordered simply the sale as a slave. One black, who was sentenced for simple larceny by the circuit court for Baltimore city in 1859, to be sold out of Maryland for five years, carried his case to the Court of Appeals, which held the sentence to be illegal, as allowing the black to be purchased by a non-resident only, instead of by a resident or non-resident, according to the chances of sale at auction.[2] In 1860 the law was changed in so far that a free black convicted of any offence for which a white man would be sent to the penitentiary, was sold either in or out of Maryland, at the discretion of the court, for as long a time as a white man would be imprisoned. The proceeds went, as before, after paying the expenses of prosecution and damages, to the family of the convict, but if there was no family, to the county or city.[3]

The number of Whites and Blacks committed to Baltimore jail for...	1852		1853		1854		1857		1858		1859		1860	
	W.	B.	W.	B.	W.	B.	W.	B.	W.	B.	W.	B.	W.	B.
For murder	21	3	56	1	11	1	28	2	51	2	32	6	28	4
For assault and battery	208	27	307	71	349	86	383	100	485	72	316	61	501	47
For felony	241	125	225	132	374	138	337	108	417	115	351	109	263	150
For drunkenness											1730	195	610	133
Peace warrants							1498	618	1880	690	1353	433	2577	460

The population of Baltimore in 1860 was 134,520 whites, 25,680 free blacks, and 2,218 slaves.

[1] How could a black sold to a Louisiana planter be helped in his claim to freedom, years after, by the sheriff's notice in a Maryland county paper?

[2] 14 Md., 412. The offence in this case was larceny of a silver watch valued at six dollars. The black was discharged, the judgment being held to be more than a technical amplification of the law. A free black sold in Maryland for a term of years would, of course, have the benefit of the law regulating the transportation of slaves for terms of years.

[3] Code of 1860, Art. 30, 194.

Such, in general, was the legal status of the free negroes in Maryland. One is not likely, in studying it, to lose sight of the influence of slaveholding; but it would evidently be most unjust to measure all this legislation by the gauge of hostility to the free black. The easy license system for the sale of liquor to free blacks in the counties, must have injured the liquor dealers only and been of real service to the blacks. The fondness of the negro for drink is well known. If an honest black was sometimes put to slight trouble over the sale of his produce, there were many others who felt no conscience to keep them from pilfering. Of the convictions in Liberia, as reported by the officials from 1828 to 1844, two hundred and ninety-one were for larceny against eighty-two for all other offences.[1] Many of the free blacks in Maryland were going to the towns, one to become prosperous and respected, while a half-dozen others stood about in the sun, working at small jobs for a week in order to live from the proceeds for a month. The idea that the free blacks were not a desirable part of the population was not confined to the Southern slaveholding States.[2]

We have touched, in passing, on plans that were advanced for the further regulation or disposition of the free

---

[1] The population had then grown to be nearly 2400. As a rule, emigrants to Liberia were the best negroes.

[2] See, for instance, the report of a committee to the Massachusetts Legislature in 1821, by Mr. Theodore Lyman, Jr. See *Niles' Register*, Vol. XX, 311; and Dr. Moore's Slavery in Massachusetts.

Dr. Chas. Deane says (Proceedings Am. Antiquarian Soc., Oct., 1886): 'It is not to be denied that the negro race, bond or free, was not regarded, here (*i. e.* in Mass.) as a desirable element of the population. They were generally ignorant and degraded, and required to be looked after and cared for as children, and strict regulations were made to ensure order among them, to see that they should have employment, and to provide for a healthy sanitary condition."

blacks of Maryland. It will be well to notice these and other plans, more carefully, in chronological order.

In 1817, a number of gentlemen of Baltimore had associated together, to further the work of the American Colonization Society; and the Assembly of that year resolved unanimously to communicate to the President of the United States and to the senators and representatives from Maryland, the opinion that a wise and provident policy suggested the acquisition of a tract of land on the coast of Africa, for the colonization of the free blacks of the country. Two years later, another and similar communication was sent to the members of Congress from the State, and the House of Delegates regretted that the State finances would not allow a contribution to the deserving efforts of the Colonization Society. In 1826, one thousand dollars was appropriated, to be given annually for the work of the Society among the free blacks of Maryland—the only plan, reads the act, which can promise practical benefit both to the country and to that class which it is intended to relieve. In 1830, the Maryland branch of the society was incorporated.[1] In 1818, a bill for the registration of all free blacks in Maryland passed the House but was rejected by the Senate. In 1821, there was some effort made in the House for a bill of the same nature. The free blacks, then growing into quite a class of the community, were looked on with growing disfavor. In a correspondence, over runaway slaves, with the authorities of Pennsylvania, the Maryland commissioners said that it seemed to them impossible in the nature of things that free blacks could be amalgamated with the whites. However liberal we may feel towards them, said the commissioners, they cannot be given the enjoyment of every political privilege, and must be in some ways a distinct portion of the community. And Pennsylvania, they added, if reports were true, had already felt the burden of a free black popula-

---

[1] Griffith's Annals of Baltimore, 223; 1817, Res. 5; 1819, Res. 58, House Journal for Jan. 3d, 1820; 1825, Res. 53; 1826, ch. 172; 1830, 189.

tion—a people usually extremely dissolute and idle, and consequently a public nuisance. A series of papers in *Niles' Register*, published in Baltimore, had already called earnestly for the abolition of slavery—"this blot, or curse," it said, which no righteous man or lover of republican institutions could believe to be permanent—but on condition that provision be made for the separation of the freed-men from the slaves, as the mixture of them was fatal to the improvement of both and at open war with the safety of person and property of the whites. A special committee of five members of the House of Delegates, on certain communications from the Legislatures of Georgia and Missouri, on colonization, in 1829, expressed the opinion that no one probably, at that enlightened day, would doubt that the existence of a free black population was a national evil, which might tend to embarrass the wholesome operations of the government: but all this preamble to their report was struck out by the House. At this same session, the House received four petitions, mostly from citizens of Somerset county, for changes in the law on manumission—doubtless to restrict the privilege—and for a tax on free blacks. These were referred to the committee on Grievances, evidently without any answer.[1]

Late in the summer of 1831 occurred the insurrection in Southampton county, Virginia. Early in the session of the Maryland Assembly, the December following, a joint committee of five senators and seven members was appointed, on the suggestion of the House that the colored population of the State had been a subject of absorbing interest, and that experience demonstrated that some legislative action was indispensable at that session. To the consideration of this committee were referred some twenty petitions and memorials, from all parts

---

[1] House Journals, 1818, 37, 116; 1821, 9; 1822, 164; *Niles' Register*, Vol. 16, pp. 177, 211; House Journals, 1829, Jan. 1st-18th, pp. 336, 547. Mr. Reverdy Johnson was probably the writer of the communication to Pennsylvania, as the House asked him to continue the correspondence.

of the State. Several of these, signed by many and highly respectable citizens—notably one from Baltimore—asked for abolition of slavery. Others desired to have manumission made conditional on the removal of the freedmen. Others, still, more stringent police regulation of the free blacks. A motion to have all these memorials printed for the use of the House, was lost by a large majority, but a thousand copies of the report of the committee were ordered. After several weeks, the committee introduced a bill on the free black population, which, after some amendments, became the act of '31 on free negroes and slaves. Copies of the bill were distributed, and it was laid on the table for several weeks by request of the committee. After careful consideration, it passed the House by a vote of forty-five to ten.[1] We are familiar with its general provisions—restrictions on the immigration of free negroes and the importation of slaves, on the use of firearms by blacks, on the sale of liquor and other dealings with them, on religious meetings; and the grant to the courts of the power to banish free blacks convicted of non-capital, serious offences, and to punish like slaves such free blacks as might be convicted of petty offences with slaves. But harder questions for the committee to answer were those relating to abolition of slavery and to the black population already in the State. That this population was injurious to the prosperity of the State, they frankly granted. Recent events had proven to the people that there must be a separation of the races. The question was to find a remedy which the State could apply, consistent with its honor, and with a due regard to the welfare of the blacks, that unfortunate class of the population. Emancipation, as it had been tried, had been a doubtful gift to all concerned; economic benefits, especially in the value of lands, would result to the State from the removal of slavery; and so the committee advised the plan of colonization in Africa, of manumission conditional, as a rule, on emigration.

---

[1] 1831, ch. 323. House Journal, 94, 114, 304, 310, 467, 544.

An annual expenditure, they asserted, of forty thousand and two hundred dollars, would remove entirely the colored persons in Maryland within a generation.[1] Such was the policy proposed for the State. Meantime, the Maryland Colonization Society was being formed by a number of gentlemen, for the removal to Africa of those free blacks who might be willing to go, and of slaves freed for the purpose. The act of 1831, embodying these suggestions of the committee, provided for the appointment by the Governor of a board of three managers, members of the Maryland Colonization Society, to take charge of the removal from the State of such blacks already free as should consent to emigrate, and of all those to be thereafter manumitted, whether they consented or not, unless they obtained annual permits to remain from the orphans' courts. Manumissions were to be reported to the board, and all sheriffs were to report a complete census of all free blacks, under penalty of two hundred dollars, and to keep the board informed of any who might be willing to emigrate. And the State appropriated then the sum of twenty thousand dollars for the expenses involved in the work during the current year, and pledged itself to further sums, not to exceed two hundred thousand dollars in all. An annual levy was ordered on the various counties and on Baltimore, in proportion to the free black population. The vote on this act in the House was thirty-seven to twenty-three.[2] The publication of these acts on negroes was ordered by the Assembly, in two of the newspapers in Baltimore and in one in every county. A resolution had already been passed, early in the session, calling on congressmen to obtain national aid, if necessary, by proposing an

---

[1] Report of committee on grievances, &c., on the colored population, 1831. The committee consisted, on the part of the Senate, of Messrs. Taney, Emory, Dennis, Wootton, Pigman; of the House, Brawner, of Charles county (chairman), Blakeston, of St. Mary's; Brewer, of Annapolis; Pearce, of Kent; Lake, of Dorchester; Carmichael, of Queen Anne's, and Handy, of Worcester.

[2] 1831, 281.

amendment to the Constitution, for removing the free blacks of the country.¹ The Maryland Colonization Society numbered among its members some of the most able and respected citizens of the State, and the abolition of slavery, as well as the removal of the free blacks, was one of the objects of the work which they now entered upon with the patronage of the State. But as compulsory emigration under the act of 1831 was not enforced—the members of the society not desiring it and public sentiment not demanding it—that work became the removal of those free blacks who could be persuaded to go, and of some of those who were freed especially for emigration. It was more costly work, too, than the committee of '31 had expected. In 1832, one hundred and forty-four—of whom some seventy-five were free born—were sent to Africa, at the cost of over five thousand dollars. This was the largest expedition. The next year eighteen were sent out, and eight thousand dollars were spent; the next year, again, fifty-seven were sent at a cost of nearly three thousand. Nor had the colonization taxes been cheerfully paid; in some counties they had not been levied by the spring of 1835. Some of the counties indeed had received no benefit whatever from the law. Of the first and largest expedition to Africa, ninety-one blacks, nearly two-thirds of all, had gone from Somerset, fourteen from Worcester, twelve from Caroline, ten from Cecil, &c., but here emigration from Worcester and Somerset had stopped, and eleven only had gone from Caroline, further, in 1835, and sixteen from Cecil in 1836. There were already requests from Somerset and St. Mary's counties to be exempted from the special tax. One black only had gone from the latter county, but its quota of the tax was two hundred and sixty-

---

¹ 1831, Res. 124. As "recent occurrences in this State as well as in other States of our Union, have impressed more deeply upon our minds the necessity" of means for such removal. A resolution of the next session asked for the appropriation of the funds from the sale of public land, for internal improvement, aid to education and aid to colonization. (Res. 28.)

three dollars yearly. Frederick county was to contribute nearly nine hundred and fifty dollars yearly, and only six blacks had emigrated from it up to 1836, when seventeen went. An act of 1834 ordered the levy courts to charge interest on back payments still due, and deficits in future were to be made up, temporarily at least, from the free school or other funds in the hands of the State treasurer.[1] In 1835, a bill to abolish the special tax throughout the State was left on the table. At the next session, the committee on Colored Population, being called on to report on the expediency of repealing entirely the act of 1831, of giving up colonization as the State policy, stated that colonization—adopted after the melancholy issue of the Southampton insurrection had warned that no time was to be lost in laying foundation for future security—still boded well. It has long been a maxim, added the committee, that the existence of separate and distinct castes in society is an inherent vice, pregnant with the most baneful consequences. The free black, dead to every generous prompting of ambition, because debarred of ultimate aim, has ever been an incubus on society. Our deepest, warmest sympathies they have, but while they remain among us, little more can be extended. A curse to our slaves, whom they are constantly corrupting, an evil to the whites, between whom and them the laws of God and nature have drawn lines never to be effaced, they must leave our shores if they would be happy and prosperous. On this report no action seems to have been taken.[2]

Meanwhile the plan was offered of requiring all free blacks to renew annually their certificates of freedom; but the committee reported—in which the House agreed—that confusion

---

[1] 1834, 197. In 1832 (Ch. 314) the appropriations to the American Colonization Society had reverted in part to the State, as these had not been drawn for several years. Certain taxes also went to the work of the State Society; as those on the introduction into Maryland of slaves who had been acquired by marriage, bequest or in distribution ($15 for every able negro, &c.). 1833, 87. See Report of Committee, 1840.

[2] See Report of House Committee on Colored Population, 1836.

would ensue and facilities for escape be given slaves, by the great number of certificates required, and that additional burdens would be thrown on the blacks, a large portion of whom were then scarcely able to procure the necessaries of life.¹ The committee was then ordered—there were thirteen votes against taking up their time over the matter—to consider the expediency of compelling free blacks to emigrate within a stated time. To drive the free blacks away, answered the committee, would be to send them to the free States, to make easier the path for runaway slaves, and to league with fanatic abolitionists. Then justice cries aloud against forced removal. However much every well-wisher of Maryland may desire to see her rid of the free blacks, at present a vicious and degraded population, yet we do not think, said the committee, that the enlightened legislators of the State are prepared, in the accomplishment of that desirable end, to steel their hearts against every consideration of justice and right. Should the proposed legislation be carried out, our consciences might remind us that the glorious result had been dearly purchased at the cost of State faith and justice; and some malignant foe of our institutions might point his finger at the Declaration of Independence and the State Bill of Rights, and call them unmeaning parchment. This report was left on the table, apparently.²

The Governor's message of 1837 spoke of the value of the colonization scheme, and stated that the attempts of the friends of immediate and general abolition to defeat the work of the Colonization Society's agents were losing force. In 1841, the committee on Colored Population summed up the work done since 1832 by the State board of managers. The total number of emigrants sent out had been six hundred and twenty-seven to Africa and twenty-five to Hayti. The amount drawn from the State had been over sixty-six thousand dollars.

---

¹ House Journal, 1835, 39, 48.
² See Report of Committee on Colored Population, 1836.

There had always been room in the vessels for more emigrants; owing somewhat to the work among the blacks of the enemies of colonization, the abolitionists.[1]

A number of slaveholders of Anne Arundel county met in September, 1841, and issued a call for a general convention of persons favorable to the protection of the slaveholding interests of the State. Delegations of twenty were to be appointed in each county and Howard district and the cities of Baltimore, Annapolis and Frederick. The convention, accordingly, assembled at Annapolis—in the hall of the House of Delegates—in the following January; but the list of members appointed give only one hundred and thirty-one—and Allegany, Caroline, Carroll and Worcester counties were not represented at all—instead of some four hundred and eighty, as called for by the September meeting.[2] The president and other prominent members urged prudence and caution: let these mark your deliberations, said the chair, the eyes of the whole world are upon us. The time was, said one member, when we had but few free blacks among us, and we entertained different feelings to them then from those feelings we hold now, when, by their approximation in numbers to the

---

[1] In July, 1832, thirty-one blacks had been sent off under the old State appropriation for colonization; adding these to those send under the act of 1831, some 800 were sent in all, at a cost of about $900.00 apiece. In one case only, we remember, was a sheriff called on, under the act of 1831, to remove forcibly a manumitted black. In this case, the fellow had had some dispute with his old master, and was carried over the line by the sheriff. Had the harsh features of the act been enforced, the results of colonization would, of course, have been very different. Under the auspices of the American Colonization Society, some 200 blacks had been sent from Maryland.

[2] See *Niles' Register*, vol. 61; Baltimore *American*. A number of the appointed delegates were not present, evidently, or at least did not remain, for on the second day there were only eighty-five. A reporter for a Northern abolition paper, who ventured there, was saved from summary punishment by the police. He was put in jail, and defended on his examination by one of the members of the convention, of Annapolis. The president of the convention was of Prince George's.

whites, we are forced to look to the shield of law to protect us. The increasing demand for relief from every part of the State calls for some action—to be, however, in a true spirit of justice to all concerned. We must at last appeal to the people, for laws have failed, and must fail, unless they have the sanction of the whole people of the State. The work of the convention was a long list of suggestions for legislation, to be presented to the Assembly then in session. The most important of these were,—prohibition of manumission except on condition of instant transportation at the expense of the manumittor, to some place out of the country.[1] Prohibition of all manumission by last will; as well as by deed, if prospective. No free blacks to enter Maryland except as servants of travelers; and strict regulations against the return of any who might once leave the State. No free black to be carried on any train or steamer out of the State, unless vouched for as a freeman by some one known to the conductor or captain; and the courts to appoint bailiffs, monthly, to watch the arrival and departure of all "common carriers," to prevent the escape of slaves. High rewards to be paid by the State for the conviction of those inducing or aiding slaves to escape; as well as rewards to be paid by the owners, according to the distance from home which the runaway had covered, when caught. The State to pay all expenses of any cases which might arise from the conflict between the laws of any State and the Fugitive Slave Law, in order to test the constitutionality of the law. No free black to be allowed to hold any real estate, or any leasehold interest running for more than a year. No sales or gifts of slaves to free blacks, under penalty of fine to the master conveying, and of sale out of the State to the black so conveyed. Every free black to give security, to be renewed

---

[1] This clause provoked some argument. One member—he who had defended the Northern reporter—opposed it as tending to entail slavery. Another said the blacks had long been invited to leave, but had refused to go. One member urged no manumission at all.

annually, for good behavior, under penalty for neglect of being hired out by a magistrate; ten dollars of his wages being paid the person who had taken him before the magistrate; and attempts to run away being provided against by a penalty of sale out of the State, if caught. After 1843, the children of all free blacks were to be bound out by the courts, from the ages of eight to eighteen or twenty, when males were to receive seventy-five dollars and females twenty-five, from the masters, on condition of leaving Maryland. All free blacks to register themselves and get new certificates, yearly, in the county offices. Sale out of Maryland or banishment, as punishment of free blacks for all offences not capital.[1] No meetings of negroes for any purposes whatever, after sunset; and fine and imprisonment—with sale out of the State for a second offence—for any black having a license to preach, who might attend any illegal meetings. A fine of one hundred dollars, half to the informer, for any retail dealer who might give or sell, in any way whatever, any wine or liquors to any negro. And an increase in the cost of a license for a traveling pedlar. Such were the recommendations of this convention, which adjourned *sine die*, on the third day of sitting, after having named a committee of five members to present memorials to the Legislature.

The House committee on Colored Population had been asked already to take some action, and leave had been granted them, two weeks before the slaveholders met, to bring in a bill "for the better government of the free colored population of the State, and for the protection and perpetuation of negro slavery therein." The memorial of the convention, duly presented a week or so after the adjournment, was read and referred to the same committee, and over a hundred copies were printed for the members and senators. , Memorials and petitions

---

[1] This clause, it is interesting to note, brought up considerable argument, pro and con. One clause called, also, for the prohibition of fire-arms and weapons to blacks.

against the work of the convention soon began to come in; the House received twenty-six, and the Senate some eight others. Public meetings were held in Baltimore, Centreville in Queen Anne's, Chestertown in Kent, and elsewhere; and a series of letters, signed Vindex, in the Baltimore *American*, called attention to the fact that the convention, which sought to perpetuate slavery and to crush down large numbers of colored men, did not probably represent a seventh of the people of Maryland.[1] Meantime the committee's bill had received many amendments in the House; and the title was changed, to an act "for the better security of negro slaves in this State, and for promoting industry and honesty amongst the free people of color." It included—so much we know—an annual registration of free blacks; the sale for a year of all those "without visible means of support" and "not of good and industrious habits," and the binding out of children whose parents were not of good character or could not honestly employ them. Every black manumitted should leave the State within twenty days, under penalty of sale by the year. Blacks could attend religious meetings after dark, provided there were present some authorized white clergyman, resident in Maryland, and at least three respectable slaveholders. And lockmen on the Chesapeake and Ohio Canal were to stop all boats whose captains were blacks. The bill passed the House, late in February, by a vote of forty to thirty-one. On the day before, three memorials against such extreme measures were received from sundry citizens of Baltimore.

---

[1] See *Niles' Register*, Vol. LXI, 368, &c.; LXII, 16, &c.
Some of these petitions were not signed by many names, and some of the meetings may not have been large; but it is safe to say that the action of the convention was disapproved by the majority of citizens. In the petitions, opposition was directed noticeably against the prohibition of religious meetings after dark. See House Journal and Senate Journal, 1841, February 1st–March 8th. The Vindex letters begin in Baltimore *American*, January 22d, 1842. There were few public expressions in favor of the suggestions of the convention.

All the petitions on the files of the House, together with one or two which came in later, were then sent to the Senate. The bill was rejected by the Senate, March 8th, by fifteen to six.

We have already noticed that Baltimore city was not fairly represented in the Legislature. The solemn claim[1] of the slaveholders' convention at Annapolis to be "a meeting of citizens of Maryland appointed in conformity with public notice to represent the wishes and feelings of their respective counties and cities, to thus constitute a general convention," may well turn us to study the matter more closely, as a matter indeed of vital importance. Under the constitution of 1776, each county was entitled to four seats in the House of Delegates, and Annapolis and Baltimore to two seats each. The Senate was a body of fifteen, chosen at large by electors, the only restriction being that nine must live on the Western Shore (*i. e.* of the Bay), and six on the Eastern Shore. This system continued until 1838. After that, and until the adoption of the constitution of 1864, each county and the city of Baltimore chose one senator; and each county, until after 1851, sent from three to six delegates, according to population, counted in "federal numbers," and Baltimore was entitled to the same number as the most populous county. After the adoption of the constitution of 1851, the smallest counties had but two members, and Baltimore was given ten. In 1840, fully one-quarter of all the whites in the State were in Baltimore city, and many more than a quarter of all the free blacks. By 1850, the proportion of both races had risen to one-third. As Delaware and New York were equally represented in the national Senate, so in the Maryland Senate, after 1837, Calvert county, with some thirty-five hundred whites, fifteen hundred free blacks and forty-five hundred slaves, had equal

---

[1] See the memorial presented to the Assembly.

weight with Baltimore—with one hundred and forty thousand whites, twenty-five thousand free blacks, and three thousand slaves. In the popular House, the delegation from Baltimore, at its largest, was less than a seventh of the members. Thus it might happen that large majorities in the Assembly would be a gross misrepresentation of the people of the State.[1]

In 1842 the House passed a bill to require blacks to take out new freedom papers, at charges proportioned to their age, but the Senate rejected it.[2] At the session following, the question was again raised, without result, of taxing all able free blacks, for the support of the State; and a bill to require them to be registered was considered, and the enacting clause finally struck out. The same questions were brought up the next year again; and a committee bill for the registry of free blacks passed the House but was rejected by the Senate.[3] But of greater moment seems the report of a special committee of the House appointed to consider evidently a proposition that the free blacks of Charles county be removed—that measures be taken to cause all the free blacks in Maryland to emigrate. At the next session the delegates from Charles county, to whom the matter had been referred, presented a lengthy report. The presence of the free blacks, they said, is deemed an evil by almost everyone, and with continued increase in their numbers, the whites must eventually amalgamate with them, or leave the State, or be reduced to slavery. All plans for removing the blacks with their own consent were destined perhaps to prove illusory, as the negro had shown an invincible indisposition to go. The testimony of the agents of the

---

[1] Constitutions of 1776, 1851, 1864; amendment of 1837.
[2] House Journal, 1842, 144, 550.
[3] House Journal, 1844, 42, 60, &c. This or another similar bill was up again in the House the next year.

Colonization Society, indeed, showed that force alone could remove them. And that the Assembly could force them to go, followed from the fact that they were legal and not constitutional citizens, and that their status could be changed or abolished at the pleasure of the legislators. In accordance with this report, a bill was introduced in the House to remove the free blacks of Charles county, but action on it was postponed, and we find no further mention of it—except that the House received a memorial against it, as well as against a bill for taxing free blacks, from nine hundred citizens of Baltimore.[1] This bill for special taxation—if we may accept the report of it in the Easton *Gazette*—required all free blacks between the ages of twenty-one and fifty, who were able and capable of self-support, to be registered yearly during the months of April and May, in the county offices, and to pay one dollar each therefor to the State. Failing so to do, they were liable to be fined between five and ten dollars, and in default of this, to be hired out. The report says that this bill was passed by the House by a very close vote: it was surely rejected by the Senate.[2] A bill for the better regulation of free blacks in St. Mary's county passed the House also, and was also rejected in the Senate. A bill to repeal the act of '31 for colonization was opposed by the committee, and was referred to the next Assembly. We find a bill to forbid the courts to give permits to freedmen to remain in the State, laid on the table and ordered to be printed, at the session of 1849.

In the constitutional convention of 1850–51, a committee of seven was early appointed, to consider all matters relating to the free blacks, and to report a plan "looking to the riddance of this State" of the free blacks, and to their coloniza-

---

[1] Reports of committees, 1844, 1845; House Journal, 1845, 58, 153, 380.
[2] Easton *Gazette*, Feb. 8th, 1845. However legitimate an object of taxation free negroes may be, adds the *Gazette*, we are inclined to look on this bill as hard and unreasonable: such provisions are liable, to say the least, to the most gross and tyrannical abuses—so palpable as to strike the attention at once.

tion in Africa.[1] Four months later, an elaborate report was made. The increase in the free blacks of the State from 1790 to 1850 had been over a thousand a year; from 1830 to 1840, when the plan of colonization was actively taken up, the average increase had been the same; from 1840 to 1850, even more. If that rate continued, the free blacks would soon exceed the whites in number, in eleven counties. Only one thousand and eleven had been colonized in Africa since 1831, at an expense of two hundred and ninety-eight thousand dollars, nearly two-thirds of which came from the State. Considering this and the vice and ignorance of the blacks, the committee recommended, to be inserted in the new Constitution, that the Assembly be empowered to pass laws for the government of the free blacks and for their removal, and be ordered to provide immediately for their registration; that no black should be capable of acquiring real estate in the future, nor of holding by lease for terms longer than one year; and that no free black should enter Maryland to stay, and no slave should be manumitted except on conditions of leaving within thirty days. When the consideration of this report was asked, some five weeks later, by the chairman of the committee, a motion to indefinitely postpone it was carried by forty-two to thirty-eight. A second attempt to bring it up later, in the same sitting, was defeated by forty-four to thirty-three.[2] This was in the convention. But we find a bill for the government,

---

[1] By motion of Mr. Jacobs of Worcester, who was made chairman, and reported the work of the committee. Two petitions were received from Frederick county for stringent legislation.

[2] Of the forty-four opposed to the report were—the entire delegations from Baltimore and Washington counties; ⅔ of the delegates from Cecil and Harford; ¾ of those from Queen Anne's and Talbot counties and Baltimore city. Of the thirty-three in favor—all from St. Mary's and Prince George's; ½ from Montgomery; ¼ from Worcester; ½ from Calvert, Charles and Kent; ⅔ from Somerset. The votes of those present from the other counties were divided—Frederick, 4 against and 1 for the report; Dorchester, 3 against and 2 for; Allegany and Carroll, 2 against and 1 for; Anne Arundel and Caroline, 1 against and 1 for.

regulation and disposition of the free blacks, before the Assembly of 1852. It gave more strict provisions for binding them out, and forbade manumission except on condition of emigration to Africa. It was put off to the next session. Then it was rejected by vote of thirty-one to twenty-two. On reconsideration, it was rejected by thirty-two to eighteen. Brought up again, it was rejected by thirty-three to twenty-one. And it was then withdrawn from the files of the House.

The Assembly was not discouraged by this gloomy report of the work of colonization, for the State appropriation of ten thousand dollars a year, which expired in 1851, was continued for six years more, to carry on the "policy of the State."[1] Again in 1852, as in 1847, some one got leave to bring in a bill for taxing the free blacks—this time, for the benefit of colonization—but we find no mention of it further. The free blacks themselves were by no means unanimous in advising colonization. A meeting of some of the most intelligent blacks of Baltimore was held in May, 1852, to consider colonization and plans for the elevation of their people; and a call was issued for a convention of delegates from the free blacks of the State.[2] According to the newspaper reports, the chief object of the preliminary meeting was to rouse greater zeal for emigration, the separation of whites and blacks being deemed desirable, and to provide pleasant accommodations for those about to sail, during the necessary tarry in Baltimore. In

---

[1] 1852, 202.

[2] Baltimore papers, May 25th, July 26th, &c., 1852. A gentleman prominent in the work of the Maryland Colonization Society, wrote in an open letter, in 1851, "The black man's heart—capable of the highest improvement, as Liberia has already proved, clings to the *natale solum* with vast tenacity, more so even than the white man feels, and the black man cannot, therefore, be expected to remove from familiar faces and familiar places, without a clinging hold, yielding only to the sternest circumstances." (Baltimore *American*, September 11th, 1851.) There had been a movement in favor of colonization in 1841 (*Niles*, LX, 227). The Baltimore *Sun* for May 17th, 1851, speaks of similar efforts among the blacks in Baltimore and in Cambridge.

accordance with the address that was issued, the convention met in July, in Baltimore. The object, as given, was to consider the present condition of the free blacks, and to adopt such measures as might tend to its amelioration. Several delegations at once asked leave to withdraw, as they were convinced that any action by the convention, instead of improving the condition of their people, would produce an agitation among them, to their injury. This was greeted with cries of approval from all parts of the house, and although the statement was plainly made that the convention had no direct connection with the work of colonization, but was for the improvement of the social and intellectual condition of the blacks, the sitting ended without accomplishing anything. In a melée without the hall, where a crowd of blacks had gathered, one boy was cut in the face with a tumbler, and a dozen men were arrested. And as the reporter of the abolition paper at the slaveholders' convention had barely escaped a laying on of hands, so here, a minister of one of the black congregations of Baltimore, a zealous advocate of colonization, had to be escorted home by the police. The next day —a strong police force being present—officers were chosen, and the resolution adopted, that all men are equal, and that free inquiry should be given to all matters affecting their welfare; and that while the zeal of those who had labored for twenty years to put the whites and free blacks of the country on a social and political equality, had been fully appreciated, the fact was evident that the condition of the free blacks as a class was less desirable than before. At this sitting and the next, there was a lively discussion as to the advantages of emigration to Liberia. Earnest and able speeches were made, showing considerable knowledge of Liberia and Hayti, but some felt that to recommend emigration would only be to destroy any good influences of the convention among the blacks. It was resolved, finally, that the "disparity of thought, feeling and intellectual advancement" which was seen to exist between the white and black races, showed that mutual prejudices could never be sufficiently overcome for the two races to dwell together in harmony and equal privileges, and that a separation from the whites—many of whom the blacks could not but love and admire—was therefore devoutly to be desired, as tending to the advantage of both whites and blacks. To these resolutions there was but one opposing voice, and the convention adjourned after having named a permanent committee and recommended the formation of local societies, to establish schools for black children, and to find out all useful information about colonization.[1] The Governor's message to the Assembly of 1858 spoke of the favorite policy of colonization, suggesting the use of further inducements to make the free blacks of the counties leave, and emancipation conditioned on immediate removal—before those who were freed might become contaminated by their new associations—or on payment of a sum sufficient to ensure the colonization of others. At that session, the renewed appropriation having expired, there was voted for the work under the managers, five thousand a year for four years, and in addition, seventy dollars for every black above ten years and thirty-five for younger ones, safely started for Africa—the entire expenditure not to exceed the previous appropriations of ten thousand a year.

In September, 1858, a goodly number of the slaveholders of Worcester county met together to recommend the calling of a general convention of the Eastern Shore, in the following

---

[1] At a national convention of colored people in Philadelphia, in October, 1855, a letter was read from a black of Baltimore eulogizing Liberia. Several members thereupon spoke against colonization, determined to demand their rights in the country where they were born; and a motion to burn the letter was carried by a large majority. So reported the Baltimore *Sun* of October 20th. The author of this letter appears to have been the temporary chairman of the convention in Baltimore in '52. The Baltimore convention adjourned to the following year, but the papers have no mention of any further meetings. See the reports of the National Colored Conventions, in Philadelphia in 1831 and 1832, opposing emigration to Liberia and Hayti, and asking the American Col. Soc. to desist from its "unhallowed persecution." Williams' Colored Race, II, 61.

November, and to pass resolutions for the strict enforcement of the laws and police regulations concerning slaves, especially to prevent runaways and the spread of abolition papers. This was to be helped by empowering postmasters in all the slaveholding States — for the resolutions looked to action by Congress as well as by the State Legislature — to open all letters and documents addressed to slaves and free blacks.[1] In response to this call, delegates from Caroline, Dorchester, Somerset, Talbot and Worcester met at Cambridge. A committee of ten reported resolutions the following day, which were adopted. It was evident, they said, to the people of Maryland that it was an impossibility under the existing laws, to control and regulate the black population in a proper manner. Attention was called to the great number of free negroes; to their habits of idleness and dissipation; to the heavy cost to the public of criminal prosecutions against them; to their well known tampering with slaves and aid in inducing slaves to abscond; and to their evil example and influence on the slaves, whom they made dissatisfied with bondage and comparatively worthless to the owners. Maryland is, and should be, a slaveholding state, true to the interest of herself and her Southern sisters. A system of legislation was needed to protect slaveholders and regulate all negroes — for their own interests as well as for the whites. Free blacks and slaves could not exist side by side, and the "vicious habits" of the free blacks, "their refusal to labor, their incapacity for self-government," leave the alternative of making them go from the State or go into slavery. Public feeling was ready for the question, and delegates of all the people should be called together to consider these propositions and make recommendations to the Legislature. A

---

[1] Baltimore *Sun*, Sept., 21st, 1858. *Niles' Register* mentions local meetings of slaveholders in Anne Arundel, Charles and St. Mary's counties, in 1845 (Vol. LXIX, 52). There was a meeting in Queen Anne's County, also, in February, 1845.

committee of seventeen was named to draft an address to be printed, before the convention, in newspapers throughout the State.[1]

In the following June, 1859, the general slaveholders' convention met in Baltimore. The plan had been to have each county and Baltimore city represented by as many delegates as each sent to the Assembly. And the meeting indeed seems to have been a large one. Allegany appears to have been the only county not represented. A meeting of citizens of Baltimore interested in the movement had been called shortly before, but so few responded that no organization was made. However, a delegation from Baltimore was nominated by the convention, the chairman stating—in response to the question of a member from Calvert, as to whom the city representatives represented—that on failure to choose members, after proper notice, the people would be voiced by those who were present. A large committee of twenty-one, from the various counties, was chosen to report action. But the committee was divided in opinion.[2] Two questions, in general, are before us, reported the majority,—first, the proposed expulsion of the free blacks from the State, and secondly, whatever legislation may be necessary to give vitality to the law of 1831, making manumission conditional on emigration. It is highly inexpedient to try to remove all the free blacks. They are indeed an evil in a slave-holding community, but the majority of them are not idle, unproductive and vicious. Their removal would be a greater evil than all the harm ever suffered. In Baltimore they number twenty-five thousand, mostly servants and laborers. Much of our soil could not be tilled without them. Then such an act of force would violate pub-

---

[1] Baltimore *Sun*, Nov. 6th, 1858. This committee of seventeen includes names from Cecil and Kent, so those counties were probably represented also. The Easton *Star* says of the convention: A number of resolutions were adopted which amount to nothing.

[2] The chairman had said, on undertaking his duties: On the slavery question every man has his own theories.

lic sentiment, which is generally just and kindly—it would not be tolerated by the people of the State. Nor should rights of freedom already vested be taken away. On the other hand, the policy outlined in the act of 1831 was wise and proper; but that law—becoming inoperative, and few blacks being willing to leave—had been almost forgotten except by members of the Bar.[1] But certain evils arising from the increase of free blacks have been almost universally admitted, and are more evident than in 1831. Slaves run away mainly through their influence, or are encouraged by them to insubordination, and the thriftless of them set evil examples to slave and free alike. They should be in well regulated subordination. It is also contrary to the policy of the State, and productive of evil, to allow them to acquire real estate.[2] The provision of '31 against the return of free blacks to Maryland is believed to be inoperative and wholly inefficient, also. Therefore, there should be no removal of the blacks then free, or to be born free; but they should be well controlled so as to be "orderly, industrious and productive"; and emancipation should be prohibited entirely, or be allowed only on condition of removal of the freedmen. The policy of '31 should be renewed with vigor. The minority report, on the contrary, advised putting an end to "free-negroism" at an early day, and "on the most advantageous terms to our white population." The free blacks should be advised to leave the State, if they would remain free; and those who wished should be allowed to become slaves to the citizens. Failing so to leave or become slaves, they and their posterity should be sold for life, and the prices be put so low, and payments so

---

[1] The committee ascribed the desuetude into which this act had fallen—to use their own language—to the imperfections of its details.

[2] It not infrequently happens, reads the report, that free blacks form thick settlements on little parcels of ground, cultivate less than can support them, labor but little for those who would be glad to hire them on liberal terms—the conclusion being that they eke out their living by unlawful means.

easily arranged, that citizens of small means might get them. Apprentices and slaves for terms of years were to be included at the end of their terms; but in all cases, a prudent discrimination should be used in favor of those who were aged or meritorious. There should be efficient police regulations for the blacks, throughout the State. The point of this report was that the labor of free blacks was needed, provided it did not come in competition with the whites; it was not just "to take the children's bread and cast it to the dogs."[1] The gentleman who presented the minority report said he did not wish to drive away the free blacks, for their labor was wanted. A member from Calvert said that the people of his county wished them to work, but they would not. A member from Frederick said that further legislation was necessary for a State half slave and half free, that a slave who would bring fourteen hundred dollars at New Orleans could not be kept with any security in the counties bordering on Pennsylvania. A member from Howard said that his county was represented simply because it was opposed to holding such conventions; there had been slaveholders' conventions, but no good results! Finally, after several substitutes for these reports had been set aside, the convention adopted the resolutions of the majority of the committee, appointed several gentlemen to petition the Assembly, and adjourned *sine die*.[2]

The message of the Governor to the next Assembly, in January 1860, spoke—as had that of 1858—of the need in many of the counties of further legislation on the free blacks. In Baltimore and the larger towns and in the Northern counties, there was little complaint against the free blacks; nor indeed was the evil of their presence felt "as it is in the lower counties, on both shores, where the community is taxed to support their idleness and vagrancy, and is subject to their

---

[1] See minority report, presented by Mr. Jacobs of Worcester.
[2] Baltimore *Sun*, June 8th, 1859. The number of delegates was over ninety.

pilfering and the ill effects of their evil example on the servile population." And the suggestion was made that every idle black be bound out for wages, under just conditions, and with freedom of choice of master and of change. The House committee on Colored Population presented a lengthy report.¹ There was, it said, an alarming state of excitement on the subject of the colored population. In the rural parts of the State, there was an evident feeling of distrust to the free blacks; the increased number of house-burnings and poisononings and other manifestations of insubordination had given alarm for the security of life and property. These feelings were clearly announced in petitions presented the Assembly, as in that of the slaveholders' convention. As to the plans to be pursued to remedy the evils, experience had shown that the free blacks would not voluntarily emigrate, and a great mistake had been made in allowing manumitted blacks to remain. The act of 1831 had been a failure.² Nothing short of an ultimate wiping out of the free blacks would meet the emergencies besetting the peculiar condition of Maryland. We think it would be "unjust, and perhaps cruel," continued the committee, to force them to leave the State; but they should be held in perfect subordination to the citizens, and made to work under their control. If it be admitted that the negroes are once absolutely free, any laws that may be passed, affecting them and not all freemen, will be regarded by them as oppressive, and will also secure for them a large amount of sympathy from the whites. By manumission the negro does not get the rights of a citizen, but " merely ceases to belong to one man, and really becomes the property of the whole State."

---

¹ Composed of Messrs. Jacobs, of Worcester; Burgess, of Charles; Dennis, of Somerset; Bryan, of Prince George's; Gordon, of Allegany; Holland, of Dorchester; Claggett, of Frederick.

² This act, said the committee, has been in operation for twenty-seven years, at a expense from the State of $280,000 and from all sources of some half million, but the free black population had grown from 52,000 in 1831, to some 90,000 or more. Of blacks born free, not over 300 had emigrated.

The free black does not like to work out on the farm, where labor is needed, nor does he look to the future. In short, "as an inferior class of our population, we owe to them the enactment of such laws as will restrain them from self-destruction, and make them subordinate and useful to our citizen population and the industrial interests of our State." The recommendations of the committee, to this end, were the repeal of all taxation for colonization; the entire prohibition of emancipation;[1] the grant to free blacks under fifty-five years of the privilege of choosing masters and going into slavery at any time; provision for the hiring out of the blacks for terms of ten years—the children to be born in future to be the property of the masters of the mothers; and a number of strict police regulations, including the right of postmasters to withhold from negroes any mail addressed to them.[2] So far the committee could agree, but some of them had wished to put the free blacks back into slavery—complete and at once. Several bills were introduced in the House. The Judiciary committee reported favorably this stringent legislation, and such further regulations as the punishment of persons for teaching negroes, and of slaves for being away from home without passes, and the prohibition of meetings.[3] Other plans were brought forward,—the prohibition of any gifts or conveyances to free blacks of either real estate or slaves, with the sale of such then held by blacks on their death; and the use of negro testimony,

---

[1] Even those blacks who had been freed on condition of leaving but had remained, under cover of a judgment of the Court of Appeals, were to be returned to their old masters.

[2] This was, in the opinion of the committee, the best disposition to make of the free blacks, "for their own good, for the welfare of the industrial interests of the State, for the peace, good order and security of society, and in furtherance of the ends of a sound and real humanity." "The restoration of them back into a state of slavery does not meet the approbation of a majority of the committee, though some of us do consider it the most humane disposal to make of them."

[3] This committee, too, was not of a mind in all things, but a bill introduced by the minority was afterwards withdrawn.

when accompanied by proof of circumstances tending to confirm it, on the trial of whites for aiding slaves to abscond.

It is not without thought of the whims and persistency of individual legislators that we draw from Assembly journals these frequent inquiries that were asked for, these repeated bills that were introduced, these occasional reports that were submitted, all in vain, with the aim of further and more stringent legislation against the blacks; but these, however worthless they may or may not have been as exponents of any public sentiment, show that the subject was kept fresh in the mind of successive Assemblies. It had been stated in the slaveholders' convention that the people were ready for action, and since that convention, had occurred the attack of John Brown on Harper's Ferry. If there ever was a time when there was a call for the enforcement of the police regulations against the blacks of Maryland, it was in the autumn of 1859. The Assembly, meeting in the January following, surely appeared ready to take some steps, perhaps long steps. There were some warnings, however, of popular disapproval. As early as October, a meeting was held at the court house of Baltimore county, small in number but of prominent citizens, and an address to the people of the county was ordered. When a petition to the Assembly for the hiring out of free blacks was circulated in St. Mary's, the Leonardtown *Beacon* stated that the citizens in general were opposed to any forcible measures. Over one thousand of the prominent citizens of Baltimore signed a petition in remonstrance to harsh measures. Some of the local papers, Southern in sympathy, deprecated the advice of the slaveholders' convention.[1]

---

[1] Also, a petition in remonstrance was received from some eighty citizens of Harford county. The Cumberland *Telegraph* stated that a number of industrious blacks, members of a beneficial society there, had withdrawn their funds from the bank and distributed it, on learning of the proposition in the Assembly to dispossess negroes of their property. See Baltimore *Sun*, Oct. 16th, 1859, and January 14th, Feb. 17th, 20th, 1860.

The Assembly finally passed four measures. The State board of managers for colonization was done away, with only two opposing votes in the House; and no general appropriation was made, but fixed sums as before were to be paid for every black sent off by the State Society, up to a total of five thousand dollars a year. Secondly, manumission was absolutely forbidden thereafter.[1] The vote on this stood thirty-eight to fourteen in the House, and thirteen to six in the Senate. Thirdly, any free black over eighteen years of age was allowed to renounce freedom and become a slave for life to the master of his own selection; if a female, any children that she might have under five years would become slaves also, while older children would be bound out by the courts. Application would have to be made by the black to the circuit court for the county in which he, or she, had lived for three years preceding, and would be granted by the court only after full examination, in open sitting, to be sure that no force, fraud or undue persuasion had been used.[2] The fourth measure was the residuum of the various plans for hiring out the idle free blacks of the counties. As it passed the Senate, the bill applied only to Baltimore, Calvert, Howard, Kent and St. Mary's counties. The House added Anne Arundel, Caroline, Charles, Dorchester, Prince George's, Queen Anne's, Somerset, Talbot and Worcester, but, at the request of the Senate, struck out Anne Arundel, Caroline and Dorchester. A board of commissioners, of three sober and discreet men, was to be appointed in each district by the commissioners of these counties, to be the commission "for the better control and management" of the free blacks. These were to summon be-

---

[1] This did not effect slaves for terms of years, to be free under deeds or wills already made or probated.
[2] 1860, 283, 322. House Journal, Feb. 16th, March 9th. It will be pertinent to add that an exemption bill, to secure persons against the seizure of furniture and other property to the amount of $300, was amended by a vote of thirty-five to thirteen in the House, so as to exclude blacks from its benefits. House Journal, Feb. 16th.

fore them on every first day of December, every free black of their district who did not have, in his or her own right, one hundred and fifty dollars of assessed property, or who did not actually reside with parents having, in addition, for every son or daughter, fifty dollars worth of assessed property. The blacks, on appearance, were to be duly warned, and then at the expiration of a month, the commissioners were to sell at auction as slaves for a year, all those who had not hired themselves out to labor for a year to industrious and respectable citizens. The hirers had to give bonds, to secure wages, satisfactory to the commissioners, and liable to suit; and if a black tried to abscond, he could be sold as a slave for life—on proof of his offence by some disinterested and reliable person, under oath —by the commissioners, for the benefit of the primary school fund. The wages agreed in the bonds were to be collected by the commissioners and paid the blacks in presence of a magistrate, after deducting expenses and the necessary contributions to a fund for the support of all those free blacks who could not be hired from age or disability. And all free black children aged from four to twelve were to be bound out to citizens, males to the age of twenty-one and females to thirty. The masters might be chosen by the mothers, if these desired, but they had to give bond, in all cases, for the good treatment and care of their apprentices. The last and most important provision of the bill was that the act was to be null and void unless accepted by a majority of the voters of the counties mentioned, at the presidential election of the following autumn. The Assembly seemed ready to leave the decision with the people. The bill passed the Senate without opposition and the House by forty-one to three. Several of the counties to which the provisions of the act were offered had large numbers of slaves, as Calvert, Charles, St. Mary's and Prince George's; others, as Baltimore county, Kent, Worcester and Somerset, had fewer slaves and many more free blacks. At the exciting election of November, 1860, the act was rejected, taking the counties together, by a vote of over three to one. And many of those who voted for president did not vote upon it.[1]

We close with the adjournment of the Assembly of 1860. In the course of the Civil War, which soon broke out, Maryland passed practically under military law. Slavery in Maryland, as in West Virginia and some parts of Louisiana and Virginia, was not included in Mr. Lincoln's Emancipation Proclamation. It was abolished by the adoption of the State Constitution of 1864. This Constitution, however—also declaring paramount allegiance to the United States, and providing that the State should not compensate former slave owners—cannot be taken as an expression of the people of Maryland. It was rejected by a majority of nearly two thousand of the forty-seven thousand and odd citizens who voted at the polls, and was ratified by a majority in all of three hundred and seventy-five votes, counting those cast in the Union camps by soldiers from Maryland, under a provision

---

[1] The vote on the act (known to some as the Jacobs' bill) according to returns given in Baltimore papers, stood—

	For	Against.		For.	Against.
Baltimore Co.	681	5,354	Prince George's	282	1,200
Calvert	242	504	Queen Anne's	125	1,467
Charles	328	471	Somerset	1,486	804
Howard	55	1,397	St. Mary's	435	816
Kent	74	1,502	Talbot	121	1,142
			Worcester	842	1,217

In Talbot, over 500 voters threw blanks on the free negro act; in Prince George's, some 450; in Somerset, some 670, &c.

The clerk of the court of Somerset county, the only county in which the act was not rejected, writes that its provisions were never applied there.

The vote of the State was nearly equally divided between Bell and Everett and Breckenridge and Lane, in favor of the latter. Douglass polled only some 5,500 votes and Lincoln some 2,000.

of the Constitution itself. The Assembly of 1861-2, severe in its blame of "the seditious and unlawful acts" of the rebellious States, yet spoke with apprehension of "so unwise and mischievous" a policy as any interference by the general government in the institution of slavery in the South; and the Constitution of 1867 declared in vain that as slavery in Maryland had been abolished "under the policy and authority of the United States," compensation was therefore due from the government to the former master.[1]

One word—and an important word—in closing. We have gleaned from various sources and marshalled together, act on act, judgment on judgment, report on report, many of them facts of little importance—except as concerning the negroes in Maryland. And we may well consider, that the average citizen of Maryland probably gave as little heed to those of them of his day, as we to-day follow the proceedings of our legislatures and courts or actually feel the working of law about us, except in so far as our own immediate, tangible interests are concerned. There was a bright and touching side to slavery which led many to think no ill of it, as there was a dark side which branded it. But all will agree to-day, probably, in thankfulness that it has gone.

Note.—We have not attempted to describe "the old plantation" of the South, for the task has been well done by some who knew it. For an interesting account of life on a large and well ordered plantation, see, for instance, "Memorials of a Southern Planter," by Susan Dabney Smedes

---

[1] The number of those who had voted in the presidential election of 1860 had been over 90,000. The vote on the Constitution of 1864 was—home vote, 27,541 for, and 29,536 against, and 61 blanks; soldiers' vote, in camps, 2,633 for, and 263 against. That on the Constitution of 1867—27,152 for, and 23,036 against. See Charter and Constitutions of the U. S. 1861-2, Resolutions 2, 3, 9, 13, 15.

(Baltimore, 1888, Cushings & Bailey). We must remember that such books deal with the bright side of slavery. On the other hand, the injustice done by the abolition literature, so called, is that it may be taken as pictures of Southern life, instead of pictures—drawn in exciting days, and often by those who were foreign to their subject—of that side of slavery which was happily the least known.

The student of the institution of slavery cannot refer too often to Hurd's Law of Freedom and Bondage, and Moore's Slavery in Massachusetts. Much of value will be found, also, in Cobb's Inquiry into the Law of Negro Slavery (1858, Phil. and Savannah).

POPULATION OF MARYLAND.

1830.

	WHITES.	FREE BLACKS.	SLAVES.
The Whole State..................	291,108	52,938	102,994

1860.

COUNTIES.	WHITES.	FREE BLACKS.	SLAVES.
Allegany...........................	27,215	467	666
Anne Arundel....................	11,704	4,864	7,332
Baltimore County...............	46,722	4,231	3,182
City of Baltimore...............	184,520	25,680	2,218
Calvert.............................	3,997	1,841	4,609
Caroline............................	7,604	2,786	739
Carroll..............................	22,525	1,225	783
Cecil.................................	19,994	2,918	950
Charles.............................	5,796	1,068	9,653
Dorchester........................	11,654	4,684	4,123
Frederick..........................	38,391	4,957	3,243
Harford............................	17,971	3,644	1,800
Howard............................	9,081	1,395	2,862
Kent.................................	7,347	3,411	2,509
Montgomery.....................	11,349	1,552	5,421
Prince George's.................	9,650	1,198	12,479
Queen Anne's....................	8,415	3,372	4,174
St. Mary's.........................	6,798	1,866	6,549
Somerset...........................	15,332	4,571	5,089
Talbot..............................	8,106	2,964	3,725
Washington......................	28,305	1,677	1,435
Worcester.........................	13,442	3,571	3,648
The Whole State.......	515,918	83,942	87,189

INDEX.

Abolition, efforts for, 52, &c., 237; Maryland society for, 52, &c., 57; society in Baltimore for, 152, 184; of slavery in Maryland, 262.

Abolition matter, spread of forbidden, 224.

Annapolis, records of Mayor's court of, 136.

Anne Arundel County Court, study of old records of, 135.

Apprentices, colored children bound out as, 198, 219; efforts to force certain free blacks to become, 260.

Baltimore, unfair representation of, in assembly, 246.

Barbadoes, notice of slave code of, 147.

Brown, John, patrols called out after raid of, 97, 111.

Carroll, Charles, efforts of, for abolition, 53, 54.

Charles county, effort to remove free blacks from, 247.

Colonization, the state policy, 66, 165, &c., 237, &c., 252, 260; decisions of court of appeals unfavorable to, 169; Maryland society, 71, 165, 235, 238; American society, 235; convention of blacks on, 250.

Conversion to christianity does not give freedom, 28, &c.

Cruelty to servants and slaves, efforts to prevent, 140, &c.; to slaves, 144, &c.

Delaware, escape of slaves to, 85, &c.

Dogs, number of held by free blacks limited, 216.

Duties on slaves imported, 42, &c.

Education of blacks, not provided for, 197.

Entertainment, of servants and slaves, restrictions on, 100; by blacks in Baltimore, must be licensed, 204.

Evidence, law of, 190, &c. See Testimony.

Exportation of blacks, efforts to prevent, 57, &c.

False imprisonment, suits by manumitted slaves for, unsuccessful, 162.

Felons, importation of, 118; testimony of, 121; numbers of, in Baltimore county, 1752, 175.

Freedom, petitions for, 36, 148, &c.; removal of trial on petitions for, 153.

Free blacks, numbers of, 175, 249; entrance of, forbidden, 176, &c., 178, 181, &c.; entrance of, allowed by special acts, 178, 180; liable to detention as runaway slaves, 183; right of suffrage once exercised by, 186; legal status of, 187, 194; property held by, 188, &c.; occupations of, 206; restrictions on trading and dealings by, 208, 211, &c.; take benefit of insolvency laws, 211; idle and indigent, bound out, 218; efforts to force, to hire out, 222; law to prevent, from quitting service, 223; punishments of, for unlawful meetings, 199; for belonging to secret societies, 200; for dealing in stolen goods, 212, for handling abolition matter, 225; laws on crimes and punishments touching, 226; sale of, as punishment, 227, &c., 232, &c.; not deemed a desirable part of population, 234, &c., 237, 240, 242, 253; efforts for increased restrictions on, 240–260.

266

French West Indies, importation of slaves from, 48; insurrection in, 96.
Friends, society of, efforts for abolition, 52, &c.; against exportation of blacks, 57, &c., 60; for unrestricted manumission, 151, &c.; against kidnapping, 184.
Garrison, Wm. Lloyd, and the Genius of Universal Emancipation, 224.
Guns and ammunition held by blacks, restrictions on, 216.

Indentured, idle free blacks, &c., see Free Blacks.
Indians, the Spaniards and the, 5, &c., 9; the colonists and the, 11, &c.; enslavement of, prisoners, 12, 19; mention of slaves, 13, 20; trials of white offenders against, 15; restrictions on, 17; conversion of, 18; trials and punishments of, 116.
Insurrections, rumors of, of papists, Indians and negroes, 91, &c., 97; in West Indies, 96; local, 96; rumors of, of slaves, 97, &c., 202. See Southampton.
Introduction of slaves to Maryland, 26.

Jacob's Bill, against free blacks, 260.
Jail treatment of blacks, 81.

Kidnapping, 34, &c., 61, 148, &c.

Liberia, 165; convictions for larceny in, 234; removal of blacks to, 239, 241, 249.
Liquor, sale of to servants and slaves, restrictions on, 102, 213, to slaves and free blacks, 213, &c.

Manumission, 55, 60, 148, &c.; not valid in prejudice of creditors, 158, &c.; allowed by special acts, 167; conditional, 169, &c., 237; by presumption, 172; by devise of property, 174.
Manumitted slaves, powers of, to secure freedom, 161; status of, 162. See Slaves for terms of years.
Marriages between blacks and whites forbidden, 32, 195.

Meetings of blacks, restrictions on, 93, &c., 100, &c., 199, &c., 205.
Military service, exemption of blacks from, 110; enlistment of free blacks in, in Revolution, 196.

New Jersey, escape of slaves to, 85, &c.
New York, escape of slaves to, 88.

Occupations of free blacks, 206.

Pardoning power, exercise of by Governor, illustrated from old council records, 130, &c.
Passes, use of, for blacks, 89.
Patrols, 97, &c., 110.
Pennsylvania, escape of slaves to, 85, &c., 88, 235.
Pinkney, Wm., efforts for abolition, 53, 152; against exportation of blacks, 57.
Population of Maryland, in 1860, 265. See also 38, 175, 249.
Prisoners, ransom of Christian, 3; enslavement of heathen, 4.
Property, of slaves, 104; of free blacks, 188.
Protection societies, for insurance of slave property, 91.
Punishments, laws on crimes and, see Servants, Free Blacks and Slaves.

Ransom of prisoners, old custom of, 3, &c.
Religious bodies of blacks, 199, 205.
Runaways, white servants, 72, &c., 78; slaves, 72-91; Indians, 74; black servants, for terms of years, 78.

Servants, black, see Slaves for terms of years. White servants, 20, &c., 72; restrictions on entertainment of, or dealings with, 100, 102; punishments of, 114, 119.
Slave code, on crimes and punishments, study of growth of, 112-126.
Slave trade, by Europeans, 4, 6, &c., 9; African, 38, &c., 40; growth of opposition to, 43, 46; prohibition of, 45.

Slavery, in antiquity, 2; early treatises on war, &c., touching, 7, &c.; basis of, in Maryland, 26–37; legalized, 37; abolished by State constitution of 1864, 262.

Slaves, introduction of into Maryland, 26; in England, 27; conversion does not alter status of, 28, &c.; increase in numbers of, 38, &c.; restrictions put on introduction of, 45, &c, 64, &c., 66, &c., lessened, 71; efforts to prevent exportation of, 57, &c.; outlawry of, for certain offences, 76, 81; punishment of, for absconding, 76, 78, &c., 81, 91, for absence from home, 100, &c., for sale of liquors, &c., 103; laws on crimes and punishments touching slaves, 117–130, 138; restrictions on transportation of, by common carriers, 82, &c.; efforts to restrict, from acting as free, 104, &c., 174; restrictions on dealing or trading with, 102, &c.; religious instruction of slaves, 108, &c.; care of old or disabled, required, 107, 149; sales of, &c., 144; issue of mortgaged, 145; owned by free blacks, 190.

Slaves, for terms of years, restrictions on exportation of, 60, &c.; restrictions on sale of, 61, &c.; runaways, 78; exportation and sale of, as punishment, 124; status of issue of, 154.

Slave-holders' conventions, at Annapolis, 242, of Eastern Shore, 252, at Baltimore, 254.

Society of Friends, see Friends.

Societies, secret, of blacks, forbidden, 200; beneficial, allowed in Baltimore, 203.

Southampton insurrection, 65, 66, 96, 99, 165, 177, 199, 236.

Suffrage, right of, once open to free blacks, 186.

Taxables, slaves, 146.

Testimony, of blacks illegal against whites, 119; of convicts, made valid against convicts, 121; of slaves made valid against slaves, 121; of white servants, 140; growth of law touching evidence, 190, &c.

Tobacco, growth of, as affecting slavery, 39.

Trades and shipping, as affecting slavery, 39.

Turner, Nat., see Southampton insurrection.

Vagrant free blacks, sales of, 218, &c., 221, &c.; committed to Baltimore almshouse, 221; children of, bound out, 198, 219.

Villeinage in Europe, 2.

Vindex letters in Baltimore *American*, against the slaveholders' convention, 245.

War, laws of, as affecting slavery, 2, 4, 7, &c.

Whites and blacks, status of issue of, 32, &c.; marriage between, forbidden, 32, 195.

www.ingramcontent.com/pod-product-compliance
Lightning Source LLC
Chambersburg PA
CBHW031951230426
43672CB00010B/2128